D0323839

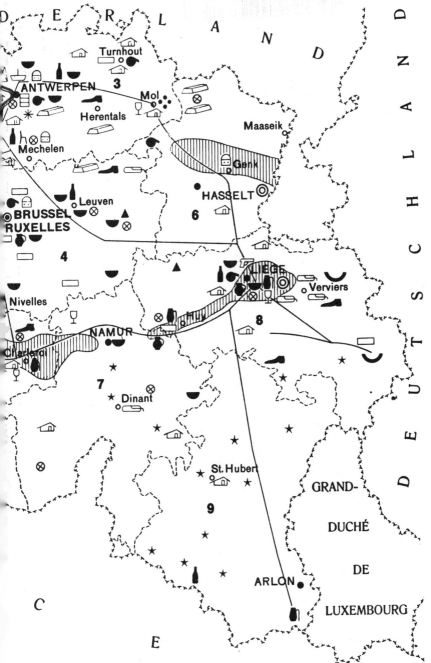

NEDERLAND

DEUTSCHLAND

Turnhout

ANTWERPEN
3

Mol

Herentals

Mechelen

Maaseik

Genk

HASSELT

Leuven

BRUSSEL
RUXELLES

6

4

LIÈGE

Verviers

8

NAMUR

Nivelles

Charleroi

7

Dinant

St. Hubert

9

GRAND-

DUCHÉ

DE

ARLON

LUXEMBOURG

C

E

Bouvier des Flandres

By Claire D. McLean

With Contributions by

Edmee Bowles
Justin Chastel
Chet Collier
Murray Horowitz, M.D.
Marion Hubbard
Diane Novak
Lil Mees
Club du Bouvier des Flandres pour la France
Club National Belge du Bouvier des Flandres

Edited by

Herm David

Cover design by

Bob Groves

Pictured on the front cover of this book are Ch. Deewal Blitzen CD and Noelle du Plateau CD, owned by Lucille and Andrew Gill. Reproduced on the back cover is a photo of the author's daughter, Chari McLean, with Ch. Deewal Thunderbuff UD.

DENLINGER'S PUBLISHERS, LTD.

Box 76, Fairfax, Virginia 22030

Claire D. McLean and three of her Bouviers—Ch. Deewal Yetta Lass, Ch. Deewal Young Husband, and puppy Arla Mae.

McLean, Claire D.
    The Bouvier des Flandres.
    Previous ed. published in 1974 as: The complete Bouvier des Flandres.
    1. Bouviers des Flandres. I. Bowles, Edmee. II. David, Herm. III. Title.
SF429.B73M32 1981   636.7'3   80-66115
ISBN 0-87714-077-4   AACR2

SECOND EDITION

(The first edition of this book was published as *The Complete Bouvier des Flandres.*)

International Standard Book Number: 0-87714-077-4
Library of Congress Catalog Number: 80-66115

*This book is dedicated
to my husband, Charles G. McLean,
and my aunt, the late Dorothy Walsh.*

Handled by his owner, Charles G. McLean, Ch. Vulcain des Clos des Cytises, left, won the 1980 National Specialty Stud Dog Class at Windsor Locks, Connecticut. Also pictured are his get, Deewal Delightful, center, handled by Christie McLean, and Deewal Donald de la Tour, owned by Bert and Pat Ennis and handled by Elliot Weiss. The get are both out of Ch. L'Esprit Fiers Xebec and bred by Donna Turk and Nancy Gamby of California. Judged by Mr. Joseph Mellor.

PREFACE

I was just a small girl when my aunt, Mrs. Dorothy Walsh, inducted me into the cult of the Bouvier by presenting me with Max. He was more than just a dog. He was my pal, and in many ways a gentle and persuasive teacher. He felt his mission in life was to guard me from all those dangers a child doesn't recognize. Whenever I went wandering off, which I did so often, Max was always there at my heels.

In a very real sense this book is Dorothy Walsh's final contribution to Bouviers. She gathered much of the material over a period of years. She believed there was a need for a book about the Bouvier and she encouraged me in my efforts. I had hoped to present her with the first bound copy, but that was not to be. However I can and do dedicate *The Complete Bouvier des Flandres* to her memory.

It seems the entire Bouvier community—worldwide—has joined in the preparation of this first true book on the Bouvier. I couldn't possibly list here all who are deserving of thanks. Whenever feasible contributions of information and illustrations are acknowledged in the text.

Every effort has been made to be both inclusive and accurate. These are objectives which, while approachable, are never fully attainable. Suggestions, additions and corrections are solicited and will be gratefully received.

If this book introduces new people to the joys and the practical advantages of a Bouvier's companionship—if it brings added enjoyment to those who already own Bouviers—then it will have been worthwhile.

Claire McLean

Chester Springs, Pennsylvania
April, 1974

The author, right, her sister, Ginger, and Max, their first Bouvier, in 1943. Bred by Mrs. Louis deRochemont, Max had small, uncropped ears. Photo by Ray Marshall.

PREFACE TO THE SECOND EDITION

It has been seven years since the first edition of this book was published, and so much has happened in that time that it is impossible to chronicle all of it; and so, for this new edition, we have dropped the word "Complete" from the title, for in essence no dog book or publication on any subject can ever reach the epitome of being "complete."

Through various newsletters I announced that the revised edition would be forthcoming and that all contributions of text material and photographs would be most welcome. To those owners, exhibitors, and breeders who were waiting for a personal invitation to contribute, I can only say that you did not need one. I could not reach each and every one of you, and if any fanciers of the Bouvier have inadvertently been left out, I regret it sincerely.

Since the first edition was so all-encompassing and universal in its content, the most important project for this revised edition was updating — and that we have done from the year 1974 to publication date. Yet, since the present is only a moment, the revised edition is already dated, for records are being broken every week and every month, new champions finish weekly, and one cannot keep up with all of the activities going on within the fancy of the Bouvier des Flandres.

A new club is being formed in Miami, another in Colorado, and serious new breeders are emerging in many of the fifty states. In a few years these breeders will be making an impact on the breed. South Africa, Peru, Australia, and England have active Bouvier owners and breeders, and Holland now boasts that the Bouvier is the third most popular breed. Mssr. Verbanck, speaking of the "Roulers" Bouvier and the Bouvier des Flandres, predicted that "the two shall merge for the betterment of both." Today, I make the same prediction regarding the "Dutch" Bouvier and the Franco-Belge Bouvier.

The Bouvier des Flandres is taking on more roles and is being appreciated more for his all-around versatility. The breed has come a tremendous distance since the days of Ch. Argus de la Thudinie — cover dog for the first edition of this book. The Bouvier has earned a reputation that not only has gained him popularity, but also, to some degree, faddism — which the lovers of the breed must work to curtail lest the Bouvier fall into the unfortunate set of circumstances that besiege all "faddist" breeds. Breeders must work foremost on the temperament of the Bouvier des Flandres, seeking out and breeding to only the most resolute and steadfast. Breeders must consider each litter a stepping stone in the breed, carefully planned and placed so that it will serve as a strong foundation for the next litter, and will lead breeders on toward the evolutionary but elusive goal of the perfect Bouvier; the perfect breed.

A few years from now, as this breed grows, as new members join the National Parent Club and the regional clubs forming throughout the United States, an even more comprehensive, revised edition of this book will be needed. Those breeders, exhibitors, and owners who are involved with some phase of activity with their Bouvier — whether it is carting, obedience training, conformation showing, or breeding — will be making the history for the next edition. If they plan well, work hard, and breed wisely, their efforts will not go unnoticed. People who deserve special recognition are those who develop their bitch or dog to the fullest potential. We all know who they are, and while there are a comparatively few of them now, from them many more should be encouraged to set goals of achievement realistic for the breed and for themselves. These are the leaders we should strive to follow, and in doing so, each in our own way, we cannot help but continue to upgrade and enhance the image of the Bouvier des Flandres.

'Til the next edition,

Claire D. McLean
1981

CONTENTS

These staunch Bouvier fanciers and club members travelled to Belgium for the International Exhibition in Brussels in 1975. Left to right: Carl B. May, Jr., John Elliott, Dr. Erik Houttuin, Carlos Suazo (kneeling), Joan Elliott, Bert Ennis, Terri Bennett, Bruce Jacobsohn, Edmee Bowles, Jeanne Suazo, Ronald Barnes, Gayle Ennis, Pat Ennis, Claire McLean, Virginia Martus, Dorothy DeSilva, and Bill Suazo.

Krepsie de la Thudinie is shown here as a young puppy with T.V. star J. Alexander, who portrayed Marshall Jay in 1961. Krepsie later became a champion and was owned by Ray and Marion Hubbard.

A rare photograph owned by Ray and Marion Hubbard of Madrone Ledge shows two Dutch girls with their "Bouvier" hitched to a cart. Circa 1900.

THE BOUVIER DES FLANDRES
AND HIS PREDECESSORS

MOST dog histories are necessarily conjecture and surmise. That is because the dog's alliance with man began long before man began to write and record the events of his emergence from the jungle. We know the alliance is at least 9,300 years old because the most careful carbon dating of surrounding artifacts in a human habitation digging in Star Carr, England places dog bones found there at 7,300 years B.C. Researchers reported man may have already domesticated some other animals.

We cannot know whether the dog was man's first conquest from the animal world, nor can we know which was the dog's first service to man. It may have been as a partner in the hunt—an enterprise in which the capabilities of canine and human still compliment each other. It may have been as a guard. A group of wild dogs bedded down near a cave in hopes of sharing in man's "table scraps" might signal by bark, howl or otherwise the approach of an intruder. The dog's service as a scavenger was necessary. The cave man who made a kill had no refrigeration. Meat he couldn't eat attracted disease-bearing insects and bacteria—and dangerous predators. In parts of India and the Middle East packs of semi-wild dogs continue to serve as the sewerage and sanitary disposal systems. The daily experience of seeing dogs eating human offal may explain the historic—and even religious—rejection of the dog by most peoples of this part of the world.

Somewhere early in their alliance against the deadly perils of their world man and dog discovered they had become more to each other than partners in struggles for survival. They discovered they enjoyed each other's companionship. The probability is that dogs were serving primitive man as hunting partners, guards, scavengers and companions. Then, we can rather safely assume, man invented a little-heralded device which made the domestication and utilization of animals possible and made an agrarian economy possible for him. He learned how to tie a knot!

The knot made it possible for man to hold an animal and to guide it into doing his bidding. Those that refused were probably beaten to death in the "guiding" process. A first factor in human selection of breeding stock was thus introduced. With his knot man could, for the first time, become a "breeder." He could select mates for the animals he held—and he surely chose those animals which most exhibited the qualities which he saw as being most useful to himself. If we are searching for the beginings of any of today's breeds of dogs we can start with the first time a man led his bitch over to the next valley so she could be covered by a stud he admired that belonged to a neighbor.

Other livestock was, by human criteria, "improved" in the same manner. But, a man can hold only a limited number of animals on a string. If he ties them out they are completely defenseless and easy prey for all kinds of marauders. Prehistoric man couldn't expand his holdings until he had developed a dog he could confidently unleash and depend upon to guard other varieties of livestock.

We will never know where or when man first confidently entrusted his livestock to the vigilance of a dog—but that is where we must date the beginings of the Bouvier and every other stock dog.

In time—and it must have taken hundreds of dog generations—man had, in various parts of his world, breeds of specialist dogs that could not only be depended upon to guard his livestock but to help him control and contain it so that it no longer had to be tied out or

penned. The process of improving stock dogs by selective breeding continues today.

Geographic isolation forced men to select breeding stock from animals easily available to them. Thus, because the introduction of "outside" blood was nearly impossible, regional "types" or "breeds", recognizable because of a certain uniformity of appearance emerged. It is interesting to note that breeds of stock dogs with the same jobs to do, i.e., over similar terrain and in similar weather conditions, although evolved independently of each other, display considerable similarity in size, weight, temperament and talents.

As man became more specialized so did his dogs. Stock dogs were sorted out into herding and droving dogs. And, there have always been some that did both jobs rather well for farmers with both sheep and cattle but only enough prosperity to support one dog.

The beginnings of the Bouvier are hardly better documented than are the beginnings of domestic dogs or stock dogs or drovers' dogs. They don't need to be. The Bouvier des Flandres of today is a proud, practical dog of distinctive, commanding appearance. He is an honest dog that needs no breed history reaching into antiquity. It would be inappropriate and beneath the Bouvier's dignity to here paste fabricated spangles onto his past.

Through all of their history the Flemings of his native land have proven themselves among the most skilled, practical animal breeders of the world. Through hundreds of years and many thousands of dog generations they utilized that skill in developing the Bouvier and his predecessors.

The development of the Bouvier into the handsome, useful and engaging companion that he is today has had its heroes and its perilous episodes. World War I, which so bloodied the meadows of Flanders, almost meant extinction for the Bouvier. At great personal sacrifice his dedicated supporters somehow managed to bring the best of the breeding stock through. Exploding shells and occupying armies, hunger and death, thoroughly tested their devotion to their native breed. Because only the best could be kept there was an *imposed* stringent selection and the net result was vastly accelerated "purification" and development of the modern Bouvier.

If we are to understand the origins of the Bouvier, if we wish to begin at the beginning, we must first know something of the people and the land where he evolved.

The Matin has either been a type rather than a breed—or a breed without type. This 1750 engraving by Moitte from a drawing by DeSeve is from *Buffon's Natural History* published in Paris. From the editor's collection.

The low countries, Holland and Belgium, are small. Together they are less than half the size of New York state—with about 11% more population (22.2 million). They comprise one of the most densely populated places on earth. The area is intensively farmed but as in most industrial-commercial societies the percentage of the work force in agriculture has been declining steadily since about 1930. Today in Belgium, for example, only about one in twenty of the work force is farming, even though farms occupy about 53% of the land area. This decline in the number of farm families has resulted in a proportionate decrease in the number of farm dogs. Some native types which survived the two world wars have either failed or are failing to survive modern agricultural technology. Only those breeds, such as the Bouvier, which have been adopted and popularized by show-minded enthusiasts have prospered.

Belgium is a country where two of Europe's ancient cultures, Germanic and Gaelic, meet. It has four languages and as many sub-cultures. The official government figures show 3,130,000 Walloons living in the southern provinces bordering France and speaking their variation of the French language, about 1,080,000 urbane Belgians living in the Brussels area and speaking a purer French, 61,000

This is the Matin as it was depicted in Eugene Gayot's 1867 Paris book, *Le Chien Histoire Naturelle*. From the editor's collection.

This more modern Matin was portrayed in *Toepoel's Honden Encyclopaedie*, published in Amsterdam, circa 1950. From the editor's collection.

The "Matin Belge" has been found in a variety of coats. He has also been known as "le chien de trait." From the collection of Miss Edmee Bowles.

Also from Gayot's *Le Chien* of 1867, another variation of the Matin, Obviously the breed served bakers as well as dairymen. From the editor's collection.

German-speaking people living along the German border, and 5,374,-000 residents of the Flemish provinces of West Vlaanderen and Oost (East) Vlaanderen where the language is a minor variation of Dutch.

The Flemings comprise about 55% of the Belgian population but, because the international boundary was drawn on religious rather than ethnic lines, they also populate the Dutch province of Zeeland. Brugge is the capital of West Vlaanderen, Ghent of Oost Vlaanderen and Middleburg of Zeeland. Ghent is easily the largest of the three.

Flanders' buffer-area status and its strategic military and economic value have made a battleground of the territory since prehistoric times. Through the centuries the Flemings have, as fiercely as necessary, persisted in preserving their language, customs, liberty and identity. They have survived Caesar and the Romans, invasions by Teutonic tribes and Islamic forces, governments of the Franks, Charlemagne and the Holy Roman Empire, and further invasions by Norsemen. They have endured rule of varying oppressiveness by the Burgundians, the French, Austrian and Spanish princes.

The sum of these brought Belgium to what it calls "The Century of Misfortune," 1621–1715. For those 95 years the country was a battlefield between the Hapsburgs and the Bourbons. Between 1715 and

16

1792 Austrian Emperors ruled through governors. There followed two years of independence before the French revolutionaries annexed Belgium in 1794. That occupation ended with Napoleon's disaster in Russia. But then he came back to spill more blood at Waterloo, about eight miles south of Brussels.

For the next 15 years Belgium was a part of the United Kingdom of the Netherlands. But there were religious and other differences and the Kingdom of Belgium was proclaimed on October 4, 1830. There followed nearly a century of neutrality, but this was violated by the German armies in 1914. Belgium again became the world's bloodiest battleground. In 1940 Hitler invaded. Again Belgium fought a delaying action and lost many men before accepting occupation. The German regime brought extreme privation and terror.

The Belgian underground undermined the Nazi rulers until the Allied armies arrived in 1944. Once again Belgium became a bloody battleground as the stubborn Nazis were fought back beyond their own borders.

The Flemings are proud and enduring, hard working and peaceful, but fierce when aroused. They are responsible and resourceful with an extremely strong sense of territory. And, that is also a rather accurate description of the dog they developed—the Bouvier des Flandres!

It is not surprising that a people and their dogs should be so similar in basic characteristics. The land makes the same demands of both.

The Flemings did not create the Bouvier by design. They had needs which they tried to fill, one breeding at a time, one puppy selection at a time, over a period of centuries.

Belgians are a practical people with practical dogs. In this rare World War I photo, a four-dog team draws a gun carriage as part of a "cart," which seems improvised from bicycle parts. The chest over the front axle probably carried the shells. From the collection of the late Janet W. Mack.

When war comes to Belgians all of their resources are utilized to repel the invaders. Here is a dog-drawn World War I ambulance cart. Note the dog's cobby body and his blocky head. he seems an intermediary between the Matin and the Bouvier. From the collection of the late Janet W. Mack.

Farmers are not ordinarily sentimental about animals. How can they be when they raise so many to be butchered as cash crops? In a sense farm dogs are both hired hands and animals. As hired hands they must earn their keep. As animals they are expendable if they do not. Selection is practical, harsh, *and effective.*

Farmers cannot afford to support overly specialized breeds of dogs. On almost any family farm, anywhere, a dog must be whatever he is needed to be. In Flanders he has had to be effective as a guard dog, watch dog, herder, drover, cart puller, butter churner, vermin eliminator—and family companion. With all of that he has had to be hardy enough to live outdoors in all kinds of weather. Again, that is a pretty good description of the Bouvier!

If we are to deal properly with the history of the Bouvier as a "breed" we must first explore a concept little known to the world of dog shows. Until quite recent times virtually all Bouvier breeders selected only for performance qualities, not appearance factors. They were interested in what a dog could do and what was in his head and heart—and not very much in what he looked like. Thus while the Bouvier has a long and honorable history, he entered this century without that uniformity of appearance which dog show folks refer to as "type." His genetics were pure for what he could do and mixed for size and color, length and texture of coat.

This concept might be easier to understand if an analogous situation is cited. Over the world there are several Border Collie registries. All but one of them require a working certificate for both sire and dam before a puppy can be registered. The breed standard is performance and there is no written appearance standard. (The exception is a tangential group of admirers seeking American Kennel Club recognition for the breed.) Most Border Collie breeders believe a conformation standard could only serve to deemphasize working qualities.

However, when priorities *must* be assigned, survival must supercede an effort to achieve perfection. As we have seen, the Bouvier would probably be as extinct today as are some of the other "breed types" of the area if dedicated "show" breeders had not at great personal sacrifice brought a few of the best specimens through two devastating wars.

Instead of being hitched in pairs these cart dogs are harnessed four abreast to haul this Belgian merchant's cart. Note the lantern for night driving. It must have been a hot day for these Matin-type dogs. The proprietor's clothing places the photo in the World War I era. From the collection of the late Janet W. Mack.

After their first appearances at dog shows very early in this century Bouviers became a minor sensation. Admirers began combing Flemish farmlands all of the way to the North Sea in searches for breeding stock. What they found was variety insofar as appearance was concerned. Using the word in another sense, they found several "types" of Chien de Bouvier, literally, in French, "dog of the herdsman."

As dog shows gained popularity early in this century prideful Belgians were anxious to discover admirable native breeds—and they did. But this effort involved them in the differences between "breed" and "type". Because they didn't understand the differences (Genetics was only in its beginnings as a science) they were understandably inclined to label "types" as "breeds." Littermates of dissimilar appearance could acquire equally dissimilar "breed" designations. International borders and national prides further complicated the nomenclature procedure. One result was that a regional, functional "type" was sorted out into several breeds.

The world's greatest dog registries still do not agree upon a definition of the term "breed." Most of them were "locked in" on their definitions and concepts before genetics became a viable field of study. If the early show enthusiasts introduced some confusion by designating "types" as "breeds" it is forgivable. But if we wish to understand the Bouvier's history we should have our own look at the situation.

It would probably be close to the truth to surmise that the first breeders of the modern Bouvier selected from a regional, functional "type," individuals of similar appearance and size; then through careful breeding, fixed those appearance and temperament factors most important to them. The result has been an animal which is now a "breed" by *anyone's* definition. That animal is the Bouvier we know and treasure today.

Some of the other "types" failed to survive the two world wars because they lacked supporters willing to make the considerable sacrifices necessary to carry breeding stock through periods of battle-ground devastation interspersed with longer intervals of hunger and privation under enemy occupation. Because the Bouvier had won the loyalties of a band of dedicated breeders the Bouvier survived— and eventually prospered.

The Bouvier fared better in Holland during the first World War because of that country's neutrality. Hitler's Nazis of World War

In the photo at top another Matin-type dog is hitched to a rather heavily-laden milk cart with big, iron-banded wooden wheels. At bottom another of the Matin-type is hitched to the Count de T'Serclaes' riding cart. From the collection of the late Janet W. Mack.

II devastated all of the Bouvier's homeland — Holland, Belgium and northern France.

That is our own, historian's, overview. It is not necessary — and probably not even desirable — that historians agree.

Specific history must be pieced together from surviving documents and photos and from incomplete published articles. Again, the wars destroyed much documentation.

Helpful is a pre-World War article in the Flemish magazine *Culture* by L. Huygebaert. So are later articles in another Belgian magazine, *L'Aboi*. Some of those who wrote on the Bouvier for *L'Aboi* were Messrs Charles Huge, A. Gevaert and Dr. Domicent. Before World War II Messrs Wolfs and Meyer wrote of the Bouvier in Dutch dog journals. Later D. W. van Brouwershaven did the same. The sporting magazine, *Chasse et Peche,* had an interested editor and carried more than any other publication of the time about the Bouvier. The French, *L'Eleveur,* also carried important Bouvier references. This use of three languages — beyond English — has also made research into Bouvier history difficult.

Huygebaert stated he drew many of his early historical references from Charles Estienne's *L'Agriculture et Maison Rustique,* first published in Paris in 1564. (Richard Surflet published an English translation in 1600.) Third and succeeding editions, including that from which M. Huygebaert worked, were co-authored by J. Liebault and J. De Clamorgan and appeared from 1574 on. The author and editor have here amplified some of the points in Miss Bowles' translation.

The word "Bouvier" is French. Many Flemings are bilingual, and especially in the border areas the Flemish and French languages are intermingled. Estienne wrote: "French was spoken especially in regard to all the 'venerie,' hunted animals, horses, cattle and dogs." In Flemish the equivalent of Bouvier would be "Koehond" or "Veedryver."

The Bouvier (our word "bovine," describing cattle, has the same Latin derivation) was a herdsman who cared for the cows and who also drove the oxcart. Therefore the dog he developed to guard and herd cows became the "Chien de Bouvier" or dog of the herdsman. The sheepdog was called "Chien de Berger" or dog of the sheepherder. The terms have been shortened to Bouvier and Berger.

Some of the Bouvier des Flandres' ancestors became known as

"Pics." For this there are two available explanations. Cattle were raised in Picardie and driven by dogs to the lush Flemish meadows. Thus it could be that because of such commercial relations between the Flanders area and Picardie these dogs became known as Picards, or Pics as a contraction. "Pic," meaning sharp-pointed, or "Picard" for harsh hair offers the alternative explanation. The word, "Bouvier," to describe dogs of this function is not encountered until 18th century writings.

In the Middle Ages "Picards," "Bergeots" and "Matins" were designations the French used for dogs used in driving, guarding and defending cattle. (Marauders included medieval rustlers and dry gulchers—even wild dog packs, lynx, wolves and bears.) The modern Bouvier des Flandres evolved from these dogs.[1] All Belgian working breeds probably trace back to the original Matins which continues as a breed—or type—in Europe. Of course it cannot be presumed today's Matin is the same as the Matin of the Middle Ages. He, too, has evolved through hundreds of dog generations.

It became a practice as far back as the 18th century to cut off the tail and to trim back the ears of guard dogs. Since these appendages were the most vulnerable in encounters with predators they were reduced to near minimums by owners since it was a virtual certainty they would otherwise be lost in encounters far from home and cauterizing materials.[2]

During the early development of the Bouvier it was customary for the head of a household to keep three kinds of dogs. The guard

---

1. Such distinctions might be too finely drawn. A sheepdog and a herding dog might come from a single litter and develop according to each dog's individual talents and the needs of the owners.
2. This is the usual explanation for the docking of ears. There is another, probably much more valid. Drop-eared dogs are prone to infections induced by ear mites which thrive best in warm humid environments. Until very recent times the best available treatment was to trim the ears back so air could circulate within the ear. This reduced the incidence of infection and promoted healing. A third reason for ear triming continues to be the belief by many breeders and owners that prick ears make a dog look more alert, more intimidating and give him "more character." A dog's tail is almost never an object of attack whether the fight is with another dog or with a predator. A tail *is* subject to injury in heavy brush and on a long-haired dog it can become a liability when laden with burrs. A dock-tailed dog loses enough of his balance to slow him a bit. Docking and ear trimming is illegal in some states. Continued practice is probably attributable to owner preference and tradition.

In the Count de Buffon's *Histoire Naturelle* of 1750 this is the way the Chien de Berger was portrayed. In the circa 1825 print below the dog was described both as "le chien de berger" and as "le matin" as if the terms were entirely interchangeable. From the editor's collection.

dog was used to protect life and property against ambushes; the Chien de Berger was used to resist predators and to manage the flock or herd. The third type was a hunting dog.[3]

The dogs destined to guard were large, (truly massive) short of body with great heads and with short, heavy necks. Their muzzles were deep, their jaws powerful. Their eyes were dark and fiery, their ears hairy and sometimes cut. They had wide chests, clublike paws. Tails were short and thick, bespeaking power. Their voices were loud and deep enough to intimidate. They were dark, presumably because they would appear more menacing by day and difficult targets by night. By nature they were ordinarily sedate. They were good watchdogs.

Only torches could provide any significant amount of light outdoors on feudal nights. The realities of the times imposed a curfew. Guard dogs enforced the curfew. By day they were kept penned or tied, often in pairs. They were released after dark to guard the manor or village. This rural police duty was left to the biggest, most powerful dogs, preference being given to those inspiring the most fear because of their appearance.

The lord, the master of the land or "baas" which meant "master" in Flemish, owned at that time, large and small herds of sheep and cattle. Their herding dogs were of many different types. Owners didn't care a great deal about looks, just that the dogs did their jobs well.

Along the two Flanders, from Antwerp to Amsterdam, from Rueben to Brabant, here and there arose a dog different from the common shepherd or sheepdog; different from the cross-breeds that were seen in the cities, and much admired and desired by their owners for their temperament and abilities. These dogs were sought out as sires and reproduced abundantly.

---

3. It appears the true situation has been misinterpreted. During feudal times—and even much later—all of the game belonged to the king or the ruling prince. Some of the highest nobility was permitted to hunt by specific license from the ruler. Penalities for poaching were extremely severe, and the lower the station of the offender, the harsher the penalty. Ownership of a hunting dog was either by royal sufferance or at extreme risk to person and purse. Cowherds were, themselves, bound to the lord and manor in feudal times and can hardly be thought of as "heads of households" as the term is used here. Some emperors, kings and other high nobility had hundreds, even thousands of hunting dogs, and guard dogs suitable for war duties, but cowherds would be fortunate if they could maintain a single dog to help them with their work.

Depicted in a miniature of a 14th century French manuscript are two Matin types wearing spiked collars and fighting wolves. They are massive headed and harsh coated. In all available illustrations early guard dogs resembled the Matins with their overall appearance of roughness with emphasis on bulk and wiry coat.

The sheep dog of this area was not as large nor as massive as the guard dog, but it was a strong, robust animal capable of speed and was used to fight and pursue wolves. People had great fear of wolves at that time and this fear was made worse by the tales told about them. The sheep dog was generally bred to be white so that it could be distinguished from the wolves, and in the belief that it would not frighten the sheep as easily.

With the Matin as the forerunner of the Bouvier, and the "Berger", it should be pointed out that not all Matins had harsh coats. Some were short coated while others had long coats. Dogs tending sheep as well as dogs accompanying ox-drivers or cattle herdsmen varied in outward appearance. Their basic skeletons were rather uniform. Bouvier heads can be recognized in paintings dating as far back as 1827.

A dog with certain Bouvier characteristics is seen in a very rare work by the artist Henry Barnard Chalen who dedicated a series of six lithographs on "The Passions of the Horse" to England's George the Fourth. In plate number four title "Affection" is a dog very much

Guyot's 1867 book described this as "Le chien du berger, petite race"—which can be translated as small type shepherd's dog. There is little difference between this and Buffon's Chien du Berger of 1750. From the editor's collection.

like that described by "Ouida" in her story of 1907, "A Dog of Flanders". It therefore seems possible that dogs evolved or changed little during this time. Chalen's dog has the erect standing small ears of a Bouvier, probably natural rather than cosmetic, a head with the Bouvier's shallow stop, but not the coat of the breed as we know it today. He is of correct size, and while more or less sleek-coated, his thick tail is feathered and he has the bone and substance of a guard dog rather than that of the hunting or racing dog. This dog seems a Bouvier ancestral type.

In the book "Les Races de Chiens" of 1894, a collection of articles previously published by Professor Reul in a veterinary journal and widely accepted during the 1890's as a standard reference on dogs, pleaded the case of the "Belgian Sheepdog" and mentioned the Bouvier. Professor Reul said of the Bouvier, "The cattle dog is for the most part a shepherd dog, or a dog that resembles him in general make-up, but who is bigger, fiercer, more aggressive and has a bolder look."

It is possible to study the works of Flemish painters in the Royal Museum in Antwerp, Belgium. One by Carl Roethard (circa 1650) depicts bear hunting and fighting with a variety of dogs. One type is a rusty brown, harsh-coated dog. Similar dogs are often found in hunting scenes by P. P. Rubens, Jan Fyt, Frans Snyders and Paul Devon. A close relationship between them, the sheep dog and the Bouvier can be seen in Jan Fyt's painting, of "Hunting the Wild Boars" in the Brussels Museum. Fyt lived 1611–1661. Some of these were rough-coated, biting hounds and sheep dogs. The rest closely resembled Bouviers. They were used by noblemen for hunting, and by butchers and other businessmen as guardians of property.

The Dutch painter, Paulus Potter (1625–1654) also painted crossbred Matins and sheep dogs from which it is thought the Bouvier evolved in primitive form. Potter also depicted one of these dogs, chained to a rustic kennel. It appears to be half Greyhound and half sheepdog.

It is sometimes suggested the Matin was crossed to the Scottish Greyhound to gain an even harsher coat for the guard dogs and Matins. The term "Greyhound" was used at that time to describe all sight hunting dogs and the large Scottish Deerhound was used rather than the Russian Wolfhound (Borzoi) or the Greyhound.

Artist Ealaisse who did many of the illustrations for Guyot's *Le Chien* in 1867 might have entitled this "The Discreet Beggars." The dogs are described by name and breed. At left is Polisson, a variety of the Brie shepherds' dog. Charmante is a "chienne de Brie"—a Brie bitch. From the editor's collection.

All varieties of dogs, including the large and small harsh-coated Otterhounds (of which no purebred specimen remains in Belgium), and the harsh- and rough-coated Barbet, (or in Flemish, *Poedelhonden* . . . poodle) had places in early domains. Greyhounds were used to pursue and attack game and predators. Barbets pursued and retrieved anything found in the country, rivers and ponds.

Characteristics of dogs chosen for the hunt are shown in a painting by Carl Roethard where one of the larger, short-bodied, big-headed Matins is taking part in a mythological hunt, "Atalande et Meleagre." This painting, in the Royal Museum at Antwerp, is also called "Chase de Calydon". Roethard depicted a powerful Bouvier type, although the coat and expression is reminiscent of the Briard. This painting suggests the Briard and Bouvier had similar ancestors. This will be explored further on.

It has been surmised that the harsh texture of Bouvier coats may have come from a Matin—Scottish Deerhound cross. It must also be understood that even though dogs were bred for specific purposes there must have been many unplanned crossings due to the crowded, informal kenneling.

While these dogs flourished for centuries in Flemish and French Flanders, in the hunting houses of the Duke of Brabant at Boitsfort and in the forest of Soignes, near Brussels, they spread no farther until much later.

In Flanders the monks of the numerous abbeys crossed the Matins with the Scottish Deerhounds and developed the Bouvier. These abbeys were mostly in desolate and lonely places where powerful, trustworthy guard dogs were needed.

It is generally accepted that the monks of St. Hubert in the Ardennes developed the Bloodhound and the Cisterciens or St. Bernards in the Alps of Switzerland, developed the St. Bernard and gave their names to their breeds. If the Bouvier does not have a patron Saint it may be because he played such a democratic role. Nevertheless, the first breeders of the Bouviers were the monks who founded the powerful Abbey of Duynen on the west coast of Flanders near Coxyde.

The honorary archivist of the town of Furnes, a lawyer named P. de Grave, gives the following information:

> The Abbey of Duynen was founded in 1107. The original buildings were destroyed by the Gueux, heretics of 1566, and later again by the Calvinists in 1577. They were demolished again in 1590 and again in 1593 after which the monks left the region only to return in 1601. This time they settled on the Bogaerts farm, parts of which are still in existence. One turret records a date of reconstruction as 1612.

Over the gates of the dwellings is displayed the coat of arms, and these gates are situated next to what may be the oldest kennel still in existence.

The farm was vast, at least 20,000 acres, and the monks exported significant parts of their crops to England. In 1237 King Henry III authorized the Abbey of Duynen to build wharfs, a fact which offers an insight into the size of the monks' commerce with England. It's probable this maritime commerce dates the monks' importation of Scottish Deerhounds and other breeds of dogs.[4]

---

4. It is just as possible that the dog used was the Irish Wolfhound, a favorite diplomatic gift of English kings.

This is the dog described by Guyot in 1867 as "Chien de Berger (grande race.) He apparently felt there were two distinct size variations, small and large. From the editor's collection.

The Dukes of Burgundy were also importing English dogs, usually hunting dogs. It is a rather ancient custom for royalty and men of rank and importance to exchange gifts of dogs.[5] High clergy had privileges often denied nobility. The Abbot of Duynen must have hunted his own vast forests as well as those of his peers in the hierarchy—as at the Abbey of St. Hubert in the Ardennes.

In an 18th century exchange of letters the Abbot of St. Hubert advised French King Louis XV to import Greyhounds from England to infuse into the St. Hubert Hounds. The Greyhound-Matin cross was more regional. No record is known of Belgian breeds being sent to England but such exports were almost certainly made. If they left any lasting imprint on the British breeds documentation is lacking. Certainly French breeds, strains and types were exploited by English breeders.

Not far from the ancient Duynen site the Bogaerts farm still stands completely surrounded by walls. There is a sort of watchtower, and a kennel which has been reliably dated as 13th century.

A bulletin of the Historical and Archeological Society of Ghent in 1904 indicating the proportions, architectual lines and material undoubtedly prove the age of this kennel as the thirteenth century.

In Flemish, the archway spanning this wall is called "moeffen"

5. Lafayette presented George Washington with fine hounds which, in part, helped to found the modern American Foxhound.

which means "cover". There is a gable inside and outside which is of interest archeologically and is also of utilitarian value. Inside this sort of fortification there were some slits through which the watch and guard dogs could scent hear and see to give the alarm to other dogs and to the monks. The sentry dogs could climb the slanting sides of the kennel to get on the top of the wide wall. The wear on the hard stone caused by the heavy chains with which the dogs were tied indicates these must have been powerful and watchful dogs. This was a job to which a dog like the Bouvier-type dog was well suited.

The French artists Desportes (1661–1743) and J. B. Oudry (1686–1755) painted many dogs. The latter was commissioned by Louis XV to immortalize hunts in which the king and his court ladies indulged, some with their Bichon lap dogs. Oudry illustrated the *"Fables of Fontaine"* in which the animals speak by action and expression and for which he was nicknamed "La Fontaine."[6] Oudry, painter to the king, was a careful and appreciative student of nature. He was professor at the Royal School of Painting and was commissioned to design the famous tapestries of Beauvais and Gobelins. Dogs painted by Oudry were authentic portraits. A favorite subject was the Matin, known ancestor of the Bouvier. Of the two Matin types, one was a smooth-coated dog with cropped ears, the other a rough-coated dog with hanging ears. Both types are depicted with spiked collars. Oudry depicts a dog with a smooth coat and thin tail killing a wolf that had attacked a defenseless peasant mother and child. Not true to life, but dramatic. Another Oudry painting depicts a rough-coated dog with a broad skull and short, smooth muzzle. It has a big shaggy tail which could come from a Briard cross. This dog could be an intermediary breeding of the Mastiff and the Bouvier or "Picards" from the French or Flemish Flanders and neighboring countries. Oudry dogs show both Matin and Briard heads. The differences in shape and coat can be clearly seen.

In Flanders, especially around Courtrai, the bleaching of flax for Flemish spinning mills was a most important industry. An advantage was the purity of the waters in the La Lys river and its surrounding meadows. The products of these mills not only appeared on the tables of the rich, but the townships offered them to dukes, clergy, and other people of importance. There are 17th century chronicles of the mayor

---

6. The Fables of La Fontaine is a French version, in poetry, of Aesops Fables.

of Courtrai presenting seventeen pairs of Damask linen tablecloths to King Albert and Isabella when they entered Courtrai on February 3, 1600. A good dog was necessary to guard valuable products such as these.

Dogs of the times also had less noble tasks such as smuggling goods. Guardians or smugglers, the dogs were much like the Bouvier and the heavy-coated Briard. The Briard originated east of Paris in the French region of "de Brie". Similar dogs were found in Belgium.

An accurate description of the Briard was given by Professor Reul in 1891, the year of the first dog show. He described them as being more or less pure silver grey with a blue tinge, double dew claws and very alert. Pierre Megnin, father of the director of "L'Eleveur", in Paris, described the Briard as a cross of the "chien de Berger" or "Beauce" or short coated sheepdog and the Barbet, or water dog.

Measurements of the Briard and the "Beauce" are generally the same. Many fanciers consider Briards to be of Belgian origin because they were there for so long.

At an exhibit in 1876 the French painter, Leon Hermann, was lauded for his painting of a shepherd near the sea with his two dogs.

An etching after Leon Hermann by C. W. Coutry indicates the artist did more than one painting on the shepherd dog theme. The dogs depicted in his "Evening Star" are either Bouviers, or Bouvier ancestoral types. The engraving was published Jan. 1, 1868 by A. Delorus, 68 rue J.J. Rousseau. From the Horowitz collection.

In the foreground is a long-haired dog lying quietly at the shepherd's feet and looking straight ahead. It is undoubtably a Briard type. The other dog, harsh-coated with a Bouvier head, stands intently watching a flock of grazing sheep.

The geographical location of Picardie, home of the Briard and its forerunner the Picard, next to Flanders on one side and the sea on the other, lent itself to the easy crossing, and the development of the Bouvier. This area was well known for its horses and cattle, which increased the demand for powerful dogs on the farms. They were needed to furnish power for spinning mills and for churns. They gave customs officials "muscle" and pulled carts among other duties.

Documentation of the Bouvier origin is fragmentary. Most of the information from this point has come from a French director of customs who had been contacted by the late F. E. Verbanck, a famed

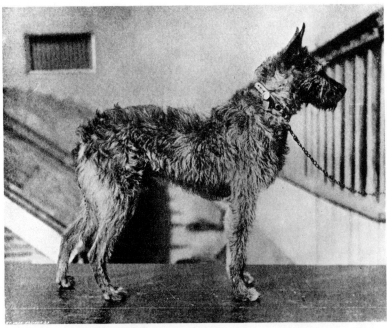

This photo of Fram from *Chasse et Pêche* via De Bylandt's 1905 *Dogs of All Nations* is proof that at the turn of the century there were Bouviers that could conform rather well to today's standards for the Bouvier des Flandres. Fram was owned by J. Jochmann of Utrecht. From the editor's collection.

breeder of Bouviers from Ghent. In letters the officer stated many records were lost during World War I. All that was found was a report of a sheepdog (Berger) and a Griffon mix and its accomplishments in about six years of service with the customs department. During this period the dog, working with its officer-master, captured about four hundred dogs being used by smugglers, many with merchandise on their backs, going alone or lying low in the woods. This dog discovered many hiding places for smuggled goods and inspired fear in the smugglers. He was described as a massive, powerful dog. In 1902 and 1903 this same dog obtained several prizes at the shows of Roubaix and Lille, but his name has not been successfully researched.

The name "berger-griffon" used to describe this dog may seem peculiar to many people but it was appropriate in terms of Bouvier evolution at the turn of the century.

Under the name of "Griffon," which in France is used for a hunting dog with a harsh coat and a large amount of Barbet or water dog blood, dogs were crossed for twenty years with sheepdogs and Picards. Confirmation of these crossings comes from an 1899 report by the well-known Dutch Griffon breeder, G. F. Leliman.

According to German authors, the Barbet or waterdog, was obtained by crossing a long haired sheep dog with a medium sized hunting dog, or "Treibhund". Leliman draws attention to the first pedigreed harsh-

From the "atlas" to Guyot's *Le Chien,* Paris, 1867, comes this engraving of "Les griffons d'arret francais"—literaly rough-coated French dogs of stop—or rough-coated French pointing dogs. A cobby body type would have to come from another source but the coat is inescapably similar to that of the Bouvier. From the editor's collection.

coated hunting dogs raised in Germany by the Dutchman, E. K. Korthals, which were shown in Frankfort in 1878. "But," says Leliman, "These dogs, Moustach I, Lina, Querida and Tampa, were French, as the catalog class name 'Griffons a Poil dur'[7] indicated. However, these dogs of Korthals came from Holland, Germany, and probably Belgium and France. In Holland, even now in the Drenthe, there are Griffons exactly the type of 'Mouche,' Korthals' first bitch, who was

7. An enthusiastic but erroneous conclusion, this illustrates how easy it is for breed histories to drift into fiction.

A Dutch herding dog, Trotteur, posed with his owner, J. Westerwoudt of Baarn for this turn of the century photo. Reprinted from *Hondenrassen*, a two-volume dog encyclopedia by L. Seegers, published in Amsterdam, 1912. From the Gerace collection.

one of the seven purebreds of 'Imperwoud'. They could just as well have originated in Hesse or Bruswick . . . their origin is unknown."

If writers of all nationalities are unable to give precise origin to the Griffons of Korthals, or Korthals Griffons as they are known today,[8] it is no wonder they can do no better for the Bouviers.

Like needs and climates can produce very similar dog breeds. When this phenomenon occurs in nature scientists call it parallel but separate development. In virtually every European country there have existed for centuries sheepdogs with long, harsh hair. Any or several of these could have been ancestors of the Belgian (small letter) bouvier. Wars and commerce brought many nationalities to and through Belgian and French Flanders and Dutch Zeeland. Herding dogs which might have been called Bouviers might have been introduced from Roulers or from Ardennes. Even Riezenschnauzers (Giant Schnauzers) from the mountainous country to the west might have made genetic contributions. To assign frontiers to the Bouvier is impossible.

Belgians have been successful, creative breeders for many centuries. Their horses and other livestock give ample testimony to their skills. In dogs they seem to have particular talents for breeding, selecting and training.

Early in the 20th century two Flemish breeders near La Lys, Paret and Moerman, deliberately set out to purify the Belgian bouvier. They, and other breeders, used sheepdogs, Matins and mixed breeds.

8. In the U.S. they are known as Wirehaired Pointing Griffons.

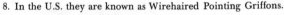

Belgian customs officers with their dogs, about 1900. Photo reproduced from Toepoel's *Honden Encyclopaedia*. Those at left and right seem to be Bouvier types. From the editor's collection.

This is recorded in the catalog of the St. Hubert Club of the North (France) for the fourth international show held at Roubais in 1905. Depicted on the cover is a customs officer leading a muzzled sheepdog. Only working dogs listed in the control books of the customs officers were eligible for showing.

Of the 43 dogs entered, 14 were short-coated. Here's the way the ten males in Open Class 237 were listed and described:[9]

441	Cartouche	brindle, white on chest, whelped 8/6/1903 out of Coco.
442	Marquis	russet fawn, June 1900, out of Turc and Sophie
443	Garcon	black, white chest, April 21, 1902 out of Gros and Lisette
444	Mousse	light gray, April 1904, out of Turc and Marquise
445	Finard	steel gray, April 1904
446	Picard	gray brindle, long hair on back and muzzle, July 16, 1903, out of Picard and Comtesse
447	Matelet	April 10, 1903
448	Brutus	brindle, March 1904
449	Compagnon	fawn, 5½ years old out of Turc and Lisette
450	Turc	steel gray, white chest, April 1903 out of Leon and Lisette

Open Class   238 included these six females:

| 451 | Marquise | steel gray, 9 years old, Prize of honor taken at Lille 1904 |
| 452 | Diana | dark chestnut, 9 years old, out of Turc and Diane |

9. Historian Huygebaert noted he was unable to reconcile sires, dams and dates of these entries as given. There are two possible explanations, both of which may be valid. Early registrations were often based upon recollection rather than records. Also, geographical areas often use favorite names for dogs. (In the U.S. these have been Rex, Prince, King and Queenie.) For example, the Lisette that whelped Compagon in 1899 might have been quite another Lisette than the entered bitch of the same name showing a whelping date of 1901.

453	Mirza	Reddish black, white chest Feb. 1904 (See 1912 photo.)
454	Lisette	gray brindle, black muzzle, Oct. 1901, out of Baron and Lionne
455	Blanche	gray muzzle with black hair, white feet, May 14, 1902 Silver medal of the Club St. Hubert.
456	Mandat	gray brindle, Dec. 1901, out of Brutus and Fatma.

Unfortunately no good photograph has been found of the entered Picard,[10] with his silver-gray, long harsh coat on his back and muzzle. His sire, also Picard, was probably one of the unknown ancestors of the Bouviers in the Paret and Moerman family. All these dogs had crosses of the sheepdog and Matin in them. Later, even after the creation of pedigrees and the Book of Origins (LOSH), in litters from "purebred" parents there were puppies similar to these harsh-coated crossbreds.

At first, and for apparent good reasons, pups with obvious faults such as spots on chests and feet were eliminated so as not to mar the reputation of their litter-mates. Some breeders, however, realized that in doing this they were also destroying some very good qualities which were needed.

In his 1905 *Dogs of All Nations* Count Henri DeBylandt noted that there were French and Belgian types of the "Chien Bouvier." Even at that early date he treated them as distinct from the "Chien de Brie" or Briard. Here are the points of the breed as he published them at the turn of the century in the same year during which the first Bouvier competition took place.

Chien de Bouvier
FRENCH CATTLE DOG.

General appearance. A strong dog, with a somewhat savage appearance, well coated with rough and hard hair. **Head.** Well made,

10. See the 1912 photo of the Bouviers exhibited at Brussels in June, 1912. The Mirza at that show may, or may not, be the same Mirza in the first recorded, 1905, Bouvier exhibition. She would have been, if the same, nine years old at Brussels. She probably is not the Mirza appearing in Betty de la Lys' pedigree on a subsequent page in this chapter. That Mirza shows a different owner — although she could have been sold. Show-minded enthusiasts were aggressively buying breeding stock during that period. Ed.

longish; muzzle not too short; skull broad and rounded. **Eyes.**
Rather small, piercing and intelligent; colour dark brown. **Nose.**
Always black. **Ears.** Erect and small. **Teeth.** Very strong and meeting evenly. **Neck.** Strong and well muscled. **Body.** Well built,
strong and elegant. **Legs.** Well boned, straight and muscular.
Feet. Strong. **Tail.** Bushy, of medium length; carried upwards but
not over the back. **Coat.** Rather long and of a good hard texture,
sometimes shorter, but profusely coated all over. **Colour.** Black,
dark tawny, or a black saddle and dirty brown on legs, belly and
underside of tail. **Height at shoulder.** From 25½ to 29½ inches.
Weight. From 65 to 75 lb.

Monsieur Paret, the Bouvier fancier of Ghent, is justly considered
to have established the foundation bloodlines of our present day Bouviers. In 1943 Mr. L. Huygebaert wrote:

> I have had the personal pleasure to judge the sire Rex (RSH
> 1766) and the dam Nelly (RSH 1892), both shown at the Inter-
> national in Brussels on May 21–23, 1910, at the Cinquantenaire
> Park, organized by the Societe Royal Saint Hubert. The Bouviers
> are only represented by two dogs. I rejoice to see this breed rep-
> resented by so few. The Bouviers are not show dogs and will not
> gain by shows when one sees what happens to native breeds. I
> only hope they will stay away from shows as long as possible. I
> remember the humiliating asterisk still placed next to the variety
> of Bouviers in the official catalogues (1927) of the new indigenous
> sheepdogs—being of too lowly origin to find a place in the stud
> books—and these were the 'gothas' of dogs. Since then our sheep-
> dogs have found a place and different types are now recognized.
> Certainly these are fine results, but alas, how many poor ones as to
> character and temperament are to be found in the shows? Let this
> be a lesson to Bouvier fanciers. If they are bent to show let there
> be no exaggerations and retain the true character of the breed and
> type of the breed. The temperament is excellent. Just look at the
> eye of Rex and Nelly. Rex is by far the better of the two—he is
> more typey. Nelly has more of the Sheepdog expression. As I
> have said at the show in Amsterdam in 1909, I repeat; the Bouvier
> should look gruff and rustic—he should be a block, not something
> elegant. I do not know whether I was right. The fact is in 1910 the
> Bouviers and different types of sheepdogs were not well-defined
> yet, but it is due to the perserverance of L. Paret with the good
> councils of the editor of *Chasse et Peche*, that finally the Bouviers
> became taken seriously. A French magazine, *L'Eleveur* drew the

attention of foreign fanciers and specializing clubs became interested."

After 1910 two tendencies were seen. The small Bouviers with natural standing ears and short tail were called, for awhile, "bergeot" by the Walloons of the Wallonie district and later called the Bouvier d'Ardennes. Concurrently with this small Bouvier, there was a larger Bouvier, one having more Matin blood. This one immediately became the more popular and also became known by different names: Bouvier de Roulers, Belgian Bouvier, or French Bouvier of Flandres.

The Bouvier d'Ardennes might as well be called the little Bouvier. He is an intermediary between the sheepdog which is relatively longer and the cobby Matin-type Bouvier. The Bouvier d'Ardennes' naturally standing uncropped ears mark him unlike other Bouviers. This characteristic suggests a closer relationship to the harsh-coated sheepdog. It was thought at the time that this Bouvier would prevail and become better known in the area for its grand cattle-driving and cart-pulling abilities.

A description of the Bouvier d'Ardennes appeared in the 1947 book, *Working Dogs of the World* by Clifford L. B. Hubbard:

> The head is moderate in breadth, and of fair length with little stop. The eyes are dark and medium in size; the ears rather small and erect. The body is rather square with a strong level back, deep chest and muscular loins. The legs are of medium length and rather heavy in bone, with round medium feet; the tail is of full natural length, set low and carried low to the hocks, usually with

A Bouvier d'Ardennes of 1913. Reproduced from Toepoel's *Honden Encyclopaedia.* From the editor's collection.

40

Boer-Sus was described as a Belgian Sheepdog in *Chasse et Pêche* and Count Henri de Bylandt's *Dogs of All Nations*, 1905. The owner was Hautôt of Brussels. From the editor's collection.

a slight final curl upward. The coat is fairly short on the head and legs, and medium on the neck, flanks, back and hindquarters, and dense, rough and shaggy. The colours vary from all black to light gray, with the darker grays flecked with black and being fairly common. Light brindles and grays with white points are also occasionally found. The height is generally about 22 inches.

The year 1910 was an unfavorable time for the development of cattle dogs and other farm dogs. These dogs were no longer a necessity as the townpeople were following the fashions. A revival was seen for police dog usage, and sought was a larger, heavier dog which would inspire more respect. The Bouvier d'Ardennes was superceded by the Bouvier de Roulers which was more massive and whose height was 27½ inches. It was accepted in a meeting held in Roulers in 1912. Here is an extract from an article published in 1912 and written by Vital Taeymans:

> The Roeselaersche Hondenclub has decided to study and discuss the propositions of the veterinarian, Dr. Louis Schaerlaeken, S.R.S.H. delegate, concerning the characteristics of the Bouviers called 'Picard'. Those present were Messrs. A. Houtard, J. Levita,

An historic moment in the development of the modern Bouvier is captured in this photo of the Bouvier exhibitors and their dogs at the 1912 Brussels show. The key to identifications is reproduced on the page opposite. Photo lent by Club National Belge du Bouvier des Flandres.

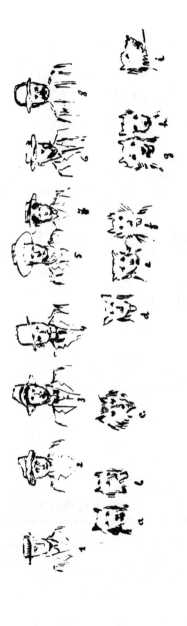

1. Marllos from Ypres
2. Smeers from Lille
3. V. Domicent from Warneton
4. Declaret from Ypres
5. F. Dubois from Lille
6. Lapierre from Ypres
7. & 8. Two amateurs from Lille

a. Maerten de la Warnave, male
b. Pic (Mssr. Smeers), male
c. Djim de la Warnave, male
d. Nicka Suprema (Mssr. M. Declaret), female
e. Spott (Mssr. M. V. Dubois), male

f. Diane (Mssr. Simoulin), female, Lille
g. Pick de Boessinghe, male ⎫
h. Mirza, female   ⎬ Mssr. Lapierre
i. Olga des Voiles (Mssr. Deruple), Lille

43

Baron J. Van Zuylen van Nyeveld of the S.R.S.H., and Messrs Orban and Taeymans as judges. After having examined the best representatives of the breed, a standard was adopted. Here follows a resume of these examinations: **General appearance:** rustic and imposing **Ears:** cropped and carried erect **Chest:** deep but not too wide **Trunk and back:** short, robust and straight (like a cob horse) **Colors:** Black, slate grey, brown, etc.

In an article published and titled *To Whom the Future*, Vital Taeymans concluded it would be with the Picards that the breed would evolve as they were larger, more calm and steady than the sheepdogs. Large dogs were most in demand. Taeymans, an administrator of the S.R.S.H., would be authoritative as to what the majority of the then-breeders wanted. And, the breeders catered to the general demand.

In 1912, M. F. Fontaine, vice president of the Club St. Hubert of the North was trying to push a smaller Bouvier under the name of Bouvier des Flandres against the Bouvier de Roulers. In France, M. Fontaine was considered a specialist and here follows his opinion: In *Chasse et Peche* of April 6, 1912 he wrote:

> In the north of France around Warneton and Ypres near the frontier, there exists a harsh-coated dog used by shepherds. This is the Bouvier des Flandres that resembles a 'Berger Picard', a product seemingly of a cross with a Matin.
>
> The Matin cross has increased size. The Berger Picard is medium size with a maximum height of 23⅝ inches and the Bouvier would be 25½ inches. I have noticed this the last fifteen years in the farm dogs as I have judged around Lille. The color of these Picard sheepdogs is black interspersed with white hairs, or dark brindle.
>
> In these agricultural shows I have also seen some Bouviers, but they were fewer, all entered in classes called 'Sheepdogs and Bouvier.' I have given an extra prize to these Bouviers to extend deserved distinction and to encourage their promotion.

This excerpt was followed by the standard, illustrated by the head of a Bouvier des Flandres with natural standing ears. The description, except for size, was about the same as for the Bouvier des Roulers. Size was set at 23⅝ to 25½ inches for males, and 22¾ to 24½ inches for females.

The Bouvier des Roulers description given by Fontaine is that of a farm and guard dog. Beyond being a herder of cattle, oxen and cows, he is listed a merchant's guard dog, a dog for defense and draught. On the farm he is also used to power the churn.

Ranked by size there was, first, the harsh-coated sheep dogs at 21½ to 23⅝ inches, the Bouvier des Flandres at 23⅝ to 25½ inches and, last, the giant Bouvier de Roulers at 25½ to 27½ inches. From these three the modern Bouvier is evolved.

The best dogs at that time, and which were most used as progenitors and recorded in the Stud Book were Champion Nic de Sottegem (LOSH 10766), Dragon de la Lys (LOSH 11776) Milton (LOSH 15936), and Goliath de la Lys (LOSH 11736). Nic and Milton are of unknown origin. During the war, in 1917, Nic was bought on a farm and taken home. Of Milton, only his sire, Brick, and his dam Lize, are known.

In 1921 the Bouvier Club de Courtrai which was affiliated with the Kennel Club Belge convened and decided that unquestionably there were two types of Bouviers. One was small, usually grey or fawn and light colored, (never black) short ribbed and with a fairly short head. Its ears were cut and its tail was docked. It was most predominently found on the farms and grazing regions situated between the La Lys river and the north seacoast. The variety was known as the Paret type after L. Paret's Rex and Nelly. It was more the shepherd type then, but has evolved into the Bouvier des Flandres. Until the time when the Paret Bouvier came by its name it was also called "vuilbaard" (dirty beard) "Koehond" (Flemish for cow dog), "toucheur de boeuf" or 'chien de vacher" meaning cowherd's dog. The standard the Club de Courtrai applied to the Paret Bouvier des Flandres was called the "Standard Domicent" after Dr. Domicent who led the investigation.

The cowherds and fanciers of the area then established that another type of cow dog "Bouvier" existed and for this type they formed the "Standard Roberfroid," named after its leading protagonist. This dog also had cropped ears and docked tails, but it was larger than the Paret type with a deeper chest, longer head and it was almost always black. Before this historic meeting, it had been referred to as the Moerman, Bouvier Belge, or Bouvier de Roulers.

As might be expected, there was a cross between these two types exemplified by a dog named "Washington Bonaparte" who possessed much of the charm of both the Bouvier des Flandres (Paret) and the Bouvier de Roulers (Moerman).

With these two main types to the front, it is unfortunate that still another cow dog of the area was never given recognition, but actually barred from the shows as undesirable. However, it was a strong type of dog, often black or dark grey with so much hair as to resemble an Old English Sheepdog. It has not, however, disappeared. On the continent it is known as the Bouvier Briarde.[11]

And lastly, but not least, came the dog of the Ardennes that seemed to contribute so much to the beginnings of the modern Bouvier, but who himself remained rather unrecognized.

It was decided at the meeting at Courtrai that the first type, the Bouvier des Flandres, was really the oldest of all the others. This type was mostly fawn or light grey—the genetic source of the fawns of today.

11. Recognized by the AKC as the "Briard."

Here are the three Bouvier types of 1912. Pick de Boesinghe and Mirza (upper left) were representative of the French type. Marius des Baies, (lower left) more massive, was typical of the type favored by Belgian breeders and judges. The debate continued until 1961. A 1912 intermediate type was the fawn Washington Bonaparte (below). Photos reproduced from *L'Elevage*, official monthly of the Kennel Club Belge.

The second type they decided was "manufactured" by taking the first and crossing it with the Matin, but that this "de Roulers" type, while bigger, stronger and always black, was not atypical and would not survive. Therefore two standards were drawn up for these two main types of Bouviers and it was decided that only the future could tell which would survive. The Bouvier Club de Courtrai at this point should have listened to the sage advise of one modest counsellor. He said: "The two varieties will have to be used in forming a single breed since one will be in need of the other if they are to survive at all." However, two Bouvier standards still existed in Belgium. The Bouvier des Flandres is recognized by the American Kennel Club. The Bouvier de Roulers is not.

Not once but twice the Bouvier was nearly exterminated by world wars waged upon his breeding grounds. Only because he served his masters so well and so loyally was the Bouvier able to survive in a few hard-core breeding strongholds in France, Belgium and Holland.

In 1918 the Bouvier made a comeback. A few families had managed to keep their dogs through the war. Sultan, belonging to Mr. Van der Vennet and to Mr. Gryson, and Picko belonging to Mr. De Poorter, and two other notable dogs, Bella and Kiss de Ramillies, escaped and left progeny leading to today's Bouviers. The one dog that did most to revive the Bouvier in Belgium lived with veterinary Army Captain Darby and was Nic de Sottegem. Nic became a champion of Belgium and was shown at the Olympic show at Antwerp in 1920. The judge, Charles Huge, wrote: "Nic is the ideal type of the Bouvier. He has a short body, with well developed ribs, short flanks, strong legs,

Ch. Nic de Sottegem, LOSH 10766, was the great progenitor of the modern Bouvier des Flandres. He was on the scene in the post-World War I era when a great sire was needed. Virtually every great Bouvier of today of predominately Belgian breeding traces back to Nic through several lines. This rare photograph reproduced from Toepoel's *Honden Encyclopaedia*. From the editor's collection.

Dragon de la Lys and his kennelmate, Goliath de la Lys, both sired by Ch. Nic de Sottegem, were worthy successors to their sire during the late 20's and early 30's. This rare photo of Dragon de la Lys is also from Toepoel's *Honden Encyclopaedia*. From the editor's collection.

good feet, long and oblique shouders. His head is of a good shape with somber eyes and an ideal courageous expression. His hair is dry and dark. The tail should not have been cut so short. I hope that the dog will have numerous progeny."

Charles Huge's wishes were realized, for when Nic died in 1926 he left a great many descendants among which we might note Prince D'or, Ch. Draga Coralie de Sottegem, Goliath de la Lys, Lyda Nefte de la Paix, Nora, Siske de Sottegem and Ch. Dragon de la Lys.

Of the early kennels the most prominent was "de la Lys". The owner, M. Gryson of St. Denis Westrem, did not hesitate to use the best he could find. His best dogs were Dragon de la Lys and Goliath de la Lys, both, as noted, sired by Champion Nic.

Many of these dogs figure in the pedigree of Actif, LOSH 16357, the top-rated dog of 1924. Here's that pedigree:

```
                                            Unknown
           Ch. Nic de Sottegem, LOSH 10766  Unknown
       Nicolo de la Lys, LOSH 11712, grey   Pickzwart, LOSH 14959
           Margot                           Mirza, M. DeBruyne, owner
   Goliath de la Lys, LOSH 11736, grey      Unknown
           Unknown                          Unknown
       Flandrienne, LOSH 11736, grey        Unknown
           Cora                             Unknown

ACTIF, LOSH 16357
                                            Unknown
           Unknown                          Unknown
       Ch. Nic de Sottegem, LOSH 10766      Unknown
           Unknown                          Unknown
   Durca de la Lys                          Unknown
           Pickzwart, LOSH 14959            Unknown
       Ch. Draga, LOSH 10773, black         Unknown
           Cora                             Unknown
```

Although the name Dragon de la Lys does not appear in this pedigree one can see the bloodlines. He is a brother, from a previous litter, of Durca de la Lys, dam of Actif.

49

In early pedigrees the name of Duduc (12872) is often seen. He was a stud used by the breeders of Courtrai and thus he appears in pedigrees of many breeders. A member of this family is Betty de la Lys (11774), kennel mate of Milton (15936), and one of the best bitches of her time. This is her pedigree:

```
                Unknown                              Unknown
        Unknown                                      Unknown
                Unknown                              Unknown
    Ch. Nic de Sottegem, LOSH 10766, black          Unknown
                Unknown                              Unknown
        Unknown                                      Unknown
                Unknown                              Unknown
                                                     Unknown
BETTY DE LA LYS, LOSH 11774

            Filou, LOSH 9569, C. Vander Heeren, owner    Pic, Moerman, owner
        Dudac, LOSH 12872                                 Charlotte, Vander Heeren, owner
            Lize, C. Vander Heeren, owner                 Unknown
    Lyda, LOSH 10278, grey                                Unknown
            Filou, LOSH 9569, C. Vander Heeren, owner    Pic, Moerman, owner
        Tata                                              Charlotte, Vander Heeren, owner
            Mirza, M. DeBruyne, owner                     Unknown
                                                          Unknown
```

Here again Champion Nic de Sottegem, of unknown origin, was a producer of top quality.

The Club National Belge du Bouvier des Flandres was organized in January 1921. In July 1923, in Ghent, well-known breeders and judges carefully examined well known Bouviers of that time. From a concensus of their evaluations of these dogs they wrote the official standard of the breed. Those who formulated this more comprehensive Belgian standard were Messrs. Charles Huge, V. Tenret, V. Taeymans, Count de Hemptinne, Captain Binin and A. Gevaert. The dogs they carefully measured and examined were Prince D'or, Ch. Draga de la Lys, Coralie de Sottegem, Goliath de la Lys, Lyda Nefte de la Paix, Nora, Ch. Dragon de la Lys, Ch. Nic de Sottegem, Trotsky, Sultan, Morki, Flandrienne and Blondine. These were the basic post World War I foundation dogs.

The very first special show for Bouviers was in Saint-Denis Westrem in 1925 and was organized by the Club National Belge du Bouvier des Flandres. The twenty-two entries were judged by L. Van Damme. In the class for junior males, first place winner was Cesar de Pont-a-rieu; first place female was Zora de Zwynaerde. In the open class for males, Bouboule, owned by Jules Rassehaert won. The open bitch winner was Molly, owned by M. Patttyn. The judge's report on Boubole read: "Magnificent type in head and expression, good shoulders, well built body and legs, also a good coat and gait—though a little stiff in forelegs." Here is his pedigree:

Bouboule de Courtrai was a winning representative of the de Courtrai Kennels, one of the pioneering Bouvier breeding establishments. In 1925 he drew a rave report from Judge L. Van Damme after winning the open male class at the first Bouvier Specialty. Photo from Toepoel's *Honden Encyclopaedia*. From the editor's collection.

```
                                Unknown                          Unknown
                   Jim de Sellier, LOSH 19345                    Unknown
                                Unknown                          Unknown
              Bobby du Sellier, LOSH 16547                       Unknown
                                Unknown                          Unknown
              Bella du Sellier, Mme Canbien, owner              Unknown
                                Unknown                          Unknown

    BOUBOULE DE CONTRAI (1924)

                                Unknown                          Unknown
                   Ch. Nic de Sottegem, LOSH 10766, black        Unknown
                                Unknown                          Unknown
              Arga de la Lys                                     Unknown
                           Pickzwart, LOSH 14959                 Unknown
                   Riga, LOSH 11754                              Unknown
                           Flandrienne, LOSH 11736              Cora
```

Nickol recieved many prizes under Judge Charles Huge and Judge Vital Taeymans. Here's his pedigree:

```
                                Unknown                          Unknown
                   Pick, M. van Damme, owner                    Unknown
                                Unknown                          Unknown
              Picko                                             Unknown
                                Unknown                          Unknown
              Mira                                              Unknown
                                Unknown                          Unknown

    NICKOL, LOSH 17522 (1923)

                           Filou, LOSH 9569                     Pic, Moerman, owner
                   Max                                          Charlotte, Doussy, owner
                           Bitch, M. Van der Venne, owner       Unknown
              Belatte                                           Unknown
                                Unknown                          Unknown
                   Vara, LOSH 10280                             Unknown
                           Mirza, M. DeBruyne, owner            Unknown
```

The concensus standard of the 1923 Ghent conference was called the "Standard Gevaert" and was patterned after the "Standard Roberfroid." (Monsieur Roberfroid was instrumental in formulating the Moerman or Bouvier de Roulers standard for the black type). The Societe Royal Saint-Hubert was emerging as predominant in Belgium.

This is the photo Toepoel used to illustrate the "Vlaamsche Koehond of Bouvier" or "Bouvier Belge des Flandres" section in his *Honden Encyclopaedia*. He did not identify the dog, but he certainly selected a cobby model with an elegant carriage and stance. From the editor's collection.

It published the "Standard Gevaert"—which differed from the Roberfroid in that it admitted all colors.

Breeding in conformity with these two standards began to produce a most formidable dog. He was very squarely built, with the characteristic massive chest development of true Bouviers. A well-chiseled head was proudly carried on a muscular neck. Becoming fixed as breed trademarks were the eyebrows, mustache and beard. Along with the alert eyes of a guard dog they bespoke the Bouvier's character and expression. The tail, placed highly and gaily carried, gave accent to a personality full of zest, fire and zeal. Four pillar-like and well-boned legs carried him without heaviness in his gait. At this time his tail was docked to about four inches and his ears cropped to a triangular contour.

In 1926, a meeting of the Kennel Club Belge at Boitsfer failed in its mission to unite the two main fractions of the breed and bring the Bouvier under one standard. Things remained the same until the K.C.B. decided to again modify procedure by having dogs judged in two classes according to color. This appeared fine until size and color conflicts were encountered. A light colored dog under the name of Bouvier des Flandres might not be the size that the Bouvier de Roulers standard demanded. A Societe Royal Saint-Hubert Belgian champion could be eliminated from the show ring at the Societe Central of

France as too big. Only size and color divided these variations. Through many debates, arguments and discussions between Belgium and France, the impasse remained. It appeared there might never be agreement.

In 1929 the American Kennel Club recognized the Bouvier des Flandres as a breed. In 1931 the AKC registered two Bouviers—the first on its books. On April 14, 1959 the AKC approved the present standard for the breed.

In 1961 the official Club du Bouvier des Flandres for France Bulletin number seven proclaimed:

> For 40 years the subject of a unified standard for the Bouvier des Flandres has caused floods of ink. Belgian judges going to France and French judges going to Belgium have concluded that there is no more difference in evaluation and that the road is now open for a fusion of the standards.
>
> The Club du Bouvier des Flandres for France and the Club National Belge du Bouvier des Flandres have discussed this problem for two years. Commissions were designated and on March 12, 1961, the French and Belgian commissions assembled and approved the unified standard of the Bouvier des Flandres.
>
> This is a memorable date in the history of the Bouvier des Flandres. We hope we have worked well for the breed.

With one standard adopted by Belgium and France breeders at last had a common ideal toward which they could cooperatively work. The Netherlands has a variation of the Bouvier standard which is quite similar and dogs registered with their National Raad van Beheer as "Bouvier Belge des Flandres" are normally accepted by the AKC for registration in its stud records.

During the 1930's and into the World War II era the general type of the Bouvier was maintained in all three of the breed's native countries, but there were variations on several points. All of the Bouviers had short, harsh coats to a degree but many were longer bodied with lighter bone than desired. In Belgium and France there emerged the type we now think of as the modern Bouvier—longer coated and cobbier. Dutch breeders have more recently followed the trend. They have used strong infusions of Belgian stock and produce first class dogs.

It was once common to refer to Bouviers with harsh, short coats as the "Dutch type." At one time all Bouviers were clothed

Fricko de Belgique dramatically illustrates the shortness of body and the sense of power and alertness which are distinctive to the Bouvier. Fricko, by Arian out of Donatienne des Coudreaux, is prominent in many Belgian and American pedigrees.

with fairly short, harsh coats—and without the undercoat which is a firmly-fixed breed characteristic today. Variations are still sometimes detectable in the Bouviers exported to the U.S. from the Netherlands. Some breeders advocate keeping the two types separate, but since both are registered as Bouviers des Flandres it is the author's opinion that with good judgement in breeding and discrimination in culling, the two types will merge to the benefit of both.

THE BOUVIER COMES TO AMERICA

THERE is probably no record of the first Bouvier imported into the the United States. The probability is that it was brought here by an emigrant family wanting a bit of its native Flanders with it in America.

There appears some mystery about the AKC's "recognition" of the Bouvier. The mystery seems to arise from attempting to understand the American Kennel Club's actions in the 1920's in the light of that body's present day procedures. Much of the terminology remains the same but concept and procedure have had some revolutionary changes.

The AKC's records indicate the Bouvier became eligible for registration in 1926. Other records show formal "recognition" in 1929. The first edition of the AKC's official *The Complete Dog Book* in 1929 had a chapter on the Bouvier with the standard of the Club National du Bouvier des Flandres—and a full page photo.

It must be assumed Americans were importing Bouviers throughout the twenties. Soldiers in foreign lands have historically brought native breeds of dogs home with them. Tens of thousands of World War II doughboys must have been exposed to Bouviers as they fought across Flanders.

Whatever the dates of the Bouviers first AKC admissability and recognition, it was not until the May, 1931 *Stud Book* that the first Bouviers were officially recorded in the U.S. There were two and both were imported by George MacCullough Miller of Old Westbury, New York.

The dogs, both grizzles, were full brother and sister from different litters. The first, AKC 780160, was Hardix (LOSH 34814), whelped Nov. 20, 1926. He was bred by Tabellion and Gand at Rue Alexis Pesnon 46, Montreuil, Seine, France. Diane de Montreuil, AKC 780161, whelped May 30, 1927, was bred by Marette and Gand.

For whatever reasons there were no further Bouvier registrations with the AKC until a single entry in 1935. Thus it appears that through the first ten years of AKC eligibility Hardix and Diane de Montreuil were the only Bouviers recorded. Popular breeds in that era were Boston Terriers, German Shepherds and Airedales. Boxers and Briards were doing little better in the United States than was the Bouvier.

The pedigree of Hardix and Diane followed classic patterns:

<pre>
                                              Ch. Nic de Sottegem
                        Dragon de la Lys
                                              Draga
      Lutin de Mouscron
                                              Piston
                        Sarah de Sottegem
                                              Coralie
</pre>

Hardix (AKC 780160) 11/20/26 and Diane de Montreuil (AKC 780161) 5/30/27

<pre>
                                              Goliath de la Lys
                        Azur
                                              Durca de la Lys
      Zette du Roy d'Espange
                                              Duc
                        Blondine
                                              Diane
</pre>

An early importer was Louis de Rochemont of New York. From The Netherlands he brought Czardas van Het Bunderbosch. Czardas, whelped in 1938, was bred by M. Widdershoven of Bunde. Imported in 1936 was Coba uit het Zuiderlicht (NHSB 25619). Whelped in 1932, she was also bred in The Netherlands by J. J. H. Klinkers. Her sire's great-grand dam was the famed foundation bitch, Flandrienne. Pedigrees of imports from The Netherlands generally reveal that

THE FIRST BOUVIER REGISTERED BY THE AKC? This is the photo which illustrated the Bouvier in the AKC's official *The Complete Dog Book* in all editions published from 1929 to 1972. The AKC does not identify its breed models, but one report, from an early American Bouvier breeder, states that this is a portrait of Hardix, the first Bouvier registered by the AKC. There appears to be no way this report can be checked. Although Hardix wasn't registered until 1931, he was whelped in 1926. He could have been mature enough in 1928 or 1929 to have posed for this picture.

the Dutch used many of the same foundation dogs that served the Belgians and French so well.

Will Judy in his *Dog Encyclopedia* remarked that it was very strange the AKC chose to recognize the Bouvier for exhibition and show purposes as the breed was seldom seen in America. He pointed out however that it was simply a matter of a majority vote in a quorum of AKC directors—in this instance four favorable directors.

During the Bouvier's early years in the U.S. Julius Bliss was the man who kept things going. He provided the communication and the stimulus for breeders and owners. He promoted the breed unselfishly, he showed and until his untimely death, imported excellent stock. He bred his imported Laraine to George Young's Bojar van

Bouvier history is captured in this photograph. At the left is Belco. When the Nazis put a price on her head, Miss Edmee Bowles had to flee Belgium with her mother. She couldn't know if she was a step ahead of the Nazis—or if they were a step ahead of her—but she wouldn't go without her Belco. In the U.S. Belco sired Dogs for Defense stalwarts and helped Miss Bowles found her du Clos des Cerberes Kennel. At Belco's left is his son by Ch. Lisa, Ch. Marius du Clos des Cerberes. And on the right is Ch. Lisa CD.

Westergoo, the first American champion. Bojar, bred in 1935 by J. Ferwerda in Leeuwarden, The Netherlands, was imported by Young. Ch. Milton, Lisa, Mary Pickford du Pandore, Sultan and Samlo figure in his pedigree. The Bojar-Laraine mating produced three notable bitches, Asta, Inga and Caprice. The last named was presented by Bliss to the then Jacqueline Bouvier, who subsequently showed her at Westminster in 1942.

In 1940 the Youngs finished a Bojar daughter, Lisa, with Miss Edmee Bowles handling her to the title. Lisa was bred to her sire, producing a large litter. Most of these puppies went on to serve in the Coast Guard's Dogs for Defense program. Again Miss Bowles was there with her great feeling for dogs and her especial knowledge of the Bouviers of her native land. She assisted Coast Guard Commander Newbolt Ely in the training of these dogs. One Coast Guard Bouvier, owned by Adam M. Butler, was killed on Salerno's beaches.

Bred to Miss Bowles' Belco, Ch. Lisa, C.D., produced Ch. Marius du Clos des Cerberes, still fondly remembered by Miss Bowles as one of the finest she ever owned.

Beeta Van Wakershof, whelped in 1944, was sold in 1948 to Mrs. L. de Rochemont of New Hampshire. She joined an import, Czardas Van Het BunderBosch, whelped in 1938, which Mr. de Rochemont had bought from M. Widdershoven in Bunda. Czardas' classic pedigree is quickly traced to such early foundation stock as Ch. Milton, Dragon de la Lys, Lydia and Arga de la Lys.

The imported Ch. Argus de la Thudinie was whelped in 1951. Bred by Justin Chastel in Belgium, he was a significant winner and

Ch. Bel Echo du Clos de Cerberes was a show winner in the 1954-55 era. Sired by Ch. Marius du Clos des Cerberes out of Ch. Ellyrdia, he was owned by Katherine Walker of Sewickley, Pa. Photo by Norton.

Ch. Krepsie de la Thudinie, imported by Ray and Marion Hubbard of Madrone Ledge Kennels in 1961. Krepsie was the first Bouvier to earn a championship in the West in fifteen years.

sire before importation to the U.S. in 1959 by Fred Walsh, New York advertising executive. Sired by Volpi de la Vallee de l'Escallion out of Ucaba, Argus made Bouvier history in the United States. A dog of commanding presence, he won a number of group placements.

Then, at 10½ years he won the large and prestigious Worcester County show with the late Mrs. Edward B. Renner judging. It was the first time any Bouvier had won an American show.

It is extraordinary when any dog past his normal prime years can take a show. Only the very soundest dogs can successfully compete at an advanced age. No domestic dog is perfectly constructed. To move well each dog must make muscular compensations for whatever defects he has in his locomotive apparatus. If they are minor he can pretty well hide them — so long as he is young enough to have the strength and muscular tone to make the adjustments. When he gets tired, or old, the defects become visible in his gaits. To gait well enough to win a show at age ten and a half, a dog would need nearly perfect moving gear. On that day Argus beat the finest dogs competing in the East. Unfortunately, his eyesight began to fail and he was retired from competition shortly thereafter.

Mrs. Renner, of Lakeville, Conn., said: "I couldn't help but admire his magnificent soundness and showmanship." Famed all-breed show judge William Kendrick pronounced Argus one of the finest working dogs he had seen. He said: "Argus' recognition in the ring should have come to him much earlier."

People who had never before heard of Bouviers saw Argus' picture in newspapers and magazines. Advertising man Walsh saw to that. Public interest in Bouviers was on the rise. And, the ice had been broken insofar as dog shows were concerned. Argus had established a precedent which demanded that judges fully and properly consider every Bouvier exhibited under them.

Statistics detail the Bouvier's lengthy climb to popularity in the United States. For the first 25 years there were not sufficient Bouviers registered with the AKC to support a viable breeding program. Only through continuing importations was the breed able to sustain a presence in the U.S. during those years. It took 40 years before the breed could average over 20 AKC registrations per year.

The "rank by breed" column in the accompanying table can be a bit misleading. In the years since 1931 there has been a significant increase in the number of breeds recognized by the AKC. If we make a mental adjustment for this factor and then consider that total AKC registrations had a sustained period of unprecedented growth between 1946 and 1980, the Bouvier's performance compared with other breeds has been admirable. It was a period when every breed had to run just to hold its rank. The Bouvier did much better than that.

A sudden spurt in breed popularity — such as might be ignited by a popular TV series — leads to irresponsible breeding for profit by unfeeling market breeders. This kind of growth destroys the work of generations of conscientious breeders. Fortunately, the Bouvier's climb to popularity has been measured and each Bouvier generation, thanks to breeders' skills and devotion, has been, in the large, better than the last.

RECORD OF BOUVIER DES FLANDRES REGISTRATIONS WITH THE AKC

YEAR	AKC Regs.	Cum. Totals	AKC Rank by Breed
1926 thru 1930	—	0	
1931	2	2	81
1932 thru 1934	—	2	
1935	1	3	93
1936	5	8	93
1937	7	15	88
1938	7	22	90
1939	2	24	96
1940	13	37	85
1941	8	45	87
1942	8	53	93
1943	2	55	96
1944	9	64	84
1945	3	67	91
1946	3	70	89
1947	—	70	—
1948	1	71	94
1949	14	85	94
1950	9	94	97
1951	27	121	92
1952	19	140	96
1953	16	156	88
1954	28	184	90
1955	39	223	88
1956	10	233	93
1957	26	259	92
1958	18	277	94
1959	44	321	85
1960	46	367	88
1961	59	426	89
1962	93	519	89
1963	85	604	89
1964	118	722	87
1965	130	852	89
1966	149	1,001	87
1967	221	1,222	82
1968	267	1,489	76
1969	330	1,819	76
1970	348	2,167	78
1971	367	2,534	82
1972	511	3,045	75
1973	585	3,630	77
1974	735	4,365	71
1975	834	5,199	67
1976	1,053	6,252	62
1977	1,204	7,456	62
1978	1,301	8,757	60
1979	1,345	10,102	57
1980	1,389	11,491	57

One of the greatest classics of dog fiction has a Bouvier as its hero. Ironically, it preceeded the Bouvier as we know the breed today. An English edition of *A Dog of Flanders—A Christmas Story,* appeared in England as early as 1872. It was authored by Louisa de la Ramé who used the pseudonym "Ouida." The story of the boy, Nello, and his dog, Patrasche, has had many subsequent editions in many languages. Here's a brief passage:[1]

Within sound of the little melancholy clock, almost from their birth upward, they had dwelt together, Nello and Patrasche, in the little hut on the edge of the village, with the cathedral spire of Antwerp rising in the northeast, beyond the great green plain of seeding grass and spreading corn that stretched away from them like a tideless, changeless sea. It was the hut of a very old man, of a very poor man—of old Jehan Daas, who in his time had been a soldier, and who remembered the wars that had trampled the country as oxen tread down the furrows, and who had brought from his service nothing except a wound, which had made him a cripple.

When old Jehan Daas had reached his full eighty, his daughter

1. The illustration is by "G. H. B." from an 1891 edition published in Boston by the Joseph Knight Co.

had died in the Ardennes, hard by Stavelot, and had left him in legacy her two-year-old son. The old man could ill contrive to support himself, but he took up the additional burden uncomplainingly, and it soon became welcome and precious to him. Little Nello—which was but a pet diminutive for Nicolas—throve with him, and the old man and the little child lived in the poor little hut contentedly.

It was a very humble little mid-hut indeed, but it was clean and white as a sea-shell, and stood in a small plot of garden-ground that yielded beans and herbs and pumpkins. They were very poor, terribly poor—many a day they had nothing at all to eat. They never by any chance had enough: to have had enough to eat would have been to have reached paradise at once. But the old man was very gentle and good to the boy, and the boy was a beautiful, innocent, truthful, tender natured creature; and they were happy on a crust and a few leaves of cabbage, and asked no more of earth or heaven; save indeed that Patrasche should be always with them, since without Patrasche where would they have been?

For Patrasche was their alpha and omega; their treasury and granary; their store of gold and wand of wealth; their bread-winner and minister; their only friend and comforter. Patrasche dead or gone from them, they must have laid themselves down and died likewise. Patrasche was body, brains, hands, head, and feet to both of them: Patrasche was their very life, their very soul. For Jehan Daas was old and a cripple, and Nellow was but a child; and Patrasche was their dog.

A dog of Flanders—yellow of hide, large of head and limb, with wolf-like ears that stood erect, and legs bowed and feet widened in the muscular development wrought in his breed by many generations of hard service. Patrasche came of a race which had toiled hard and cruelly from sire to son in Flanders many a century—slaves of slaves, dogs of the people, beasts of the shafts and the harness, creatures that lived straining their sinews in the gall of the cart, and died breaking their hearts on the flints of the streets.

Patrasche had been born of parents who had labored hard all their days over the sharp-set stones of the various cities and the long, shadowless, weary roads of the two Flanders and of Brabant. He had been born to no other heritage than those of pain and of toil. He had been fed on curses and baptized with blows. Why not? It was a Christian country, and Patrasche was but a dog. Before he was fully grown he had known the bitter gall of the cart and the collar. Before he had entered his thirteenth month he had become the property of a hardware-dealer, who was accustomed to wander over the land north and south, from the blue sea to the green mountains. They sold him for a small price, because he was so young.

In all probability *A Dog of Flanders* did inspire some Bouvier importations into both the United States and Canada. But we find no record of these importations prior to World War I. There are unconfirmed reports of importations circa 1920 to Michigan with stock spreading from there into Canada. However, since such imports left no continuing line they have left no imprint upon the history of the Bouvier.

Among the earlier American breeders and promoters of the Bouvier were Mr. and Mrs. George Butts of Springfield, Ill. Their imported Ch. Coquin de la Thudinie was the first Bouvier to win a working group first in an American Kennel Club show. They also imported Ch Draga de la Thudinie. Bred to Coquin she produced Chef de Truffe. Miss Bowles purchased Truffe and finished his championship in grand style by winning best of breed at Westchester in 1962.

It might be useful to pause here to point out how difficult it is —and how important it is— to win a working group placement in an AKC show. Take two, large, representative and recent shows. They had a total of 6,296 dogs entered in classes with group-eligible potentiality. Of the six AKC groups the sporting had 20.9% of the dogs, hound had 14.6%, terrier 9.4%, toy 10% and non-sporting 11.4%. The working group, with 33.76% comprised over one-third of the show honors-eligible entries. This is about average. These figures show it is more than half again as difficult to win a working group placement as one in the sporting group; 2.31 times harder than in the hound group; three times harder than in the non-sporting group; 3.4 times harder than in the toy group and 3.6 times harder than in the terrier group. Stated more simply, working groups with more than one-third of the competition have four group placements while the remaining two-thirds of the competition have 20 group placements to share. Dogs in other groups average a two-and-one-half times better shot at a group win. And, before a Bouvier can win a show he must first win the working group.

Evert Van de Pol, Miss Bowles, Miss Virginia Bull and Miss Janet Mack of New York City, as well as Dorothy and Fred Walsh of Flem-

This photo produced publicity for Bouviers during their earlier days in the U.S.. Evert Van der Pol sold a brindle male pup to a dog food promoter. He was one of a litter which produced Ch. Ciscoldo, Ch. Rialto and Ch. Ellydria. He was called Calo because that was the brand name of the dog food. He did his bit with the cart and stories were put out that he was 31 inches high, weighed 140 pounds—and ate six pounds of Calo daily. AKC records indicate Ch. Ciscoldo and Calo were the same dog. There was an ad painted on the front of the cart. Van der Pol wrote Janet Mack: "It was a misleading advertisement, so I've blotted it out."

ington, New Jersey, were all interested in the promotion and better-ment of the breed and worked together to this end for some time. Their first dogs, most all of which were from The Netherlands, had the very short harsh wiry coats that is still seen in the Dutch strains today. Van de Pol imported Silta. She was then in whelp to the Dual Champion of Holland for four years in succession, Ch. Basko Aleida v.d. Zaanhoeve. From this litter she produced the first and second west coast champions, Ciskoldo and his litter sister, Rialto. Another puppy from this litter, Ellyrdria, was sold to Miss Bowles. She also became a champion. Silta won 12 points and a C.D.

Miss Bowles then moved toward French and Belgian breeding. She imported Wandru des Coudreaux from France in 1958 and Re-mado's Katleen from Belgium in 1960. Van de Pol imported Bona-parte van Darling-Astrid from the Netherlands and sold him to the Walshs' Deewal Kennels. Bonaparte became a champion but sired only one champion, Deewal Toronto.

In 1959 the Walshes joined the move toward Belgian-French breeding. They imported Argus de la Thudinie, Faussette l' Ideal de Charlerei, and Hardy l' Ideal de Charleroi. These were followed later by Hion de la Thudinie, Kaline du Posty Arlequin, and Irca de la Thudinie. Mrs. Marion Hubbard of Madrone Ledge acquired her first import through Miss Janet Mack. From Belgium's de la Thudinie kennel came Krepsie de la Thudinie, who became the third West Coast champion and first one there in 15 years.

Even in those days of much milder inflation, dogs sold to America were quite high — except for Argus. He was purchased for $125.00. Hardy was $300.00 and Faussette l' Ideal de Charleroi was $500.00. It must be remembered that Argus, who figures into many pedigrees today, was 8½ years old when imported. He was used often as a sire in Europe, and even after his arrival here, his campaigning and best in show, he produced several litters before his death at age eleven.

Evert Van de Pol, who had been inactive in breeding and showing for several years, imported a dog from the Netherlands named Quintus Astra V.D. Ouden Dijk; a dog that has gone best of breed and has earned points at western shows.

An early friend of the breed and the president of the Bouvier des Flandres Club of America was Evert Van de Pol of San Francisco. Also instrumental in forming the early club were Miss Edmee Bowles, Mr. and Mrs. Louis de Rochemont, Julius Bliss, and George Young.

Ch. Bonaparte van Darling-Astrid was an excellent example of the Dutch stock which was imported and bred from in the years immediately after World War II. Bred by H. M. Vougelers at Ostvoorner in 1953, he was imported by Evert Van de Pol and later sold to Deewal Kennels. Photo by Shafer.

Bliss was the first Bouvier breeder of record in the United States. Later on Mr. and Mrs. Fred Walsh and Mr. and Mrs. Butts, Mr. and Mrs. Butler and others tried to keep the club together and functioning.

Miss Janet Mack of New York City was a strong influence and a hard worker for the breed. She imported Erlo de la Thudinie, who quickly became an American champion. Erlo was a producing sire and the foundation of the Bouvier branch of Miss Mack's famed Grenadier Kennels. Erlo sired many litters, but his litter whelped by Ch. Kaline du Posty Arlequin owned by Seymore Levine of Putnan Valley, New York, made the news pages of the New York Times. Kaline had 18 puppies in September 1962, of which 15 survived.

James Neylon imported Ch. Konard du Rotiane and Remado's Jasmine from Mssr. Dauwe. He bred Remado's Jasmine to Deewal import Ch. Hion de la Thudinie in 1964. The mating produced Ch. De Ney's Grosser Knabe, who became number three Bouvier in the nation in 1966, when he took a Group first.

Another early import was Etoile Des Coudreaux from Mme. A. Sornin de Leysat Corbier's kennel. Whelped in May 1955, Etoile, imported by Col. Duke, sired several litters. His quality puppies attracted the attention of several people who became serious fanciers. One such mating was to Trixie in 1958. She was owned by Dorothy E. Taylor. Trixie (Deewal's Max — Escaut de Belgique) whelped a large litter that included Ch. Deewal Nicole and Devil of Story Book. Ch. Deewal Nicole bred to Ch. Argus de la Thudinie produced Ch. Demon Ripp.

The de Rochemonts were instrumental in getting Fred and Dorothy Walsh interested in the breed. Mrs. Virginia Bull became a very active member and breeder for a time. Her Peerkja O'River Oakes was an early champion. Mrs. Edith Sturges O'Conner worked for many years on behalf of the club and Bouviers.

A second attempt to form a strong working Bouvier Club of America faltered and the club became inactive. There were too many miles between owners. They were spread far apart, and communications were lacking. Owners were still few in number — and there was a need for a real catalyst.

Ch. Deewal Benjamen, shown here with Tommy Glassford.

Am. and Can. Ch. Shirwal Yorick ("Jester"), sired by Am. and Can. Ch. Uriah Bras de Fer and out of Deewal Victoria, is owned by Wally and Shirley Seger of Shirwal Kennels.

Ch. L'Esprit Fier's Zachariah, handled by Charles Gamby, was awarded Best of Winners by Chester Collier at the Rio Hondo Kennel Club Show, January 1978. Zachariah was owned by Diane B. Schanz.

THE ROLE OF THE BOUVIER CLUBS

IF it is to progress in quality and in popularity a breed, such as the Bouvier, needs a rallying point for its enthusiasts. Breeders and exhibitors need a base for cooperative efforts. These are just two of the reasons why breed clubs are formed. There are others.

Pioneering one of the rarer breeds to popularity can be a rather lonely undertaking. And, no matter his financial, mental and physical resources every breeder *needs* an opportunity to directly compare his stock against the creations of others active in his chosen breed. Without the opportunity of competition he cannot know if he is progressing or regressing. He cannot know how far he is ahead or behind.

Breed promotion and propagation cannot be a one man or one kennel undertaking for this very reason. In England before World War I one wealthy enthusiast almost succeeded in gaining ownership of *every* quality Flatcoated Retriever. The breed lost its momentum and almost became extinct.

Breed clubs can generate promotional literature. They can be available to answer questions from the public, to make referals to prospective puppy buyers, to formulate and establish a breed standard, to sponsor competitions within a breed, to assist in an exchange of information between breeders and owners—possibly through a breed publication—and become a social outlet for people with a common interest.

71

The Bouvier des Flandres was slow in gaining momentum in the United States until a permanent breed club was established.

Evert Van de Pol made a valiant effort to launch a national Bouvier club in the early fifties. At that time the AKC's policy required a club to gain a local foothold before it could expand to a national membership and influence. Van de Pol's Bouvier des Flandres Club of America was national in name only. The AKC restricted its activities to an area within 60 miles of San Francisco. It held only one AKC sanctioned event—a "Plan A" match in Petaluma, Calif. on January 13, 1952.

Active with Van de Pol in the BFCA were Miss Edmee Bowles, Mr. and Mrs. Roberts Butts, Jr. of Springfield, Ill., Mr. and Mrs. Louis de Rochemont of New York, Hollywood and New Hampshire, Mr. and Mrs. George Young of New Canaan, Conn. and a few other pioneers. Dorothy Young was secretary. Van de Pol lived in California. Most of the rest were on the east coast. Distances apparently were too great—and the time for a national Bouvier club had not come. The BFCA faltered and became inactive.

In November of 1962 Carl May, Jr. and John Elliott discussed the need for a national Bouvier club at the Back Mountain Kennel Club dog show. They felt the time for such an organization had arrived.

May and Elliott compiled a mailing list and sent invitations to an organizational meeting held in connection with the Philadelphia show in December. Seventeen people attended. A committee of Miss Edmee Bowles, John Elliott, Carl May, Jr., Mrs. Edith Sturges O'Connor and Fred Walsh was appointed to draft a constitution and by-laws—and otherwise get things started. It conducted a survey of breeders and owners so the club could cater to the real wants and needs of prospective members. Invitations were then mailed for a first annual meeting on Feb. 11, 1963 in conjunction with the Westminster show in New York. After Westminster's entry of 11 Bouviers had been judged, 21 breed enthusiasts met at the Picadilly Hotel. Fifty-four charter members were enrolled.

The organizational name selected was the American Bouvier des Flandres Club. Elected the first president was Mrs. Edith O'Connor. Miss Edmee Bowles became the initial vice-president, Joan Elliott the secretary and Carl May, Jr., the treasurer. Elected to the board of governors were Mrs. Virginia Bull, Gerald Jacoby, James Neylon and Fred Walsh. John Elliott was chairman.

The time was right. Within six months the club membership had

Carl May, Jr. with John Elliott was responsible for calling the organizational meeting of the American Bouvier des Flandres Club. He's shown here with the best of opposite sex Bouvier at the ABFC's first specialty in 1965. Selected over 44 entries was Ch. Giaconda du Clos des Cerberes.

grown to 72. In October the AKC gave tentative approval to the club's constitution. A first sanction match under "Plan B" was held the same month at Fred and Dorothy Walsh's Deewal Kennels in Flemington, N.J. There was an entry of 32. After the AKC-imposed six month interval, in April 1964 the second "Plan B" match was held. The AKC then approved a "Plan A" match which drew 43 entries in October of 1964. Right on schedule, in April 1965, the second "Plan A" match was held. The ABFC thus completed all of the prerequisites for the offering of an AKC-recognized specialty show. It was almost exactly three years from the first organizational meeting in Philadelphia to the first specialty in the same location. Exhibitors responded with 44 entries, and specialties have been held continuously since.

RITA

The Societe Royale Saint Hubert records her as Lumina, LOSH 86108, a brindle bred by J. Josis of Cuesmes, Belgium from Cleps de la Ville des Doges — Herbelotte du Prefeuillet and whelped March 26, 1937. The AKC records her as Lumina, A270003, owned by Virginia de Rochemont. To the de Rochemonts she was Rita who warned them immediately whenever their young Louis showed symptoms of insulin shock. She so infused the de Rochemonts with appreciation for Bouviers that they continue as owners and breeders. Also, in appreciation, they commissioned Holden D. Wetherbee to execute this etching of Rita, of which only six prints were pulled.

The American Bouvier des Flandres Club became a member club of the American Kennel Club in 1971. The name and address of the ABFC's secretary are listed in each issue of the AKC's official publication, *Pure-Bred Dogs,* under "Member Clubs." Another means of obtaining the secretary's name and address is by request to the American Kennel Club at 51 Madison Avenue, New York, N.Y. 10010.

Terri Bennett's Ch. Jumbouv's Athena, Elsie Guseila's Ch. Pouky Jones CDX, and Betty Jane Gogolin's Ch. Dareventure's Delta Dawn. This candid shot was taken in the mountains in Pennsylvania on the way home from a Bouvier Specialty.

Bouviers from Am. and Can. Ch. Deewal Victor out of Ch. Delanda's Jan'ette Racquel CDX are shown here winning Best of Winners and Best of Opposite Sex. They are Dejoy Kedar CD and Dejoy Kelda CD, respectively. Behind them, left to right, are Glen McVicker, Lenord Kruse, Glen Sommers, Dennis Criss, and Bob Hastings.

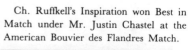
Ch. Ruffkell's Inspiration won Best in Match under Mr. Justin Chastel at the American Bouvier des Flandres Match.

Bruce Jacobsohn finishing Ch. Ishtar du Clos des Cerberes under judge Vance Evans.

Ch. Wittebrug Thor of Oakridge, below, winning Best of Breed at the Golden Gate Show in February 1979.

Ch. Zina, above, is owned by Jane Kramer of Virginia. Zina was sired by Deewal Noah out of Zabeth CD.

Rex Cepheous of Standfast Farm, below, winning Best of Breed at the Heart of the Plains Show, September 1978. Handled by Richard Byrd.

Delanda's Bernadette, by Ch. Delanda's Garcon Brave out of Delanda's Flaxie II, winning first major. Owned by Donna M. and Roy E. Larson.

Below: Mariposa Miracle Mouchette CD (Ch. York de la Grande Maison—Delanda's Keepsake) winning Best of Winners. Owner-breeder handled by Allyn Byrd.

Ch. Delanda's Kizzie, above, owned by Marily Graves of Colfax, California, was sired by Ch. Delanda's Apollo out of Delanda's Flaxie.

Ch. Deewal Challenger finished his championship here at eleven months of age. He was sold to Diane Schanz of California.

Iakof de la Buthiere, below, was bred by international judge George DesFarge of France.

EUROPEAN KENNELS

THE European kennels which are of the greatest interest to Americans and Canadians are those which developed and bred from the foundation dogs, and those that have exported worthwhile breeding and show stock to North America. In most instances those who guarded and refined the breed were also prominent among those who sold good dogs to America. Many of the names encountered in the chapter on Bouvier history will be recorded again in this chapter dealing with important and helpful exporters.

Many extended pedigrees of today's winning dogs show the names of Yoja and Ucaba and others carrying the suffix of Victor Martinage, "de la Ville des Doges."

It would be impossible to overly honor the contributions of the late Florimond E. Verbanck of Ghent who used the suffix, "de Royghem." His diplomacy in keeping French and Belgian breeders working together was only one of his contributions. Like Victor Martinage, he was a highly respected international judge and a dedicated breeder, exhibitor, guardian and promoter of Bouviers.

M. Verbanck had an excellent command of the English language and he gave wise counsel to several generations of North American Bouvier fanciers. A faithful correspondent, his help was always available for the asking. And, he was a gracious host to the many Americans who made the pilgrimage to his kennel. He was in his 83rd year in 1971 when he retired from breeding and shows.

The late Florimond E. Verbanck of Ghent was friend and counselor to virtually all Bouvier breeders in Belgium and the United States during recent years. An early American Bouvier des Flandres Club specialty's best of breed trophy was dedicated in his honor. He was secretary of the Club National Belge du Bouvier des Flandres until well into his 83rd year. It was M. Verbanck who responded to most queries from overseas. He translated for other breeders who did not have a command of English and he infused many with his enthusiasm for and dedication to Bouviers.

Verbanck paid a towering tribute to Justin Chastel of Thuin, Belgium. He said Chastel had "created the modern Bouvier"—that Chastel had bred a distinctive line of such quality that it had, little by little, become the standard of "type" for the breed.

Justin Chastel began his show career in 1932—as a losing exhibitor. His successes began after he purchased, in 1936, a three-year-old bitch named Albionne de Biercee. Her sire, Follie du Ci Blanc, was widely considered the best male of his time. Follie had lost an ear in a fight so Chastel was able to buy him, also.

Then, exhibiting the kind of objectivity which distinguishes outstanding breeders, Chastel passed over his own celebrated stud to use a male he considered a superior mate for Albionne. From her litter by Klaas du Pandore he kept one male, Lucifer de la Thudinie—and thereby launched a great kennel.

Bred back to his dam, Lucifer produced Mirette de la Thudinie. She was soon established as one of Belgium's top ranked Bouviers. Then the Nazis overran Belgium. Mirette was sent to stay with a

Justin Chastel and his son with, respectively, the winning team and the winning brace at a Brussels show about 1957. De la Thudinie has been deep in quality Bouviers for nearly three decades.

Justin Chastel of de la Thudinie, left, with his friend and mentor, the late Florimond E. Verbanck.

farmer friend in the hope that the blight of war would spare both people and dogs and better days would come. Breeding was beyond contemplation. No one could know how long the war might last. Finally, in 1944, Chastel brought Mirette home.

Chastel knew what he liked and he had the courage of his convictions. He selected for Mirette a stud he fancied but which had never been shown. Adolphe Meeus' Joris de Ble d'Or and Mirette produced Soprano de la Thudinie. At the first post-war show in Binche Soprano was something of a sensation. He won the CAC in males and his dam did the same in the classes for females. Soprano went on to an international title and highly rewarding victories. From that point on de la Thudinie dogs have won consistently for M. Chastel and they've won wherever Bouviers have been shown.

Poisoning, the details of which were not disclosed, killed twelve young dogs of the Chastel kennel in 1969. This slowed Chastel's show exhibiting until 1971—but it didn't stop him. His Quarine de la Thudinie won a RCACIB at Paris in 1970. In March of 1972 his Tina de la Thudinie won the CACIB in Paris. At the same show Uhlan de la Thudinie was rated the top young male and Tina received the same award in the young female class. Tina won another CACIB soon after in Luxemburg and went on to defeat the only Bouvier rated ahead of her in Paris.

M. Chastel has assumed at least a part of Florimond Verbanck's role as advisor to those who feel a need to write to "headquarters" for information about Bouviers. However he is not conversant in English as M. Verbanck was.

Edward Moreaux of Brussels, now deceased, made his I'Ile Monsin kennel name famous worldwide. His breeding won at European shows over a period of many years. A recent AKC champion from his kennel is Poukydel I'Ile Monsin. Whelped in 1966, Poukydel was imported and is owned by Isaiah V. Oglesby of Michigan.

Because he came upon the scene some years after Chastel, Felix Grulois, also of Thuin, had the opportunity to build upon Chastel's success. His "du Posty Arlequin" suffix has become as famed in North America as it is in Europe.

Grulois' first exports to the United States came in the early 60's and proved significant more as producers than as show campaigners. Ch. Kaline du Posty Arlequin was prolific; in one litter she whelped 18 living Bouviers—and raised 15 of them. Ch. Nota du Posty Arlequin was an excellent producing dam for Robert Abady.

Int. Ch. Soprano de la Thudinie (Joris du Ble d' Or—Mirette de la Thudinie), top was the post-war foundation sire for Justin Chastel. He was a sensation on the bench—even greater as a producer.

Ksar de la Thudinie, right, had a wet coat when he was photographed immediately after competing in a working trial. In 1968 he was champion of France.

Saga de la Thudinie, left (Rico de la Thudinie—Quattiona de la Thudinie) was whelped in 1969, the year Chastel lost a number of dogs in a poisoning incident She was owned by Serge Shire.

One of Grulois' first Bouviers was Idole du Posty Arlequin. From Ch. Job de la Thudinie she produced for him Linouche du Posty Arlequin — dam of several outstanding winners, some of which were sold to the United States. Eliane de la Thudinie was also purchased from Chastel. Like Idole, she was bred to Job and this mating did much to establish the du Posty Arlequin line. In the litter was Liska du Posty Arlequin, who became the dam of one of the top bitches in American Bouvier history, Ch. Odelette du Posty Arlequin. Eliane also produced the dam of Johane du Posty Arlequin when bred to Bonzo l'Ideal de Charleroi. And, Johane is the dam of the top-winning Bouvier, Chester Collier's Naris du Posty Arlequin.

Naris was sired by one of the greatest champions of the continent, Ch. Marc de la Thudinie.

As might be presumed, neighbors Chastel and Grulois have worked together for many years and the latter credits Chastel with important guidance and instruction. To some extent they still intermingle breeding lines.

Grulois, his wife and their three children do not have an enormous kennel from which to operate. But, because the kennel is in their backyard, they have every opportunity to study closely each of their 20 or so adult Bouviers. (Not all are breeding stock. Some are canine pensioners.) So it is really from a quite modest base that Grulois has achieved so much.

Naris has now retired to grace and guard the Collier's Irvington-on-Hudson home, but his success as a campaigner created a heavy demand for du Posty Arlequin Bouviers. Grulois resisted any temptation to inflate his breeding program and thereby capitalize on the situation. Some of the dogs he sold to America since have made fine show records. One is Ch. Picolette du Posty Arlequin. Another is Ch. Raby du Posty Arlequin. Two that have been fruitful producers of quality are Ch. Sadine du Posty Arlequin, imported and owned by Dr. and Mrs. Arthur Pedersen, and Tania du Posty Arlequin, owned and appreciated by Miss Bowles.

The late Auguste Franshet bred some of the earlier notables. His Ike de Belgique and Fricko de Belgique are sires prominent in many modern pedigrees.

Charleroi, near the French border, is a city with a great dog show. Interest in pure-breds runs high there, and Lebon used the name for

Calli des Coudreaux was bred by Madam Sornin de Leysat of Montfermeil, France. He won the CACIB in Paris in 1956.

Whelped in June 1970 Tania du Posty Arlequin (Rico de la Thudinie—Praline du Posty Arlequin) was imported by Miss Edmee Bowles in 1972, shortly after this photo was taken.

Four excellent fronts are evident in this unposed photo of Demoiselle, Eliane, Irca and Hulotte de la Thudinie. Demoiselle was the dam of Ch. Hion de la Thudinie. Eliane became an important foundation dam in the breeding program of Felix Grulois' du Posty Arlequin kennel. Irca later became an AKC champion.

his "l'Ideal de Charleroi" kennel of winning Bouviers. Bonzo l'Ideal de Charleroi is in the pedigrees of many outstanding dogs. He sired Konard du Rotiane. Konard's dam was Hosca l'Ideal de Charleroi, a great bitch of her time.

The name "du Ble d'Or" was established by Adolphe Meeus of Belgium. His most notable stud was Joris du Ble d'Or, who sired International Ch. Soprano de la Thudinie. Soprano was an outstanding producer. He sired Ucaba, Victor Martinage's dog. When bred to his daughter, he produced Zolla de la Thudinie, dam of the first important American sire, Ch. Coquin de la Thudinie. Coquin, in turn, sired Ch. Chef de Truffe.

The "des Coudreaux" prefix belongs to Madam Sornin de Leysat of Montfermeil, France. She has campaigned her Bouviers successfully over most of Europe. Their progeny are prominent in many American pedigrees.

Ch. Wandru des Coudreaux was another of Miss Bowles' imports. She was a litter sister to Wanda des Coudreaux—and Wanda was the dam of the 1953 champion of the year at the Paris International show, Ch. Ygor des Coudreaux. Among Ygor's get, the most important to American breeders was the aforementioned Coquin de la Thudinie, imported by Mr. and Mrs. George Butts of Springfield, Ill. Coquin was the first Bouvier to win an AKC Working Group.

Joan Butts was among the first of the American breeders to travel to Europe in search of Bouvier breeding stock. Some notes she made in the '50s reflect the inclination of American breeders of that period to look to Dutch breeders. However, this was about the time she imported Coquin and Draga de la Thudinie from Justin Chastel, the first breeder on her list.

Of Florimond Verbanck she wrote: "He is secretary of the Belgian Bouvier Club. When I wrote several Belgian breeders, he replied for them because none spoke English. He does." Her notes continued, "Mr. and Mrs. Vacheniius de Jongh, Hasseltsestraat 27, Scheveningen, Holland. He is a retired ship captain and speaks English. She does not. She runs obedience classes in and around Scheveningen, a suburb of The Hague.

"Dr. Vervoorn-Malinosky Blom, Roelofsstraat 54, The Hague, Holland. She is a veterinarian, speaks fluent English. Our last puppy from her.

"S. v.d. Waardt, Buurtweg 88a, Wassenaar, Holland. I believe he is

Kaline, Irca, Job and Ketty de la Thudinie comprise a formidable quartet of Bouviers.

Quelly, Pia, and Quiar de la Thudinie were whelped in 1966 (Pia) and 1967 as indicated by their names. Quiar was exported to Deewal Kennels.

Ringo de la Thudinie was "Rouge Pommier" at the 1971 Bouvier Specialty Show on the Paris estate of Gilbert Thorp in June 1971. A study of this photo can demonstrate better than any words the desired cobbiness in Bouviers.

Victor Martinage's Yoja (LOSH 152360) was one of the few Bouviers ever to win an international show in Europe. She did it in March 1952. She was by Tory de Groeninghe out of Trika de Groeninghe. Here Martinage wins the "grand prize" with her in Utrecht, The Netherlands. Photo by Jolas, Gravenhage.

Florimond Verbanck called Ygor des Coudreaux, left, and Almyre des Coudreaux "a magnificent brace of Bouviers." Both were bred by Mme. Sorin de Leysat, then of Corbier, France. Ygor was whelped August 30, 1950, and Almyre less than six months later. Both were owned by Rene Canay of Seine, France. Photo by Dim.

Rika du Clos du Petit Neuf Pres, above, was the granddam of Ch. Lutteur du Val de Rol. "Rika" was a recommended producer in France.

Malou du Val de Rol and Mirande du Val de Rol are from Marie Niquet's du Val de Rol Kennel in France. They were sired by Ch. Vulcain du Clos des Cytises.

a police or customs officer. He lives in the remodeled stables of a huge estate. Derby from him. One of the best looking litters of Bouviers I have ever seen. He speaks no English but knows Mr. de Jongh who can reply for him. Wassenaar is also a suburb of the Hague.

"Mrs. W. Neyenhuisen, Kromstraat 62, Oss, Holland. I have not met her and really know nothing about her or her Bouviers.

"Dr. Bernard Bourinet, Rue Lacapelle 68, Montauban (Tarn-et-Garonne), France. This veterinarian has the du Maine-Giraud line. He speaks only French but has a friend who can write in English.

"Mme. Sornin de Leysat, Avenue Vancanson 19, Montfermeil, S. et O., France. I doubt that she has an understanding of English. At least my several letters have been unanswered."

In Europe the title "champion" means considerably more than it does in the United States and Canada. Competitions there are held under the Federation Cynologique Internationale which is based in Brussels. Titles are not structured on the number of dogs defeated but on judicial evaluations of quality. Progression toward a championship can be made only at pre-designated shows. Show-qualified dogs of functional breeds—including Bouviers—must also win a working certificate before they are designated "champion."

This procedure places a strict limitation on the number of champions that can be made in any breed during a given year. So difficult is show championship qualification that exhibitors seek the working certificate qualifications as preludes to serious bench campaigning, there being little point in pursuing a championship unless a dog can go all of the way. At the designated national shows all of the best dogs are usually in competition, including entries from several neighboring countries seeking qualification for the even more difficult title of "international champion."

Even the championship *qualifying* designations are highly respected because they are difficult to achieve and because they are not awarded unless the judge feels he has found deserving quality. Puppies can change as they mature so they are ineligible for all official designations of quality. If an adult entry is the best of its sex and breed and if of approvable quality it can be awarded a C.A.C. which translates as a "certificate of aptitude to championship."

Even more coveted and thoroughly indicative of quality is the title, C.A.C.I.B. (certificate of aptitude to international beauty championship). It is available only at first class shows—in France, for example, at the Paris International.

Because of these high standards, only a few Bouviers have achieved national or international championships under the FCI.

Some of the breed's early champions such as Ch. Nic de Sottegem, Chastel's Int. Ch. Soprano de la Thudinie, Ch. Konard du Rotiane, and Madame Leysat's Ch. Ygor des Coudreaux have already been mentioned. So have Ch. Milton, Ch. Draga Coralie de Sottegem, and Ch. Dragon de la Lys. Other early giants included Ch. Francoeur de Liege and Verbanck's Ch. Volpi de la Vallee l 'Ecaillon.

Later Belgian Bouvier champions include Chastel's Ch. Riva de la Thudinie, Ch. Job de la Thudinie (1963), Ch. Marc de la Thudinie, and Ch. Olaf de la Thudinie (1965). His Ch. Ninette de la Thudinie was exported to Carl May, Jr., and John Elliott. She was the last Belgian champion Bouvier to come to America. Ninette had won Best in Show at Brussels.

Orlof de la Sapience lives in Larrauri, Vizcaya, Spain. He was shown December 9, 1979, at the Madrid Dog Show by Mrs. Miate de Arana.

Deewal's Nantes d'An Naoned, co-owned by John Cooper and Claire D. McLean. Handled by John Cooper.

Ch. Zito Ten Roobos, co-owned and finished by Wally Seger and Claire D. McLean, was sold to Gold Creek Bouvier Kennel.

IMPORTING A BOUVIER

NORTH American Bouvier breeders have been extremely dependent in the past upon imported dogs to improve and replenish their breeding stock. The greatest winners have been, almost exclusively, imported dogs. Now western hemisphere breeders may be at a turning point.

Bouvier popularity on this side of the Atlantic has had a very healthy growth. There are sufficient quality Bouviers here that universal objectivity and close cooperation between our breeders could project homebred Bouvier quality the equal of any. There are already some indications that such a shift is underway.

But, there is no need for any countries without quarantines to be insular in their breeding programs. Jet flights make the shipment of dogs across boundaries and oceans quick, relatively inexpensive, accessible to virtually all and, theoretically at least, safe and humane.

We can, in fact, look ahead to enjoying the fruits of research by Dr. Stephen W. J. Seager at the University of Oregon sponsored by the AKC, and the work of other scientists. Dr. Seager is already, by using improved and carefully controlled laboratory techniques, achieving a pregnancy rate equal to natural from matings via frozen and stored semen. Semen banks and such other techniques as egg removal, storage and implantation, ovarian transplants and in-laboratory fertilization promise future breeders tools whose potentialities dazzle the imagination. For example: Dr. Seager is looking ahead to the day when eggs might be extracted from a prize bitch in the United States, then frozen and stored. Semen from a Belgian stud could be similarly frozen and stored. Sufficient semen and eggs could then be flown to, say, Australia. (By storing the material for the required quarantine period while the donors are closely observed it could be established that neither was a carrier of rabies or other communicable disease — so fulfilling the purposes of Australia's quarantine.) In the country where stored semen and stored eggs meet they could be thawed. The eggs could then be fertilized in a laboratory and then placed in the body of a healthy host mother. Thus a puppy could be whelped in Australia from a dam in North America and a sire in Europe.

This and other projections of today's researches will virtually eliminate time and international boundaries as handicaps to breeders. But, they are slightly into the future as anything more than laboratory experiments. They *do* inform us of the direction of future breedings. They *do* tell us dog breeding will be conducted on an international scale and they portend international registrations (with more uniform concepts and requirements) and international competitions (with more uniform concepts and rules). Breeders who prefer to be rather ahead than behind the times might be well advised to be thinking internationally *now*.

In former times selections for importation into America were made by agents for the purchaser — either a resident of the exporting country or an American professional who traveled abroad on buying trips. A few men made careers in such trade.

Now jet travel, inexpensive in time and money, has put Europe within the reach of all who can afford to realistically contemplate dog importation.

Americans and Canadians are now traveling to Europe by the millions. Most exhibitors and breeders have made at least one trip. Many of these trips have included pilgrimages to the more famous of Europe's kennels. And, the temptations to bring a dog or two home have made importers of thousands.

The author is a part of this trend. In 1973 she, with her husband, traveled to the homeland of the Bouvier to see, to visit, to research — and in hopes of finding a bitch to improve her breeding program.

There is magic in the word "dog." Between people of good will it can be an international "open sesame" to cordial hospitality and new

The author visited the Brussels home of the late Edward Moreaux's widow, he of L'Ile Monsin fame. Above right she photographed Justin and Mme. Chastel with Uberty de la Thudinie. At the Van den Rekels kennel in Holland, left, she found a warm welcome and more good Bouviers. Below, one of the last known photographs of the late Florimond Verbanck, at author's left, with Justin and Mme. Chastel in their home.

De la Thudinie Bouviers share a common exercise run and must therefore be compatable. Quiar de la Thudinie was posed for the portrait at center with breeder Justin Chastel when the future AKC champ was just maturing. At bottom is a view of another exercise area just inside the kennel entrance. The dogs observe visitors closely but they are too well-mannered to compete in raising a fuss.

A recent import to reach America from the noted du Val de Rol Kennel of Marie Niquet, is this bitch, Naomi du Val de Rol, who made many wins in Europe, including CACIB's.

friendships. Among appreciators of Bouviers there is an instant opportunity for rapport. Such was our experience.

Our search for Bouviers and Bouvier history began in Brussels. After some difficulty we located the widow of Edward Moreaux, he of L'Ile Monsin fame. The gracious lady proudly showed us photos, ribbons and other mementos of the kennel's great dogs and their triumphs. The dogs had gone to Justin Chastel's de la Thudinie kennel in Thuin—and that was our next stop.

At Chastel's lovely villa we saw quality Bouviers in abundance. Our first impression was of cleanliness and neatness in and about the kennel. Then we were nearly transfixed by the personalities and the quality of five bitches he showed us. His most prized bitch, Tina de la Thudinie, was not for sale at any price. His Belgian Ch. Riva de la Thudinie was equally treasured. We were taken with a bitch he was then breeding to a young male he esteemed very highly, Tapin de la Thudinie. Silette de la Thudinie's personality, her Bouvier character and her sweet nature captivated us. We could not believe Silette was attack trained until M. Chastel demonstrated her prowess to us. In conformation and bloodlines she offered much that we wanted to add to our breeding program. After brief negotiation she was ours.

Whist des Bois des Saules was, possibly, Europe's winningest fawn in the early '50s. He totaled three CACIBs, 19 CACs and 13 RCACs.

Tina de la Thudinie is the current pride of Justin Chastel's kennel. He has refused to put a price on her and has, in fact, declined some very generous offers.

Happiness for an American Bouvier buff is attending the Bouvier specialty match on the estate of Gilbert Thorp near Paris, especially if it is a beautiful, sweater-weather day—just right for dogs and people.

While in Thuin we were not about to miss the opportunity to meet Felix Grulois and see his du Posty Arlequin Kennel. The Gruloises were gracious and the Bouviers were abundant. The establishment is smaller but of equal quality to that of M. Chastel. Puppies were peeking at us from around corners and displaying all of their winning ways. We were especially impressed with a young bitch, Ultima de la Thudinie, who has since taken several prizes at Belgian shows.

In the Flemish countryside we visited the De Brochian Kennel, where we thought the Bouviers very good in temperament and type. There the top winning campaigner and brood bitch is Querida de la Thudinie, who has been rated "excellent" at shows. Her daughter, Undine de Bronchain, is a young adult full of promise.

Mr. and Mrs. de Blanders have been breeding Bouviers for many years under the tutelage of Justin Chastel. Their "Ten Roobos" suffix is encountered in the pedigrees of many quality Bouviers of today. For examples: Milord Ten Roobos and Quitus Ten Roobos.

A delightful day was spent with Miss Julia Von Vorst at her Ouden Dyk Kennel. A Bouvier breeder for over 40 years, she has exported many fine dogs to North America. She exported Ch. Boris von Ouden Dyk to the Millers in Michigan, one of the earlier quality Bouviers in that area. Evert van de Pol, inactive in Bouviers for several years, has had a resurgence of interest and is showing his imported Quintus von Ouden Dyk.

While in The Netherlands we took the opportunity to visit the Van de Rekels Kennel of Miss Vermuellen in Soest.

Miss Vermuellen showed us a big three year old male, Breston Xandra v.d. Rakkers. Sired by Arnaud Wally v.d. Rekels, he was out of Xandra Peggy v.d. Rakkers. Their pedigrees are exclusively Dutch. They show no infusions, at least not recently, of Belgian bloodlines.

The Dutch customarily use the name of the dam in a registered name. Exandra Peggy v.d Rakkers' name indicates she is out of a Peggy, in this instance Peggy Herta v.d. Rakkers.

The Belgian and French breeders give all puppies whelped in a given year names beginning with the letter of the alphabet designated for that year. These follow in alphabetical sequence. Dogs with "U" names were whelped in 1971. In 1972 names such as Vlada, Vertu, Vonike, and Victor were used. Some American breeders have chosen to follow this rather sensible custom.

We journeyed through the countryside of Holland and Belgium, down through Normandy and into Paris. There we attended a Bouvier specialty match held at the magnificent villa of M. Gilbert Thorp.

Many Bouviers were assembled on the green, sunlit lawns of the rolling grounds — all parading at the ends of leashes held by proud owners. Here we saw the bloodlines of de la Thudinie and du Posty Arlequin in abundance. Mr. and Mrs. Gelineau of Le Blanc have established the Du Clos Des Jeunes Plantes suffix. They are generally considered the most successful Bouvier breeders in France. Their stud, Ch. Quarl du clos des Jeunes Plantes (Karl de L'Ile Monsin-Ninon des Casseaux) won the best male and best Bouvier awards. The top rated female Bouvier was Twiggy du Posty Arlequin, owned by a Miss Nicolle, also of Le Blanc. Victor Martinage judged the males and D. Le Lann judged the females. Between them and with the assistance of Mr. Thorp, they chose the best in match.

With our homeward trip approaching, we felt excited and anxious to get our new Bouviers home. Justin Chastel made all arrangements for necessary[1] papers, health certificates, vaccines and pedigree forms. We notified the airline we would be traveling with one mature Bouvier bitch and two puppies.

In August Silette de la Thudinie whelped eight puppies. They are registered as being imported "in uttero" with Justin Chastel properly listed as their breeder. We kept Deewal Victor and Deewal Victoria. The Hubbards of Madrone Ledge took Deewal Vlinder. The James Seghers of California purchased Deewal Vonika de la Thudinie. Miss Anne Ebert, also of California, took another of Silette's hopefuls. Deewal Volt went to Miss Teresa Troy and another pup was flown to William Marshall in Denver. The eighth pup went to Alger Ashley of Michigan.

---

1. There should also be a bill of sale or equivalent showing the sale price of the dog. The U.S. still has a ridiculous import duty on dogs not intended for breeding purposes. Since this is just about the only possible reason for importing a dog of value, the duty is only rarely collected with justification. Except that it is almost always collected at the point of entry — and then refunded when the proper papers are filed in proper form in proper sequence and on schedule. Customs should be notified of intention to file for a refund and the proper forms secured and executed *at the time of entry.* The Treasury Department has told the House Ways and Means Committee this levy costs the Treasury more to handle than it produces in revenue. The Agriculture Department has informed the same group that the duty is a pointless expense to administer. However, the law remains on the books. (Ed.)

Usti van de Cerbershof, owned by Bob and Trus Stevens and Stan Kohn.

Ciska Flandrienen van Dafzicht, also owned by Bob and Trus Stevens and Stan Kohn.

Ch. Kitalee was awarded Best of Winners and Best of Breed at a show in Texas in the fall of 1977. Peter Knoop judged.

The recommended producer of France, 1976, Ch. Vulcain du Clos des Cytises, won CACIB in Europe at several shows. He was imported by Deewal Kennels, Reg., in 1977, and has produced a line of outstanding champions.

BELCO AND I

by Miss Edmee F. Bowles

The story of the Bouvier in America is characterized by the
story of Miss Edmee Bowles and her Belco. Both were
natives of Flanders. Both served in the struggle against the
Nazis, first in Belgium, then in France, and finally in the
United States. Together they took up a new life here and
stayed to demonstrate to all who would look or listen the joys
and advantages of a Bouvier's companionship. Their arrival
was the beginning of Bouvier popularity in the United
States. Miss Bowles has been an active and successful
breeder, trainer and exhibitor during all of the years since.
She has worked selflessly with dedication, ability and enthusiasm.

During the last several decades Miss Bowles has been advisor, translator, worker in breed promotional campaigns,
club member, and official. Virtually every American Bouvier
breeder has known her as a source of excellent stock, as a
friend, and as a delightful companion.

The terrors of World War II are matters Miss Bowles
has pushed to the back of her mind. She prefers happier
memories, but her story is so much the story of the Bouvier's
emigration to America that she was persuaded to tell it here
in her own words. Editor.

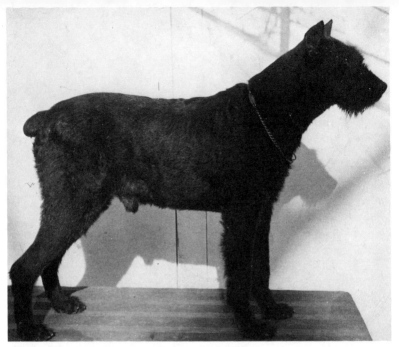

Belco is credited by Miss Edmee Bowles with several times saving the lives of her mother and herself during their escape from the Nazis across Belgium and France and into Spain and Portugal. When Miss Bowles and Belco arrived in the United States in May, 1942 they became the forerunners of — and important factors in — the Bouvier's popularity growth in America. Whelped in November, 1935, Belco died in 1947. This photo was taken in 1942.

I was born in Antwerp, Belgium. My mother was Belgian and my father English and Scotch. World War I drove us from our home to England. After the armistice I stayed to complete my. art studies. I was also interested in breeding and feeding experiments.

In 1932 I returned to Belgium, rejoining my mother who had bought a property in Schilde, about ten miles east of Antwerp on the main road to the German border. The area is known as Campine. It is a flat land with many pine woods.

The old farmhouse had been blown up during world War I. A new villa, Norman style, had been built on an elevation. It was of solid brick with huge chimneys. The house had two secret hiding places. Its builders had remembered the first World War when the Germans took all the valuables — silver, copper and even woolen blankets.

We had about five acres in the front of the house which we laid out with a vegetable garden and fruit trees. A long driveway, about 200 yards, led to the highway where the Belgian army had built a new blockhouse. The drive was bordered with an old copper beech hedge on one side and a wide border of flowers that bloomed from early spring until late fall on the other. Many a motorist would stop to admire the vista with the large meadows, dotted here and there with our prize goats and Westphalian geese.

We had a splendid view from our veranda. A large bell hung on the wall. Beyond were the wide rustic gates, the garage, buildings for stock, stables, a barn and the tenant farmer's house. Then there were more meadows and pine woods. Here our dogs ran freely to guard the property. There had been many robberies and trouble with poachers. Several gamekeepers had been injured and their dogs killed. Next to us was about 2,000 acres belonging to the Baroness of Schilde.

The Dutch Sheepdog we acquired with the house had been beaten almost to death. At first I had some Belgian Sheepdogs, German Shepherds and a couple of Bouvier des Flandres puppies, Dash, a female and Dombey, a male. There was also a terrier that was never home when he was needed.

My Bouviers grew into large, rustic dogs with rough coats, beards, mustaches and whiskers. I was impressed by the way these dogs of Flanders stayed home and by their effectiveness in herding cattle, even when working alone. Little by little the Bouviers superseded all the other breeds. They took over all the chores. The Bouvier is tough when necessary but he isn't mean or trecherous. His presence is a deterrent to wrongdoers. He commands respect with his dignified and determined demeanor.

In the village we formed a club, "Watch and Guard." I was manager. Various breeds came for training. First there were the usual obedience lessons: heel, forward, right and left by word or gesture. Then: jump, scale walls, find the man or object, defend, disarm, bring the man back and, of course, announce. Each dog had to be staunch to gunfire. I took my young Bouviers along and let them watch the older dogs working. They took to the training naturally.

When I acquired Belco he was just ten months old. No one foresaw his illustrious future. He had just recovered from distemper. He was a stoic, an observor and bystander. Other club members made fun saying: "That dog! He would not even say 'boo' to a goose." Dash had won the silver medal as the best working and attack dog. She saw to Belco's training.

Belco learned about the responsibilities of being a Bouvier one day

Miss Bowles has always been aware of the advantages of dramatizing the capabilities and the nature of Bouviers. She has put on many demonstrations at dog shows and other events. She obtained a Belgian dog cart and used it in publicity efforts and charity drives. Here three of her early favorites, Ch. Ellydria, Ch. Marius du Clos des Cerberes and Elfrieda du Clos des Cerberes are seen in a three-dog hitch.

when I drove to a nearby village. While in a shop I left my little niece in the car and the care of Dash and Belco. I was told later what happened. Some young hoodlums tried to get in the car. Dash knew *she* could handle the situation, but it seemed she thought Belco should face up to the situation. Belco wasn't making a move so she pushed, tugged and nipped until the light hit him. He lurched at the hoodlums with a roar!

As the hoodlums ran off Dash sat back. Her body language seemed to say: "At last it has penetrated his thick skull." From then on Belco recognized his duties and took them seriously. Interestingly, he was thereafter the unquestioned leader but he always deferred to Dash.

One morning we found one of my prize turkeys dead on the roost showing little sign of violent struggle. There was only a small puncture in the skull. Our tenant farmer suggested a weasel. That night, shod in high riding boots and armed with a club and flashlight I, with my faithful followers, laid in wait for the killer. Making my rounds I saw a huge, solitary rat. He was standing on his hind legs, hissing and prefering a fight to flight. He defied the dogs. They hesitated and I gave the command: "Attack!" The rat curled himself around one dog's muzzle. It was over like lightning. Before the rat could bite the other dogs destroyed him. He was about the length of a Dachshund. Rats are cunning. I once saw one on his back cuddling an egg while another rat was dragging him by the tail.

The summer of 1939 brought portents and the fear of war. Hitler's defiance and his tank-rattling tested the will of Europe's other powers. They let him retake the Saar which Germany had lost to France in a League of Nations plebiscite. German troops occupied the Sudetenland and annexed Austria. At Munich there was another yielding. Then—the invasion of Poland and the war was on.

France was foolishly dependent upon what it thought was the impregnable Maginot Line of fortifications. It mobilized but there was decay within its government.

In Belgium, also, there was general mobilization. Hitler had said he would never invade Belgium. Some, even in our army, believed him—probably more out of hope than logic. Most of us did not. The Nazis had planned and worked carefully. There was infiltration of both thought and people. Spies, collaborators and saboteurs were among us.

Because our house was the highest point in a flat land reaching toward the German border it was quickly commandeered as an artillery observation post. The guns were placed two miles further back. I quickly became involved. Riding my bicycle with my dogs accompanying me I did not attract attention as I gathered information from which military maps could be corrected for exact fixes of strategic points. Sometimes I would borrow the commander's horse for these expeditions but mostly I cycled. If Dash or Belco got too tired they would jump into a box on my carrier and ride with their front paws on my shoulders.

The infantry soon followed the artillery. About 12,000 strong men took up positions on our grounds and surrounding properties. By then I had more Bouviers. All ran freely except four grown ones that were posted at strategic points.

Trenches were quickly dug, some without consideration of water levels despite my cautions. These were soon waist deep in water. Other units respected my knowledge of our grounds and their trenches were, by comparison, comfortable. The main network of trenches was only 25 yards from our house. A quarter mile further there was an anti-tank canal. Trees in the woods were cut two feet above the ground leaving another tank barrier.

The first floor of our house was reinforced with, first, a layer of tree trunks and then sand bags. Branches and thickets were employed as camouflage for machine gun emplacements and ammunition storage units. Infantrymen were billeted in civilian homes in the village. Two officers lived in our house.

Three men were on duty at each post on a 24 hour watch. The sentries all wanted the help of a dog or puppy, especially during the night watches. No one could come near a Bouvier on sentry duty without the warning of a low growl or nudge. Sleepy soldiers were alerted to the approach of the watch officer on his rounds.

The rolling kitchens, still drawn by horses, were used to feed the men. Each company had its mess call eagerly answered by our Bouviers. They would stand at attention waiting for their share of the chow.

We needed coal for heat and cooking but there were no more deliveries. We improvised a sled and harnessed my dogs to go to the village for supplies. Zulma, our white donkey, refused to move and just sat down!

On May 11, 1940, everyone owning a car was requisitioned to evacuate the old and the sick. When I presented myself I was assigned to go with the secretary of the Town Hall and take the archives of the village to a secret vault in Antwerp. These were huge, leather bound books with brass fasteners. Luckily I had reinforced springs and heavy duty tires which, in peacetime had been used to absorb the weight of a trailer to bring grain from the docks. During scarcity, this stood in good stead when I had to drive in ploughed fields to avoid shell holes. All the chrome on the car had to be painted with a special blue paint. We also had to drive without lights during black-outs. On my return, when crossing the bridge in Wyneghem where I left the Secretary, I saw a plane in the canal. I proceeded home, alone with Belco.

It was three a.m. when I arrived home with Belco as bodyguard. There were many difficulties as the password to go through the lines had been changed. Several times I was challenged by a sentry pointing his rifle with fixed bayonet. It was a very uncomfortable feeling, especially when I could see a nervous, shaky hand on the trigger. After only two hours' rest I was ordered to leave for the coast as the bridge between was mined and scheduled for demolition.

There is hardly anything more fun than being a Bouvier pup. This du Clos des Cerberes fellow believes the world was put here for him to enjoy. Later he will learn about and assume responsibilities. The Flemish bakery cart asks for a bit of understanding. The dog is so hitched that he can help push — but it would seem he could, if inclined, just keep pace. Certainly his presence would deter swipers of sweets while the baker is away making deliveries. Puppy photo by Howard Kling. Cart photo from the collection of the late Janet W. Mack.

My mother and I hastily loaded the car and trailer with mattresses and blankets. I also took my bicycle. Later it was my only means of transportation. We also included a good supply of eggs. We left another 2,000 eggs for the stationed army as their supplies were overdue.

I chose Belco to accompany us. Dash was getting older and the younger ones had not had as much training or experience.

When we arrived at my sister's house in Antwerp the cook told us the family had already gone to La Panne on the coast. Bombs were already falling. We left some of our silverware, preferring a good supply of eggs. We took a large supply of gasoline in cans which had been brought from the tanks for us. My brother-in-law was manager for the Atlantic Refining Company in most countries in Europe. He had ordered large supplies of sugar to be dumped in the tanks at the approach of the German army. This would not only make the gas useless for refueling their tanks but it would jam the motors of their vehicles.

The slow exodus to the coast took nearly two days for what was normally only about three hours' drive. The roads were blocked by army and civilian traffic. Refugees were in all conditions. They moved by car, bicycle, wheelbarrow and on foot, besides anything on wheels that would move. Ghent already had been bombed and there was no room anywhere. We drove through the iron gates of the château. We introduced ourselves and begged for a night's lodging. Belco and some eggs, a rare commodity then, were an "Open Sesame" as they were often to be on our long journey.

We rejoined some of the family at the coast. Then we were ordered to move to France. Our point of entry had been closed.

After some arrangements we joined the Bell Telephone Company convoy ordered to Paris with their special equipment. When crossing the border I ordered Belco to hide under the mattress to avoid further delay with customs. French troops on the crossroads separated us from the rest of the convoy so we about did a "tour" of France; Calais, Abbeville and Dunkirk were included. We had to keep taking shelter, whenever possible, from planes dive-bombing or machine-gunning the civilians. At one time going bumper to bumper along a lane bordered by trees on one side, open fields on the other, we jumped out of the car leaving Belco to guard it. We ran toward a cluster of trees and landed in a manure heap. Returning to our car we saw many people walking about in dazed condition. One young couple held their dead baby in their arms. They heard crying and stopped. There was another baby beside its dead parents. After some hesitation the couple exchanged babies.

We headed for Clermont-Ferrand where we had friends. Our car was impounded and we spent three weeks there. We hid our trailer, supply of gasoline and tools in the garage of our friends' summer cottage. During this period I kept busy. Depending upon my bicycle for transportation and Belco for protection I tried to help the refugees who were arriving in most pitiful conditions. The Germans came closer and closer until they were in Vichy, just three miles away. Luckily for us the Germans stopped there to enjoy the wines and champagne. That gave us a few hours to get away.

Refugees were ordered to remain where they were but I was afraid to encounter the Germans and I had better reason to fear them than I knew then. I found out much later that our tenant farmer had betrayed me and that there was a price for my capture.

Always the Bouvier booster, Miss Bowles here donned an authentic Flemish milkmaid costume, hitched her great favorite, Ch. Marius du Clos des Cerberes, to a cart and got their photo in one of America's great newspapers. Philadelphia Evening Bulletin photo.

Smuggling is an ancient profession. Almost as old is the device of training a dog to carry the booty across the border. Belgian customs officials countered by training *their* Bouviers to contravene the canine contraband carriers. At the Valley Forge show in 1953 Miss Bowles, in an authentic customs uniform of 1900, demonstrated both facets of this training. Loaded with tobacco Ch. Marius did the smuggler dog crawl. His kennelmate, Ch. Ellydria, "captured" him. Photo by Shafer.

The leaving was difficult and dangerous. From our cache I took two heavy cans of gasoline and strapped them onto my bicycle. Belco helped me push the load up the hill and I brazenly "liberated" our car.

I hurried back to the châlet where I made inquiries how best to get out of town. It was important that we discipline ourselves against panic. We waited until dark before loading up. I had become a familiar sight with my bike and my dog but this was a different matter. Every detail had to be anticipated. The policeman on duty that night was paid to look the other way. We had to cross the mountains by moonlight. The route over Mount Dore, 6,000 feet up, was by a narrow, winding road.

Traveling without lights we headed for Perigueus on the way to Bordeaux. At that port on the southwestern coast of France we hoped to rejoin my sister, her husband and daughter. Cars were abandoned everywhere along our route. Some were wrecked. Many had become totally useless when they had consumed their last drop of gasoline.

We hoped to be in time to board the Manhattan for the last trip from France to the United States. But enroute we were told the Germans had surrounded Bordeaux. We selected Bayonne as our best alternative. It is the next furthermost town on the Bay of Biscay. We again went east for a visa to Cahors, an ancient Roman town. There we found more confusion, people shouting and pushing. Officials at the headquarters pushed everyone out of the building.

I went to the back of the building and crawled in through a window. Then I stood calmly at the desk. Because I was so calm it was assumed I belonged. When the post commander arrived I was able to depart quickly.

I had left my mother in the car with Belco. Even during what must have been a time of great stress for him a man felt he had to stop for a moment. He said: "Oh, a Bouvier. I owe my life to a Bouvier in World War I. I was left for dead in the trenches. The medics, accompanied by a Bouvier passed me over. They found no sign of life but the Bouvier insisted. On the chance the dog was right they took me into the medical station. That was twenty years ago."

After many more adventures and urged by the peril of our situation we reached Bayonne. As usual there were no accommodations available. The French had signed an armistice. That seemed only to create more confusion, if such was possible. We had to sleep in the car, my mother on the front seat, Belco and I on the back seat. I was awakened from an uneasy sleep by Belco on the attack. He lept to the front seat and grabbed a man pointing a revolver at my mother. There was another man on the other side of the car. I never saw two men run so fast! We would not have been the first casualties of plunderers in those lawless days.

We had to remain in the Pyrenees for 18 months. Food was extremely short and we had to exist on 900 calories a day. It was during this period that Belco again saved my life. While cycling on a mountain road an oncoming truck, loaded with overhanging bags, swerved onto my side of the road leaving me barely a foot between it and a drop over the edge. I laid flat on the handlebars. Belco was leashed at my right. By pulling as hard as he could he kept me from falling under the wheels of the truck. The truck went on, leaving me in a heap on the road. Belco helped me home.

Finally, after three months in Portugal, we were able to embark for America. We arrived safely in May of 1942.

Belco and I gave training exhibitions for Dogs for Defense. We helped to train trainers for the Coast Guard's K-9 Corps. The Coast Guard had obtained the fine female, Ch. Lisa. From her Belco sired puppies for Dogs for Defense. Further, he and Lisa helped to raise funds for the program by pulling carts with collection boxes.

Belco died when he was 12 years old, brave and loyal to the end. I had him embalmed and brought him here to Collegeville, Pa.

We were never reimbursed for the military occupation and damage to our home in Belgium. What was not demolished by V-bombs was stolen. I had had a price on my head but thanks to Belco we were always a step ahead of the advancing German army. They searched for me to the end. I lost everything I owned except Belco. He lives on through his descendents, never forgotten.

European photographer DIM has captured Bouvier intensity and character in this head study of Dalila de la Fontaine au Roy. This daughter of Whist de Bois des Saules out of Youlande des Coudreaux was whelped in January 1956 and was a winner in Paris and elsewhere.

Miss Bowles walks her Roland du Clos des Cerberes in the snow at the entrance to Belco Farm.

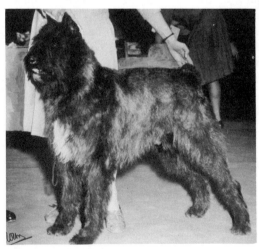

Ch. Chef de Truffe became an important winner and sire for Miss Bowles. He was bred by Joan Butts (Ch. Coquin de la Thudinie—Ch. Draga de la Thudinie). He is pictured here as he won Best of Breed at Westminster in 1962. Photo by Brown.

EARLY KENNELS IN AMERICA—1930-1974

Blueberry Bank Kennels

THERE was no blaring of trumpets, no roll of drums to celebrate the arrival of the first Bouviers in the United States. The first dogs may have come here with returning World War I doughboys. If so there seems to be no record of their residence here. Certainly they had no lasting impact on Bouvier history in America.

Of those Bouviers arriving in the late 20's and the 30's there are some bare facts as represented in the AKC records of their registrations. The owners are mostly gone or untraceable. Show records don't tell us much because there were few entries. Because it was almost impossible to find competition in the breed, owners of the time usually found dog shows a zestless exercise. Such was the experience of Mrs. Virginia de Rochemont, one of the very few people of that era who still has an interest in Bouviers and vivid recollections of the dogs she and her family have enjoyed since the late 30's.

In the 1930's and 40's Louis de Rochemont was a very busy and influential man. He was the driving force behind Pathe Movietone News and he was a cofounder of the March of Time. In pre-television days these were two of the world's most important opinion molders. Newsreels were a part of every movie program and the March of Time in its movie and radio versions had a virtual monopoly on dramatization of the news.

115

This is Louis de Rochemont's account of how he and Virginia de Rochemont came to be pioneer Bouvier owners and breeders in the United States. "At the age of three our son, Louis de Rochemont III, was diagnosed as diabetic. His doctor told us: 'Listen, you must get a dog for this child.'

"We turned to my brother Richard for advice, as he was then the dog lover and owner in our family. Richard was living in France where he had Bouviers and he procured for us and shipped a trained female Bouvier we called Rita. She at once took charge of young Louie. She slept with him. He was subject to insulin shock. Whenever he began to wiggle and waggle she would come into our room and wake us. We always kept orange juice ready and, with Rita's warnings we were, time after time, able to keep the child from going into a coma.

```
LUMINA RITA, LOSH 86108, female, whelped Mar. 26, 1937, Breeder - J. Josis

              Demosthene, LOSH 36211          Bolton, LOSH 36208
        Freton, LOSH 52949                    Lidiane, LOSH 27904
              Rita, property of M. G. Carette Unknown
  Cleps de la Ville des Doges, LOSH 52960     Unknown
              Doudou du Grand Marais, LOSH 36162  Bruno de Rebecq, LOSH 28646
        Franchette, LOSH 47280                Viviane, LOSH 36162
              Esperance de la Roselle, LOSH 40390  Bolton, LOSH 35208
                                              Viviane, LOSH 36162

LUMINA RITA, LOSH 86108

              Stop du Genie, LOSH 18068       Brillant, LOSH 12939
        As du Prefeuillet, LOSH 23832         Sora de Ramillies, LOSH 9586
              Olivette de la Lys, LOSH 19383  Goliath de la Lys, LOSH 13021
  Herbolette du Prefeuillet, LOSH 54890       Dinah de la Lys, LOSH 13281
              Stop du Genie, LOSH 18068       Brillant, LOSH 12939
        Ottara, LOSH 54703                    Sora de Ramillies, LOSH 9586
              Corona, LOSH 48350              Triumph de Pont-a-Rieu, LOSH 19905
                                              Sara, owned by M.E. Decroes
```

"Lumina Rita, our first Bouvier, was whelped in 1937. Since she was already trained when she came to us that must have been in 1938. We bought our best Bouvier, a fine big, gray fellow, Czardas van het Bunderbosh, just before the Nazis marched into Holland. He had been judged 'the Queen's champion' and he came to us on the last Dutch ship to sail for New York. Strangely, we did not get the bill for him until after V-E Day."

Other importations followed the war. Virginia de Rochemont became interested in breeding. There was one litter of 16 but all did not survive. A number of Bouvier puppies were bestowed upon appreciative friends. One even went to movie mogul Jack Warner, the man whose earliest successes were Rin Tin Tin pictures. A de Rochemont Bouvier appeared in the film, "Outward Bound."

Like Evert van de Pol on the west coast, the de Rochemonts plan

Family portrait is of Ch. Aurega du Clos des Cerberes winning the brood bitch class at the specialty in 1968. Aurega's on the left with George Edge. Altaire and Bunji were nine month old pups. At middle left is Aurega when she went BOS at the '67 specialty. Zorina du Clos des Cerberes, right, was the second bitch to win a west coast show title. Imported Ch. Remando's Katleen, bottom left, and her daughter, Ch. Elaine du Clos des Cerberes, right, were also outstanding producers. All photos except Zorina by Gilbert.

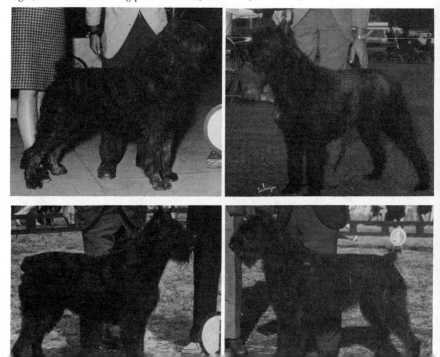

to resume breeding Bouviers. When they were interviewed Virginia de Rochemont said: "Bouviers are right for these times. They are the kind of dog people want and need today."

De Rochemont added: "We love all dogs but we think Bouviers are especially wonderful. We plan to breed them again. Our kennels at our New Hampshire home, Blueberry Bank, are nearly ready and I've made inquiries to obtain new breeding stock."

Among the breeds in the United States during World War II Bouviers must have had the highest per capita enlistment in the Dogs for Defense program. De Rochemont Bouviers also served in the Coast Guard.

Du Clos des Cerberes

In the previous chapter Miss Edmee Bowles told the story of flight from her European home just ahead of the Nazis—and of how she, her mother and her Bouvier, Belco, arrived in the United States and made their home in Collegeville, Pa.

A man from the Philadelphia area, Commander Newbolt Ely, was placed in charge of the Coast Guard's war dog program. For him Miss Bowles trained both dogs and trainers. So she could also breed Bouviers for the Dogs for Defense program she obtained a bitch, Lisa, from George Young of New Canaan, Conn. Lisa was a daughter of the first AKC Bouvier champion, Boojar van Westergoo, a Dutch import.

Early in 1958 Miss Bowles purchased Wandru des Coudreaux from France. In 1960 she imported Remado's Katleen from Belgium. Then she bought Chef de Truffe from Robert and Joan Butts of Springfield, Ill. These became the du Clos des Cerberes foundation dogs. From them has come a long line of obedience and show winning Bouviers—and many more that were successful as family companions.

Chef de Truffe (Coquin de la Thudinie - Draga de la Thudinie) finished his championship title with a five point major and 23 points. He was nine times best of breed from the classes. His sire had 30 group placements including one first—often showing under judges who had never before seen a top quality Bouvier.

Belco and Ch. Lisa produced Ch. Marius du Clos des Cerberes, one of Miss Bowles' all time favorites. He was the Westminster best of breed each year, 1945-50. He was also a group placer. Miss Bowles had bought Ch. Ellydria from Evert van de Pol. Bred to her he pro-

Above: The five points she won as Best of Winners at the ABFC's first Specialty in 1965 went a long way toward Del-Poppy du Clos des Cerberes' AKC show title. Club co-founder Carl May presented the trophy. Owner Mrs. Carrie Adell was prideful. Handler Pat Marcmann watched the photographer, and the late Albert Van Court, who judged, held the ribbons. Photo by Gilbert.

Mrs. Ingrid Kornheiser shows her bitch, Ch. Aries du Clos des Cerberes, as a young female before she finished. Aries went on to produce many champions for the du Clos des Cerberes Kennels of Edmee Bowles.

duced Bel Ami du Clos des Cerberes. Bel Ami sired seven champions including Ch. Sapho du Clos des Cerberes.

Through all the years the unquenchable Miss Bowles has been an imaginative and active press agent for Bouviers. She either made or imported costumes and other props which were used in photographs that won Bouviers space in newspapers and magazines all over North America.

Miss Bowles' Bouviers continue to win. In 1971 Ch. Jaspar du Clos des Cerberes went from the open dog class past all the champions competing to win the American Bouvier des Flandres Club's annual specialty show. A homebred, he's by Ch. Altair du Clos des Cerberes out of Brabo du Clos des Cerberes.

In 1972 Miss Bowles imported Tania du Posty Arlequin, then in whelp to Sim de Bronchain. She has, at this writing, great hopes for all of the litter of eight—and especially for the two which she kept. Miss Bowles is always seeking new challenges—and better Bouviers.

Madrone Ledge

Ray and Marion Hubbard had had Saint Bernards, Poodles, an Irish Wolfhound and a Bedlington Terrier. They were visiting San Francisco's Golden Gate show in 1953 when they had their first real encounter with a Bouvier. They were captivated by the combination of gentleness, character and authority. The dog on the bench was being exhibited by Bouvier pioneer Evert van de Pol—and they sought him out and purchased Cere Bere, a bitch by Bonaparte v. Darling-Astrid.

Cere Bere didn't know enough about automobiles and highways. She was killed in 1957. Later the Hubbards replaced her. Through Miss Janet Mack they imported a three-month-old bitch, Krepsie de la Thudinie. She became the first Bouvier to win an AKC championship on the west coast in 15 years. Krepsie was a pale silver with a black mask. Her kennel name, Flax, was descriptive. At that time the Hubbards were still living in Ross, California. There was a degree of frustration in showing Bouviers on the west coast at that time due to a dearth of breed competition. Only Mrs. Dorothy Stern of Goleta, Calif., with two dogs (one from Evert van de Pol and a Dutch import) was providing competition.

The Hubbards bought Beiard D'l'Vons. Bred to Krepsie he sired a litter of fawns and light brindles.

In 1965 Madrone Ledge moved to Sands Point, Long Island. A year later the Hubbards imported the littermates, Pebbles du Posty Arlequin and Pepita du Posty Arlequin. Both completed AKC show titles.

In 1966 Mrs. Hubbard, with help from Miss Mack, rescued Grenadier Coquette of Walden from a girls' school where she had been given temporary shelter when abandoned. She was one of two puppies whelped in 1962 by the then ten-year-old Coquette de la Thudinie. The dam was a litter sister to Ch. Coquin de la Thudinie that had been imported by the Butts of Springfield, Ill. Grenadier Coquette of Walden first went to Mrs. Hubbard, Sr. on the west coast and it was there she won her AKC title.

Chet Collier of Irvington-on-Hudson, N.Y. bought Coquette and began showing her, along with his Madrone Ledge Blazen.

In 1967 Marion Hubbard attended Belgium's Charleroi dog show. She came home with Odelette du Posty Arlequin and word of a spectacular dog named "Naris."

In 1968 Ray Hubbard toured Belgium kennels. Shortly afterwards he purchased Picolette du Posty Arlequin. Odelette became the top winning Bouvier bitch in 1968 and 1969 and won the largest specialty in 1969 under the noted Belgian breeder and judge Victor Martinage. In 1971 Picolette became the first bitch to win the working group and a best in show. She also won the ABFC National Specialty at Philadelphia.

Madrone Ledge Socrate, at two years of age, became the first American-bred Bouvier to win a best in show. The following weekend he added best of breed at the 1971 Specialty in Philadelphia.

Ray and Marion Hubbard share in the challenge of breeding, training and showing better and better Bouviers. Their energies and devotion to the breed are, in appreciable measure, responsible for the Bouvier's healthy growth in North America.

Redfox Kennels

Life's greatest pleasures are often unplanned. In 1960 Carolyn and Charles Markham of Bartley, New Jersey bought their first Bouvier for companionship and as a measure of security in their automobile agency. Deewal Bonne Amie became much more than that. The daughter of Ch. Argus de la Thudinie-Ch. Deewal Nicole at her first show went from the puppy class to reserve winners bitch. She finished her championship before she was two years old.

Bred to Ch. Rostan du Clos des Cerberes she produced a litter of eleven. Of these three, Ch. Redfox Lariat CD, Ch. Redfox Velvet Lassie CD and Ch. Redfox Clonmel won a total of five AKC titles. By then the Markhams had enthusiastically undertaken the Bouvier challenge.

Carolyn Markham bred her Lassie to Ch. Picard des Preux Vuilbaard and kept a puppy she called Redfox Liberty Bell. He went on to become the first Bouvier to win American, Canadian and Mexican titles.

Clonmel was bred to Virginia de Rochemont's Jingles of Blueberry Bank in 1965. He produced Ch. Redfox Smokie, the first Bouvier to win American, Canadian and Bermudian CD's—and all with distinction.

The Markhams imported Ch. Quina de la Thudinie produced just one litter before she died of intestinal complications. From her litter by Lariat she produced Redfox Quina Tubbina. That was in 1967.

Ernest Topoliski of York, Pa. bred his Blandford's Bianca to Smokie. In that litter were Ch. Babka de Saint Roch and Ch. Babette de Saint Roch. In 1971 from imported Sia du Posty Arlequin Smokie produced Redfox Whisp of Smoke that won nine points before she was 17 months old and went on to reserve winners bitch at the 1971 specialty.

Meanwhile Carolyn Markham's commitment to Bouviers had been expanding beyond that of owner, breeder, exhibitor and obedience trainer. She had hired a professional handler the first time she had shown Bonne Amie. In 1967 the AKC licensed her as a "limited handler" after an apprenticeship under W. Harry Manning.

Kennel names hopefully become something of a breeder's trademark. Sometimes they are capriciously chosen. Sometimes they find their origins in foreign languages—as with French and Bouviers. These can be difficult to spell and even more difficult to remember. The Markhams chose Redfox for reasons beyond its distinctness and rememberability. They had shown horses for some years before dis-

Ch. Redfox Lariat CD was a home-bred. Sired by Ch. Rostan du Clos des Cerberes, he was out of Ch. Deewal Bonne Amie. The judge in this photo is James W. Case and the handler W. Harry Manning.
All photos by Gilbert.

Redfox Clonmel was just past his second birthday when he completed his show title at the Mid-Hudson show in July 1965. Maxwell Riddle judged and W. Harry Manning handled.

Ch. Deewal Bonne Amie (Ch. Argus de la Thudinie - Deewal Nicole) es-tablished herself as the matriach of Redfox Kennels in Flanders, N.J. On this Feb. 1965 day in Hartford owner Carolyn Markham handled and Frank Foster Davis judged.

Ch. Quina de la Thudinie was pho-tographed winning three points at Bucks County in 1969 just six weeks after whelping 14 puppies. Mrs. Charles G. Markham, co-owner of Redfox Kennels handled. The judge was Henry Stoecker.

covering Bouviers. Redfox was their fabulous open jumper that competed until he was 33 and lived to the age of 36.

Blandford Kennel

In past years, one of the strongest Bouvier forces in the Midwest has been the Blandford Kennel of Agnes and Pat Miller in Mt. Clemens, Mich.

Blandford's foundation stud and top winning show dog was Ch. Boris van de Ouden Dijk, imported from Miss Julia Van Vorst of The Netherlands. "Nikki's" winnings in the Midwest were important steps in helping Bouviers become better known in that part of the country. In 1968 he was the top winning Bouvier in Canadian shows, the best stud dog class at the ABFC Specialty in 1969. The latter is a competition where a sire is shown with his get — and Nikki sired many winners before his death in 1971. One son, Blandford's Raoel, was one of the youngest Bouviers to win both American and Canadian championships. Raoel was also the 1969 second-ranking Bouvier in Canadian shows and best of opposite sex (to best of breed) at the 1969 ABFC Specialty.

A Blandford bred Bouvier was the first to win a Canadian show. Ch. Blandford's Basko, owned by Mr. and Mrs. Harry Dyk of Norlock Kennels, Kleinburg, Ontario, won the 1972 Canadian National Sportsmen's Show. He's by Nikki out of Penny the Pooh.

Des Preux Vuilbaards Kennel

The 120 plus breeds recognized by the AKC are such a diverse lot that there is a pure-bred dog for almost every conceivable human taste and need. Even within Bouviers there is opportunity for a wide range of opinion and expression through ownership, breeding, and training, and in show and obedience competitions.

Robert Abady of Des Preux Vuilbaards Kennel is an individualist with strong opinions on many subjects — and especially on Bouviers. Like the Europeans, he believes Bouviers should be attack trained. He sees the Bouvier as a law and order adjunct. In a controversial *Sports Illustrated* article he was quoted as saying it takes about a year to train his Bouviers to attack and that he selects only the most stable dogs for this work.

This homebred brother-sister combination became double holders of AKC titles. Ch. Redfox Lariat CD and Ch. Redfox Lassie CD had this double win at Westminster in 1967 under Judge Peter Knoop. Lariat was best of breed and Lassie winners bitch. Carolyn Markham handled.

Ch. Giaconda du Clos des Cerberes was best of opposite sex at the ABFC specialty in 1965. Pat Marcmann handled for owner Carl B. May, Jr. Both photos by Shafer.

If the success of Abady's breeding program was measured only by the success of Des Preux Vuilbaards Bouviers on the bench — admittedly a standard some might be expected to reject — the record would be outstanding.

Abady was born in Curacao, the Dutch West Indies. At 21 he traveled to Germany and Holland. There he first came to know the Bouvier des Flandres. In 1963 he bought his first Bouviers and settled on a Quebec farm. Later he became discouraged with his stock, discarded what he had, and moved to Stormville, N. Y. For breeding stock to meet his high standards, he traveled to Belgium. There he bought Nota du Posty Arlequin and two other bitches. His great triumph, however, was the acquisition of Ch. Marc de la Thudinie. Justin Chastel is quoted as calling Marc the greatest dog he ever owned. Marc was best in show at both Brussels and Charleroi. He continued his winning ways in the U.S., but it was as a stud that he made his greatest contribution here.

For Abady, Nota produced the outstanding winner and sire, Ch. Prudhon des Preux Vuilbaards. Among his many winning get are Ch. Hanover's Alon and Ch. Hanover's Ardanne, owned by Dr. Clifford and Joyce Bodarky.

Bibarcy Kennels, Reg.

Art and Mary Pedersen were well indoctrinated in dog breeding and dog shows when they first welcomed a Bouvier into their home. Bibarcy's first winners were Collies. Soon after, they added Miniature Schnauzers. Their Collie bitch Bibarcy's Blueberry a la Mode was not only best in show quality, she did win a show.

The Pedersens bought their first Bouvier for their son in 1964, but she failed to survive an outbreak of encephalitis. Being dog-wise, they knew the right time to buy a puppy is when the right puppy is available. At Deewal Kennels they reserved a puppy from Ch. Deewal Argusette by Ch. Job de la Thudinie.

Their patience paid off. Bibarcy's Job's Daughter became one of the top producing Bouvier dams, and eight of her whelps won

Owned by John Cooper, Coopers Babette des Bibarcy was the dam of Champions Bouvchon's Wee Babette Trote and Coopers Rocky des Bouvchon.

Only thirteen months old when he completed both American and Canadian championships, Ch. Blandford's Raoel exemplifies "desirable cobbiness."

Ch. Koala du Clos des Cerberes CD, left, was Best of Opposite Sex at the October 1977 Superstition Kennel Club Show. Owner-handled by Diane Novak.

Ch. Delanda's Black Orchid, below (Ch. Terry du Posty Arlequin—Redfox Flaxie) is owned by Shirley and Jorge Landa.

AKC show titles. Five came from one litter by Ch. Deewal Demon Ripp. The other three were from a litter sired by Ch. Deewal Homer.

Job's Daughter's most spectacular scion is Ch. Bibarcy's Soldat de Plomb, who in a short time won six bests in show. Plomb was the second American-bred Bouvier to win a show. He was the first dog of American-bred parents to do so.

A 1969 litter by Ch. Pebbles du Posty Arlequin - Ch. Bibarcy's Cassandra produced two more show titlists, Ch. Tambour de Ville and Ch. Bibarcy's Tourterelle. Also in 1969 the Pedersens imported Sadine du Posty Arlequin. She became an AKC champion in 1971.

For many years Dr. and Mrs. Pedersen maintained his practice, their home and kennels in Council Bluffs, Iowa. Their move to Gaffney, S.C., in 1971 established a Bouvier "beachhead" in the South, and in 1978, Bessamer, Alabama, became their home.

Hilgrand Kennels, Reg.

Murray and Shirley Horowitz of North Woodmere on Long Island in New York registered their Hilgrand Kennels in 1967. Their foundation Bouviers were Ch. Deewal Hardiesse and Ch. Deewal Grand Prix. They bred Deewal Samantha, the first Bouvier to win an AKC sanctioned match at the Suffolk County Kennel Club in 1967. The Horowitzes declare Samantha was given the Deewal prefix as their tribute to the encouragement and assistance they had received from the late Dorothy Walsh.

The Horowitzes brought Ralph and Sandi Goldman of South Salem, N.Y., into the Bouvier ranks when they sold them, as a puppy. Ch. Hilprize Kelli Sandra (Ch. Job de la Thudinie - Ch. Deewal Hardiesse). The Goldmans, in turn, bred Ch. Vlaanderen's I'm Kelli Too (Ch. Prudhon des Preux Vuilbaard - Ch. Hilprize Kelli Sandra). Kelli Too was at one time the youngest Bouvier ever to attain an AKC championship. Whelped March 27, 1973, she finished at the Philadelphia show in stiff competition on Dec. 9, 1973. She was just 258 days old — or just a bit over 8½ months! It was an especially gratifying accomplishment for the Goldmans, since the dam died shortly after giving birth.

The Horowitzes showed Ch. U Oliver des Preux Vuilbaard (Ch. Noceur de la Thudinie - Taquine des Preux Vuilbaard). He has

129

many best of breeds and six group placements to his credit. A show career represented quite a change of life-style for Oliver. Shirley Horowitz found a classified ad in a community newspaper offering a young adult Bouvier for sale. Curiosity prompted a phone call. It was explained the family could no longer keep their pet. When the Horowitzes heard the pedigree, they had to see the dog. When they saw, they bought. The Horowitzes had Ch. Nomura Wave and Ch. Chainte Vicaire on the show circuit. However, it is as scholars of all of dogdom that the Horowitzes are best known. Their cynological library is one of the most comprehensive and judiciously assembled in North America. Some of their prints, bronzes, and other art pieces depicting Bouviers are pictured in the chapter on the Bouvier in Art.

Bras De Fer Kennels

Sometimes a first dog's successes will so infect his owners with "showitis" that their involvement and delights will grow and grow. That's the way it happened to Frank and Lil Mees of West Chester, Pa. The puppy they bought at Robert Abady's des Preux Vuilbaards Kennel was too young to take home. When he arrived, they named him Nic. It wasn't until his papers arrived that they discovered his registered name was to be Prudhon des Preux Vuilbaards. That was in 1966.

Less than a year later at the Bouvier National Specialty in Philadelphia, Nic, at 13 months, went from the American-bred class all the way to best of winners — over Odelette, the winner in the open bitch class and the rest of the class females — and over the winner of the open dog class. *And* the winner of the open dog class that day was an import with considerable potential — Naris de la Thudinie. The judge was the late Albert E. Van Court.

In July 1968 Vuilbaard offered Frank Mees a bitch that was failing her opportunities as a brood bitch. They bought the Ch. Job de la Thudinie bitch, Oriane, a fawn. After patient treatment for a low-grade vaginal infection, they bred her to Nic. Oriane pro-

This head study of Genadier Aleida of River Oakes CD might be used to illustrate many desirable factors such as character, intensity, careful grooming, proper ear set and trim and coat quality. Aleida was owned and trained by Virginia Bull of New Jersey.

Ch. Ripeau Bras de Fer, above, was owned by Mr. and Mrs. Jay Arnold of Northfield, N.J. Although not bred by Vuilbaard, she was from Vuilbaard stock, which in this instance was three-quarter Chastel. She was by Prudhon out of Orianne. Photo by Gilbert.

Ch. Picard des Preux Vuilbaards was by Marc de la Thudinie out of Nota de la Thudinie—and that made him a full brother to Ch. Prudhon des Preux Vuilbaards. Photo by Gilbert.

Ch. Ur des Preux Vuilbaards was owned by Mr. and Mrs. Fred Joyner of Port Tobacco, Md.

duced several outstanding litters. In her first was Ch. Ripeau Bras de Fer owned by Mr. and Mrs. Jay Arnold of Northfield, N.J.

Until Naris passed him, Nic was the winningest Bouvier in AKC history. He had 93 best of breeds, eight group firsts and 29 additional group placements.

A Nic daughter, Ch. Bougie de Feu Allure, owned by Mr. and Mrs. Walter Herec of Detroit, won her title at the age of nine months. (That was the record until her half-sister (via Nic), Ch. Vlaanderen's I'm Kelli Too, shaved some weeks off it by finishing at 258 days.) Considering the strength of any AKC working group it is amazing that Allure was also a group placer at 11 months of age.

There can be no conclusion other than that Nic's daughters have shown their quality young. His Ch. Tamara Bras de Fer was the first American bred bitch—and the second, imported or U.S. bred—to win a working group. She was only 22 months old at the time of that triumph.

Bras de Fer Bouviers are noted for toplines, temperament and type. They are always formidable show ring competition.

A son of Nic's, Ch. Duxbury House's Ulrich, went all the way from the junior puppy class to best of winners at the December 1971 specialty.

Deewal Kennels, Reg.

Editor's note: This is the corner into which the author painted herself when she undertook the labors of writing a much-needed book on Bouviers. No "Complete Bouvier" book could be complete without a history of Deewal Kennels, but the author is the owner of Deewal. Her aunt and uncle, Fred and Dorothy Walsh, made her heir to the AKC registered name because they were confident she would carry on very much in their own style and manner.

As an author writing about Deewal none of her alternatives were attractive. She could have affected an insincere humility about what Fred and Dorothy Walsh achieved as importers, as exhibitors, as breeders, as Bouvier boosters,

Ch. Deewal Hardiesse was the first show titlist for the Hilgrand, Reg. kennel of Dr. Murray and Shirley Horowitz of Valley Stream, N.Y. Photo by Gilbert.

Picking from this litter of ten was very nearly a sure thing. Five of these puppies became AKC show Champions, making Ch. Bibarcy's Job's Daughter the top producing dam for 1969. The sire was Deewal Demon Ripp. The owners are Dr. Art and Mary Pedersen of Bibarcy.

Ch. Bibarcy's Casanova was one of Bibarcy's prides. Owned by Dr. Art and Mary Pedersen, he was bred by William A. Pedersen.

Ch. Ivan D'an Naoned CD, relaxing on grooming table.

Ch. Deewal Thunderbuff UD and owner Dr. Don Pruitt.

Sire of champions, import from France, and current stud dog at du Clos des Cerberes Kennel, is Ch. Lutteur du Val de Rol, below.

as sportsman and sportswoman and as responsible citizens
of the canine community. She could have attempted ob-
jectivity about a subject in which she has a deep personal
involvement—and that is obviously impossible. Or, she
could have just plain bragged on her own.

None of the above happened. I've written the Deewal
section in this chapter. And now objectivity demands that
I report I met Fred Walsh once, just long enough for a
handshake. The same for Dorthy Walsh and the author.
Argus de la Thudinie is a different matter. The one time
I saw him he was in a working group ring at a show near
Reading, Pa. With his presence and his quality he de-
manded and got the group first. I didn't believe any judge
could have missed him. The BIS judge, a testy AKC direc-
tor, wavered—then gave the show to a Poodle handled by
Ann Hone Rogers.

That one experience made an Argus fan of me so I won't
pretend objectivity when writing about him. H. D.

Louis de Rochemont gave the Bouvier "fever" to Fred and Dorothy
Walsh. In 1943 he gave them a Bouvier named Max. Their conver-
sion into Bouvier boosters had begun but its completion would take
nearly a decade. A next, and logical, step was to acquire a companion
for Max. Appropriately she was named Lassie. The pair led a happy
existence as farm and cattle dogs at the Walsh's residence near Cam-
bridge, Md.

The family moved to Croton, N.J. There Poodles and Quarter
Horses became their absorbing interest—but Bouvier fascination
was building. In 1952 the horse barns were converted into kennels
and Bouviers were cast in starring roles. Dorothy Walsh continued
breeding and showing the Poodles but it was undeniably Bouvier
time at Deewal.

Serious Bouvier breeding at Deewal began with the purchase from
Evert van de Pol of Bonaparte von Darling Astrid, one of the early
American show champions. He'd been bred in Holland by H.L.M.
Veugulers. From the de Rochemont Blueberry Bank Kennels came
a gray and black bitch, Wallonne (Polox - Beeta van Wakershof.)
AKC records show a litter from this mating whelped on June 10,
1948. Wallonne was mated to Miss Bowles' Ch. Marius du Clos des

For many years Fred and Dorothy Walsh were found in the Bouvier benching area during Westminster time. This photo was taken in the basement of the old Garden in 1960. Ch. Argus de la Thudinie attended Dorothy Walsh while Deewal Nicole directed her Bouvier charm at Fred Walsh.

For many years Dorothy Walsh put her abilities and her energies into popularizing Bouviers. She wrote thousands of letters to people who inquired about Bouviers, made innumerable phone calls and became a dynamic center of Bouvier activity.

An airview dramatizes the scope of Deewal under Fred and Dorothy Walsh. In the center foreground is the kennel. Nearby is the home of kennel manager Jack Van Vliet. Note the enviable acreage under fence. Photo by Stephanie Rancou.

Cerberes and they produced Deewal Yhelot. She was bred to Miss Bowles' Bel Ami du Clos des Cerberes. The Walshes campaigned a pup from the resultant litter and she became Ch. Deewal Zita. Bonaparte's only champion for Deewal came from Zita—Ch. Deewal Toronto.

Fred H. Walsh was a decisive man. Bouviers were so few in North America that there was little choice of breeding stock. Like the good advertising man that he was, Walsh researched the problem. He gathered all of the material he could about the European kennels and their Bouviers. He decided to go to the Belgian route.

He imported Argus de la Thudinie that had won first prizes at Binche, Warve, Ypres, Vieux-Dieu and Brussels. Walsh was able to buy him because he was nearly eight years old and because he had been widely enough used at stud in Belgium that his blood was abundantly available there. In an era when it was a brave group judge who would give a Bouvier a good look Argus averaged a group placement every six weeks during his active career here.

Walsh imported Faussette l'Ideal de Charleroi, a prize winner at Brussels, Warve and Lille because he felt she would make a good nick with Argus. Hardy l'Ideal de Charleroi and Irca de la Thudinie also made the trans-Atlantic trip to Deewal. All became AKC Champions except Hardy. He sired eight AKC show titlists. Argus had seven AKC champions in a shorter stud career in the U.S. One of his AKC champion sons, Erlo de la Thudinie, had been whelped in Belgium in 1955.

Later the Walshes imported Argus' grandson, Hion de la Thudinie. He was a winning campaigner and sired seven AKC champions. After Hion came the Belgian champion, Ch. Job de la Thudinie, a top AKC producer with 13 champion get at this writing.

After a medical accident took Fred Walsh in 1963 Dorothy Walsh continued breeding activities with the help of Jack Van Vliet who was serving as Deewal's kennel manager. She imported Quiar de la Thudinie in 1970. Ch. Quiar won best of breed at the Westminister show in 1972 just before Mrs. Walsh passed away. At the September 1972 specialty, Quiar was selected best of opposite sex by another breed pioneer, Carl May, Jr.

It wasn't all breeding for show qualities and campaigning their Bouviers in the ring. The Walshes had far too much depth and social conscience for that. Through the years their pride was the service

When you are a youngster having a Bouvier puppy is like having your own
~ve and playful Teddy Bear. Chari Raye McLean has always had Bouvier play-
~ates. Now that she is entering young womanhood the author's daughter is an
~complished junior showman.

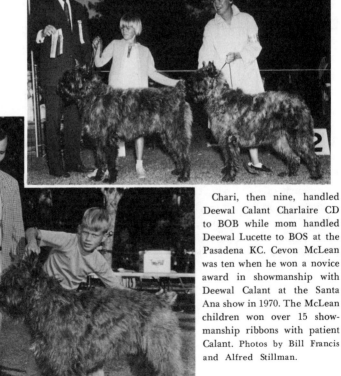

Chari, then nine, handled
Deewal Calant Charlaire CD
to BOB while mom handled
Deewal Lucette to BOS at the
Pasadena KC. Cevon McLean
was ten when he won a novice
award in showmanship with
Deewal Calant at the Santa
Ana show in 1970. The McLean
children won over 15 showmanship ribbons with patient
Calant. Photos by Bill Francis
and Alfred Stillman.

Deewal-bred and Deewal-donated Bouviers were giving to the blind. The Walshes worked with The Guiding Eyes for the Blind at York-town Heights, N.Y.

At Deewal, adaptability and suitability for service to the blind was at least as important a breeding consideration as show conformation. At this writing 36 Deewal Bouviers have survived Guiding Eyes' stringent screening process, have successfully mastered the training program — and have served as eyes for the unsighted.

Ch. Deewal Argusue, C.D. was the highest scoring dog in an obedience trial among 185 dogs. The AKC's highest obedience degree is Utility Dog. The first Bouvier to attain it was Deewal Merveille.

Deewal won the ABFC specialty in 1966, 1967, and 1974 with, respectively, Ch. Job de la Thudinie, Ch. Deewal Lorenzo, and Deewal Victor.

In addition to membership in the American Bouvier des Flandres Club Dorothy and Fred Walsh belonged to the Societe Royale de Saint Hubert and the Club National Belge du Bouvier des Flandres in France.

Deewal's proudest moment came when the American Bouvier des Flandres Club voted to offer a challenge trophy in honor of Dorothy Walsh.

Hanover Farm Kennels

Although the Hanover Farm Kennels of Dr. Clifford and Joyce Bodarky were successful in breeding and campaigning show Bouviers, the Bodarkys felt obedience work was the natural forte of Bouviers. For a number of years they averaged better than one new C.D. per year, each of their own training and handling.

Perkiomenville, Pennsylvania, was home for Ch. Hanover's Alon, Ch. Hanover's Ardanne, Ch. Hanover's Beatrix, Ch. Hanover's Belle Amie, Ch. Hanover's Charleroi, and Ch. Urex Bras de Fer. Dr. Bodarky said that what started in 1965 as a limited hobby with the purchase from Miss Edmee Bowles of Ch. Sarita du Clos des Cerberes and Liska du Clos des Cerberes, C.D., became an intensive and extensive undertaking. Both Bodarkys attributed a great part of their success to their emphasis on socialization. The ten or so adult dogs and the puppies all had freedom of access to the house and all of them spent their share of time in the house.

Ch. Bibarcy's Admiral Ben Boo finished at seventeen months under Harry J. Thomas on September 3, 1977. Owned by Roy D. Larson and Mary Tripp, "Ben" was sired by Ch. Bibarcy's Yankee Peddler out of Ch. Bibarcy's Witch of the West.

Ch. Bedelia du Clos des Cerberes won three points and took Best of Winners at the Fort Bend Kennel Club Show, February 1979. The handler is Nancy Jane Pincus.

Ch. Delanda's Apollo, below, by Ch. Ruffkell's Invincible and out of Urana des Preux Vuilbaards.

Scott Jewell, finishing his bitch, Ch. Gemstone Brandy, above, at Butler County Show, 1980.

Am. and Can. Ch. Deewal Yetta Lass, below, top bitch for 1977.

Ch. Delanda's Oly, above, owned by Jorge and Shirley Landa of Delanda Kennels.

Windsong's Yankee Rogue, below, handled by Richard Dixon to Best of Winners in Kentucky, 1978.

Above: Azuree' Du Maas, owned by Mr. and Mrs. Roy E. Larson, winning second major.

Ch. Terry du Posty Arlequin, below, owned by Jorge and Shirley Landa.

Above: Am. and Can. Ch. Titne du Posty Arlequin, by Nicko du Posty Arlequin out of Lorita du Posty Arlequin.

Ch. Dominic's Bold Image, affectionately known as "Hot Shot."

AMERICAN BOUVIERS AND
THEIR OWNERS — 1974 TO PRESENT

During the years that have passed since the first edition of this book was published, much has occurred in the lives of the breeders and in their kennels, and in the breed in general. There has been a tremendous surge of popularity in the breed. In overall AKC registrations, the Bouvier des Flandres has moved from seventy-seventh place in 1973 to fifty-seventh place in 1979. California and Michigan now hold the record for entries in shows.

Several very spectacular young show dogs and promising producers have been added to our ranks, and, sadly, several great dogs, top producers, and beloved companions have passed on. In 1978 death claimed the all-time top Bouvier, Ch. Taquin du Posty Arlequin, and a litter mate, Tania du Posty Arlequin, died a year later.

In 1978 we saw the demise of American and Canadian Ch. Deewal Victor, a victim of bloat. This dreadful disorder also claimed the life of Ch. Quelly du Plateau, owned by John Cooper of Bouvchon Kennels, and of Bon Ami Nomura (dam of Ch. Beaucrest Ruffian), owned by Roy and Pat Schiller of Beaucrest Kennels. The top producing sire of all time, Ch. Prudhon Des Preux Vuilbaards, died in December 1979 at the age of thirteen. His famous daughter Ch. Hilprise Kelli Sandra died in 1973, but fortunately she left a legacy and a line of some of

Vlaanderens Franc E Styne, left, was bred by Joyce Lak and Sandi Goldman, and owned by Sandi Goldman and Marilyn Meshirer. "Franc" was sired by Ch. Vulcain du Clos des Cytises out of Ch. Vlaanderens Emilie L'Etoile.

This seventeen-month-old bitch, right, finished her championship with her owner Gloria Molik of Alderaan Bouviers handling. Her name is Ch. Foxfire's Allegria, and she was bred by Bridget Guy.

the most important Bouviers in the United States — champions and foundation dogs that have established Ralph and Sandi Goldman's Vlaanderens line as prominent and successful.

Among other great dogs that died during this time were Miss Edmee Bowles' Ch. Jasper du Clos des Cerberes and Bill and Jeane Suazo's Ch. Dom'nique du Clos des Cerberes. Jasper's champion offspring numbered seventeen by the end of 1979, while Dom'nique was best known for her Best of Opposite Sex win at the 1974 National Specialty Show in Detroit.

Another Bouvier that died suddenly in 1979 was the great American and Canadian Ch. Sigurd de la Thudinie. Imported from Belgium as a pup by Paul De Rycke of Bolshoy Kennels in Canada, attack trained and a Best in Show winner there, Sigurd was sold to Claire McLean and Don Pruitt, who finished him to his American championship. Sigurd sired ten American champions and several Canadian champions, including Ch. Thunderbuff's Butler, who recently became a dual champion, and who was owner handled to a Group first by Anita James. Sigurd is a litter mate of Ch. Silette de la Thudinie, the top producing bitch in the breed, and of Satan dit Senior de la Thudinie, a Bouvier who has provided much of the foundation to Mssr. Gelineau's du Clos des Jeunes Plantes Kennel in France.

A tragic accident claimed the life of American and Canadian Ch. Urex Bras de Fer, C.D.X., and leukemia took the life of his brother, Ch. Uriah Bras de Fer. Another brother from that same litter, Ch. Uris Bras de Fer, sire of the all-time top winning bitch, Ch. Bo Peep Des Ours, is also deceased. These three brothers did more to carry on the Prudhon line than any other Bouviers Prudhon produced.

The Ch. Deewal Victor legacy continues to go on through his highly acclaimed son Ch. Timlor's Bairgnhomme, winner of two Specialty Shows and of two Best in Show awards, breeder-owner handled by Loryce Hiesel, and through his grandson Ch. Beaucrest Ruffian, winner of thirteen Best in Show awards, handled by Roy Holloway. When we think of the other outstanding Bouviers that have left us — too numerous to mention here — we realize how short the life span of the Bouvier is: ten to thirteen years, at best. Yet, a lifetime of love, fun, companionship, and loyalty is crammed within those years for us. Most of us would not have it any other way.

I also must sadly note that several of our very successful and important breeders of yesterday either have halted their breeding programs temporarily or have stopped them altogether.

The owners of Gold Creek Kennel with their foundation bitch, Ch. Deewal Autumn Dream, above. Second from left is Wendy Weil with the youngest Weil member. Fourth from left is Mrs. Mary Jo Plante.

Ch. Dax du Clos des Cerberes, above, bred and owned by Mrs. Jane Self, Jillax Bouviers, Richmond, Texas.

Am. and Can. Ch. High Sierras Amiel de Bolshoy, above, finished his American championship under Mr. Skarda in 1978 at the Dog Fanciers Show of Oregon. Handler Mr. Glen McVicker, owner Mr. Eugene Hoenig of Wingard Bouviers.

Ch. Yana des Preux Vuilbaards, below, going Best of Opposite Sex at a show in the summer of 1977. Yana finished her championship two weeks after this show.

While extremely active as promoters and exhibitors, Dr. and Mrs. Horowitz of Hilgrand Kennels are not breeding Bouviers to the extent they once did. Instead, they encourage others and participate through their successful campaigning of Bouviers that encompass much of what fanciers, judges, and breeders desire to see representing the breed in the ring.

Dr. and Mrs. Horowitz list Ch. Deewal Hardisse and Ch. Deewal Grand Prix first among their Bouviers. Those two are followed by Ch. U Oliver des Preux Vuilbaards, Ch. Chanterie Vicaire, Ch. Nomura Wave, and Ch. Maijeune Babiliard. The Horowitzes currently own and show Ch. Bo-Peep Des Ours, the all-time top winning bitch bred by Lancaster Wray and handled by Douglas Holloway. (Douglas Holloway is the son of Roy Holloway, who is well-known for handling Chet Collier's Ch. Taquin du Posty Arlequin to the all-time top winning spot.)

The breed has suffered because such successful breeders as Joyce Bodarky of Hanover Kennels and Carolyn Markham of Redfox Kennels have curtailed their breeding activities. Joyce and her husband, Cliff, now live in Florida with their beloved Ch. Hanover's Ardanne ("Annie"), a Bloodhound, and several Brussels Griffons which Joyce breeds and shows. Fortunately, Carolyn remains involved in breed activities by handling for several clients, including Mr. and Mrs. Kroese, who own Ch. Jumbouv Benjamin Bear. Mrs. Ingrid Kornhieser, who did so well with the Jumbouv Bouviers (named for her famous and much loved Ch. Sir Jumbo du Clos des Cerberes), is handling a Special — Ch. Astarte du Clos des Cerberes — and is active in Tibetan Terriers. Her husband, Robert Kornhieser, passed away in 1980. He was much loved and respected among Bouvier fanciers, and is missed.

One no longer sees many young puppies coming from Mr. Robert Abady's des Preux Vuilbaards Kennel. I understand that he has curtailed his kennel activities because of other business activities that take up most of his time. However, the mark he made on the breed — the notable line of Bouviers he produced and the superb dogs that carry his kennel name — has done much to bring the Bouvier to the attention of the public.

While still active in the American Bouvier des Flandres Club, particularly in heading the Constitution Committee, Mrs. Lil Mees of Bras de Fer Kennels has devoted much of her life to the breed, but

Am. and Can. Ch. Deewal Banner de Quiche, above, handled to Best of Breed at the Pontiac Kennel Club Show by Mr. Robert Astolotz. Owner, Louise Pacquett.

Ch. Voodoo des Preux Vuilbaards, below, taking his twenty-third Best of Breed in Portland, Oregon, 1977. Handler, Glen McVicker. Judge, Maxwell Riddle.

Ch. Wabouve des Preux Vuilbaard, above, finishing her championship at the 1977 Detroit Specialty under Mr. Chet Collier.

Ch. Deewal Charger, below, is by Ch. Vulcain du Clos des Cytises out of Am. and Can. Ch. Deewal Yetta Lass.

for the last few years she has not engaged in breeding. I am sure she feels there will never be another dog like Ch. Prudhon des Preux Vuilbaards ("Nic"), and I agree that there probably never will be. Although bred to only ten bitches in his lifetime, Nic produced twenty-six American champions, including Ch. Bras de Fer Ursus, U.D., as well as several other dogs with obedience titles. At this writing, it appears extremely doubtful that another Bouvier will ever equal Nic's feats. One of his daughters, Ch. Tamara Bras de Fer, won the National Specialty twice.

Another Bouvier fancier who did some very successful breeding and showing and then moved on to other ventures is Carol Wyatt of L'Esprit Fier's Kennels in California. She not only promoted Ch. Uriah Bras de Fer to prominence as a top winning Bouvier, but also bred several of the more important litters in California at a time when strong, new, high quality bloodlines were badly needed there. Almost every Bouvier in California can be traced to the breeding done by Carol Wyatt.

Just as it is with sadness that we note that many of the familiar and popular fanciers of the early years are not so active as they once were, it is with joy that we announce that in most cases their ranks have been filled with new, enthusiastic, dedicated breeders and exhibitors who take quite seriously their responsibilities to the breed.

In California, Willie Hasson of Wiljamark Kennels, Bridget Guy of Foxfire Kennels, and Judy Codd of Dominic Kennels are numbered among the few people who shipped their bitches back to Ch. Urex Bras de Fer, C.D.X., and by so doing, produced dogs that are winning today. The bitch Ch. Croix de Guerre Xena, owned by Mr. Hasson and Ms. Guy, is a top producer on the West Coast. Mr. Hasson also shipped a bitch back to Ch. Jasper du Clos des Cerberes and Ch. Beaucrest Ruffian. Puppies from the resulting litters have done much to bring the best of the East to the best of the West. Mary Ellen Fostick, Judy Codd, and Denny Criss are Westerners who shipped bitches back East to American and Canadian Ch. Deewal Victor, and Donna Turk and Nancy Gamby may make an impact on the breed with the litter from their Ch. L'Esprit Fier's Xebec which was sired by Ch. Vulcain du Clos des Cytises.

Mr. and Mrs. Robert Stevens, along with Mr. Stan Kohn — old-timers in the breed in California — have imported Bouviers and are now breeding and showing Bouviers from their own line as well as their imports. Diane Schanz of Capistrano has bred several litters

Ch. Kutah Ouden Dalerdyk, above, bred by Ann Greer and Larry Moon, is one of the top winning bitches of all time.

Below: Ch. Standfast Recaro, fawn son of Ch. Deewal Victor and Ch. Pepper of Standfast Farms.

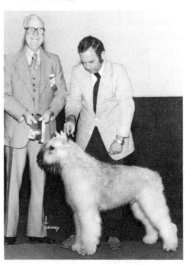

Below: Ch. Deewal Cambria Romasto taking the breed win in January 1980 at the Palm Beach County Dog Fanciers Show. Handler Clay Cody.

Shown above with owner Alex Saunders and assistant Lana Saunders is Zarko's Karl v. Sylvahof, Best of Breed in Canada.

which may make an impact on the breed. Phyllis Oja Jones of Sausalito, California, is rightfully proud of two litter mates she bred: Ch. Arwen of Rivendell and Ch. Ajax of Rivendell, C.D. These two homebreds are by her imported Ch. Arita Vedette v. Dafzicht.

The Dafzicht Kennel name, which is showing up in California and Texas, belongs to Mrs. Anne Semmler of the Netherlands, who is carrying on for her deceased father. Bouviers currently rank third in registrations in Holland, so it stands to reason that in America we will be seeing more and more Bouviers imported from Holland. And, as I said earlier in this book, the two types will blend and become one.

Another Bouvier merits mention because he is dominating the show scene in Northern California. He is Ch. Wittebrug Thor of Oakridge, owned by Mr. and Mrs. Anderson of Concord, California. Having finished at eighteen months of age, Thor has become very popular in only limited showing and has made an enviable record. We also must mention Mr. Fritz Dilsaver's Ch. M. Bonnafont de Silverado, a dog who has defeated enough Bouviers to earn his place as one of the twenty-five all-time top winners in the breed. Bonnafont is a litter mate of Ch. Kutah Ouden Dalerdyk, who was Best of Opposite Sex at the 1980 Specialty Show. These two Bouviers together have defeated more Bouviers than has the top winner for the year 1980.

Herchel Copeland and Gloria Molik are owners and exhibitors noted for Ch. Duxbury House Ulrich and Ch. Shirwal Yankee Doodle, respectively. These Bouviers, top winners on the West Coast, are listed in the all-time top five. Both won first in the Group and can be found in the "Blue Book" section of this book.

The success of Denny and Joyce Criss of Dejoy Kennels in the Seattle, Washington, area is without compare. Their first litter, by Ch. Deewal Victor out of their beloved Ch. Delanda's Jan'ette Racquel, C.D.X., has all but made history, for it included four champions and three obedience title holders. And from Denny's pick bitch from that litter, Ch. Dejoy Kelda, C.D., bred to his Best in Show winning Ch. Delanda's Jacques Rauol, C.D.X., came Ch. Dejoy Ozette, another superb bitch who finished with three majors at eleven months of age.

Also in the Washington state area, joining the Crisses with many years of breeding experience, are Jorge and Shirley Landa, whose Delanda prefix has been well known and well respected for many years. Coupling their Bouvier activities with a beautiful big boarding kennel, the Landas raise and train Bouviers that have dominated the Northwest for many years. They literally have pioneered this area

Ch. Chessman Sur Qui Compter, whose name means "without compare," was handled to his championship by breeder-owner Diane Novak.

Handled by Cathy Thistle, fifteen, Ch. Deewal Colette des Ours, above, finished her championship with five majors. Owner, Lionel M. Mapp, MD.

Bred by Mr. Chuck Huntress and owned by Catherine MacDonald, Standfast Rival, below, was sired by Ch. Deewal Victor out of Ch. Pepper of Standfast Farm.

Ch. Deewal Amulette, above, owned by Sherry McDowell, winning Reserve Winners Bitch at the 1978 National Specialty at Pasadena. Pictured with judge George DesFarge and the author.

and have introduced the public to the breed through their excellent articles for the local newspapers and through a continuing series they write for *Dog World*. One must not forget that it was the Delanda breeding that launched Dejoy Bouviers so that Delanda garnered the first Group win and the first Best in Show award in the Pacific Northwest. Joining the Landas with much success in the field of Bouvier training are Gene and Marjory Hoenig of Wingard Kennels, who place emphasis on obedience and attack work. Importing much of their basic stock from Paul De Rycke of Bolshoy Kennels in Canada, they had the distinct honor of coming from the classes to Best of Opposite Sex at the 1978 National Specialty in Pasadena, California, under Mr. Desfarge, the respected French judge. The Hoenigs' Ch. Heve de Bolshoy was the second Bouvier bitch in breed history to make such a win.

Eddy (Evelyn) Maas of DuMaas Kennels had a sensational litter of Bouviers in Oregon in 1976 when she bred her marvelous Ch. Voodoo des Preux Vuilbaards to her Ch. Yana des Preux Vuilbaards. Of the ten pups, six of the litter have either finished or have major points. Voodoo accumulated more than twenty-four Best of Breed wins in very limited showing over a two year period. One of the pups is Ch. Aviance DuMaas, owned by Cheryl Marshall of Portland, Oregon. Another is Ch. Azuree DuMaas, who has become one of the foundation bitches for the kennel of Roy and Donna Larson in Texas.

Colorado is the site of much interest in Bouviers of late, and the 1981 National Specialty Show is scheduled to be held there in June in Colorado Springs.

Gold Creek Bouviers in Elizabeth, Colorado, is the joint effort of Wendy Weil and Mary Jo Plante. For their foundation stock they purchased the imported Ch. Zito Ten Roobos, and from Deewal, Ch. Deewal Autumn Dream. A litter by Ch. Deewal Young Husband and another by Zito have increased the Bouvier population in that area substantially, along with others whelped by Ch. Delanda's Cheyenne Buff (X Ch. Delanda's Jacque Rauol, C.D.X.) owned by Susan Miller of Cheyenne, Wyoming, and one whelped in Big Piney, Wyoming, by Ch. Deewal Dejoy Krista (X Ch. Deewal Charger), owned by Dr. and Mrs. William Close of Sandhill Kennels. These new breeders join with such long-time breeders as Mr. and Mrs. William Laird of Laird Kennels, who have been breeding Bouviers in Elizabeth, Colorado, since 1942 — and who owned "Topsy," the fifth Bouvier to be imported to America. Douglas and Michaelanne

Mr. Vincent Perry awards points to Deewal Dejoy Krista, above. Owners, Dr. and Mrs. William Close. Handler, Corky Vroom.

Ch. Croix de Guerre Xerif, below, finished in May 1977 and was sired by Ch. L'Esprit Fier's Wilhelm out of Blandford's Ursula CD.

Ch. Vlaanderens Emilie L'Etoile, above, is one of four champions in a litter by Ch. Taquin du Posty Arlequin out of Ch. Vlaanderens I'm Kelli Too.

Arwen of Rivendell, below, makes a five point major win under judge Ralph Goldman. Owners, Laurence and Susan Poplack. Breeder, Phyllis Oja Jones.

Johnson, who own Sunrise Kennels, are another very influential couple who have been "in" Bouviers for some time and who have imported stock to enrich the genetic pool in the Midwest. Offering at stud Ch. Urus de la Buthiere (CACIB) and Ch. Lexy de la Buthiere, both imports from the kennel of Mr. Desfarge, the Johnsons' Rocheuses Bouviers are of a quality that makes the competition at shows very keen. In just a few years the entries in the Rocky Mountain area have increased more than one hundred percent.

Moving east, we find that Dr. and Mrs. Don Pruitt of Thunderbuff Kennels have bred a successful litter in Evansville, Indiana, and that Mr. and Mrs. James Faulkner of Fallcroft Kennels in Yorktown, Indiana, have been active in the breed since 1964 and continue to raise and train Bouviers for obedience, tracking, and guard work. Mrs. Faulkner has produced a bronze Bouvier statue that at one time was available for purchase. At present, Wendy Weil of Elizabeth, Colorado, is offering a bronze Bouvier statue in a sitting position.

In Texas we find the Jillax Kennel of Jane Self, active and busy with breeding and showing. Offering Ch. Dax du clos des Cerberes at stud, Jillax Bouviers expects to have many litters carrying the blood of both Dax and Ch. Lutteur du Val de Rol in the future. Mrs. Judy Odom, best known for her handling and exhibiting of Ch. Ivan d'an Naoned, is now breeding, raising, and training several of his offspring, and — like all of us — looking for that new star on the horizon.

The Bibarcy Kennel of Art and Mary Pedersen in Bessemer, Alabama, is Bouvier dominated — as it always has been. The Pedersens' permanent place in breed chronicles was assured by their utterly fantastic success in making their Ch. Bibarcy Soldat de Plomb the top winning American-bred Bouvier (a title only recently topped again by Ch. Beaucrest Ruffian, owned by Roy and Pat Schiller). The Pedersen's most notable dog since "Sarge" has been Ch. Bibarcy Yankee Peddler, and he has been followed by Ch. Bibarcy Adonis. Through their efforts, Dr. and Mrs. Pedersen have literally educated the dog-showing South to the Bouvier des Flandres and have brought several dedicated and ardent new fanciers to the breed. Mrs. Marie Anderson of Montgomery, Alabama, has established Roma Bouviers and has Ch. Bibarcy's Yerma as her first champion and foundation bitch. John Cooper of Bouvchon Kennels in Durham, North Carolina, has quickly established himself as a most serious breeder, exibitor, and handler, getting his start from Bibarcy. His skill as a groomer is widely known and his Bouvchon Kennel has the respect of

The only Bouviers in Peru, South America, are from the Sandhill Kennels of Mr. and Mrs. William Close; they are Sandhill Accolade and Sandhill Goblin, both sired by Ch. Deewal Charger out of Ch. Deewal Dejoy Krista.

Another Vulcain son who has finished his Canadian championship and placed in the Groups in Newfoundland is Can. Ch. Deewal Celtic Warlord, pictured at right. Celtic Warlord is owned by Steven Andrews.

Sire of eight champion offspring, Ch. Deewal Demon Ripp, left, was owned by Mr. and Mrs. M. J. Barnabic and sired by Ch. Argus de la Thudinie out of Ch. Deewal Nicole.

his peers. Mr. and Mrs. Larson of Texas claim Ch. Bibarcy's Admiral Ben Boo as a catalyst to their growing interest.

Mr. and Mrs. Garnett Sauls of Atlanta, Georgia, have done limited breeding and have established the Kocomo line. Having finished several champions herself, Mrs. Sauls enjoys the challenge of breeding, owning, and handling. Mr. and Mrs. Larry Cox of Maryland have done some successful breeding over the years, and the Nomura name can be found in the pedigrees of some of the top winning dogs of today. Most notable of the dogs with their kennel name is Ch. Nomura Wave.

The kennel that probably has made the greatest impact on the breed in the last six years is Timlor, owned by Tim and Loryce Hiesel in Califon, New Jersey. They have come a long way since Ruffkell's Beau Ombre, C.D.X. Their foundation bitch, Ch. Wendy de la Tour, was bred by Bert and Pat Ennis, who bred, owned, and promoted Wendy's litter mate, Ch. Whizbang de la Tour. Wendy proved to be the Hiesels' most prolific producer. It was, however, Deewal Ti Ti (a Quiar daughter) who gave them their most famous litter — their "Barney & Bailey" litter. Their success with that one litter has led them to become the most formidable of exhibitors as well as breeders of great accomplishments.

The Maijeune Kennel of Carl and Gladys May has also continued to produce Bouviers that make competitors shudder at ringside. Mrs. May, like Mrs. Hiesel, does a highly professional job of grooming and handling, and the two of them monopolize the East Coast with showmanship and professionalism that are a hard combination to beat. Often coming from the Bred by Exhibitor classes, these two experts are then frequently found in the Group ring.

Maijeune is probably best known for the top winning dog for numbers of Bouviers defeated, Ch. Maijeune D'artagnan — always owner-handled by Niron Conrad. Besides "Dart," there are Babiliard, Boutineere, Ichor, Dulcinee, Destinee, Callinerie, Ezekeal, Gottfried, Gigi, True Glory, and Harmony, to paint the Maijeune picture. One might say it all started with Ch. Madrone Ledge Venus and Ch. Madrone Ledge Valerie, and the Mays' friendship with Ben Getty, the importer and owner of Ch. Ulfio de la Thudinie. Ulfio produced two champions for Deewal Kennels — Icon, owned by the Hudaks, who breed Vacher Bouviers, and Isabella, owned by Colonel and Mrs. Art Lusby of California. Ulfio adds four more from the breedings of Carl and Gladys May as well as one, Ch. Queque Joyce

Owned by Richard Lake, Can. and Am. Ch. Jenbedon's Tuff Tully, left, sire of several champions, combines the Blandford line with a Dutch line.

Mrs. William Hayes shows Fallburn's Judo, left, which she co-owns with Mr. Paul De Rycke. Bred by Mr. and Mrs. David Wiggins. Judo's sire is Ch. Smokey de Bolshoy and his dam is Fallburns Bruges Sierra.

Alex Saunders, owner of Zarko Kennels in Canada, shows his imported bitch, Grisette Barry V.D. Sylverhof, left, to a five point win at the London, Ontario, show in 1977.

Solo, for Tom and Susan Griffin. Incidentally, during previous marriages, Gladys was known for her Glad-Stan Bouviers in California when she was Mrs. Rutherford, and Carl May for his Maidan Bouviers.

Madrone Ledge, the kennel of Ray and Marion Hubbard in Potomac, Maryland, has continued to produce a line of winning Bouviers, and in the last six years has added many notable dogs and notable accomplishments to its list. The breeding that brought the most lasting positive effects was the mating of Ch. Odelette du Posty Arlequin to Ch. Quiar de la Thudinie. The litter which Madrone Ledge produced through this breeding helped Odelette to hold the record for top producing bitch of all time until her total of nine champion offspring was exceeded by Ch. Silette de la Thudinie's current record of twelve. Yet, the bitches that Mrs. Hubbard found most significantly helpful to her line were the wonderful Champions Vonnie and Zolla. Vonnie was spayed after a litter by Ch. Deewal Victor, and tragically, Zolla died during a Caesarean section which produced puppies by Ch. Yago van de Buildrager, a sensational import owned by Fred and Madeline Joyner, formerly of Port Tobacco, Maryland. The five champions from the Odelette X Quiar litter are important in that two have gone on to become excellent producers for the kennel of Jack Van Vliet, who inherited Ch. Madrone Ledge Tosca, C.D., and Ch. Madrone Ledge Taussant, C.D., from Dorothy Walsh. Special mention should be made of Ch. Madrone Ledge Tamboryn, C.D.X., who attained her titles in California. With Tosca and Taussant both earning their Companion Dog titles, and five champions in the litter, it ranks as second most famous litter in the history of the breed. Odelette bred to Prudhon produced Ch. Madrone Ledge Valerie, Viking, and Vonnie for Mrs. Hubbard, and, as noted, Valerie went to Maijeune. Viking sired the Best in Show winning Ch. Nomura Wave, who, when bred to Madrone Ledge Winterset (a litter of one pup by the incomparable Ch. Picolette du Posty Arlequin), produced the "Z" litter of which Madrone Ledge is so proud: Zolla, Zoe, and Zege. At present Madrone Ledge has several impressive litters carrying the foundation bloodlines and incorporating the bloodlines of popular imports such as Ch. Yago van de Buildrager and Ch. Ivan d'an Naoned.

The du clos des Cerberes Kennel of Edmee Bowles has continued to produce, and probably has produced more Bouviers than any other kennel in America. Yet it maintains the very high and consistent

161

quality of Bouviers that the public has come to expect from "Belco" over the past forty years. In Bruce and Rose Ellen Jacobsohn, Edmee has found two able and enthusiastic assistants. Since the demise of Ch. Jasper du Clos des Cerberes, the stud force has been headed by an import from France who came to the kennel quite by accident and good fortune when Lutteur du Val de Rol was waylaid on his way to New Caledonia. Never getting any farther than Belco, Lutteur was "just what the doctor ordered" for Edmee and Bruce, who were look-ing for a line to complement the great Jasper and who knew a "good" Bouvier when they saw one. With some difficulty and a certain amount of negotiating, they were able to get this young French dog for themselves. He soon proved his prowess both in the show ring and with the bitches, for he quickly became a champion and the sire of ten champions.

Lutteur is a son of Ch. Vulcain du Clos des Cytises, who was im-ported by Deewal Kennels. After many years of being competitive and at opposite ends of the spectrum, the du Clos des Cerberes line and the Deewal line are more compatible. Lutteur was loaned for some time to Jane Self of Jillax Kennels in Texas, and his blood will be plentiful. Lutteur's ten champions have made their titles across America. They are: Capone, Banshee, Claudette, Cayce, Caliphe, Bedelia, Chessman, Sharduke, Brioche, and Bohannon.

Deewal Kennels have continued to make an impact on the Bouvier scene, not necessarily in terms of top winning dogs, but in terms of a consistent line of high performing champions and high quality Bouviers — whether for the show ring, for breeding, for obedience, or for overall companionship. The Deewal guarantee and prefix are much sought after and yet are selectively and prudently used by owners Claire and Charles McLean. If it were not for their many im-portant imported Bouviers of selected bloodlines from highly esteemed European kennels, the genetic field for Bouviers in America would be lacking.

Since 1954, Deewal has imported a total of thirty-six Bouviers — twenty-eight since 1972. Of the total imports, nineteen have made championships — thirteen since 1972. Two have earned Companion Dog titles as well.

Ch. Silette de la Thudinie (whose purchase and importation are described in the chapter titled "Importing a Bouvier") is an example of the exceptionally fine stock the McLeans have imported, and Silette's get are among the noteworthy Bouviers the McLeans have made available to American Bouvier breeders.

Silette produced three litters before she was spayed — one by International Ch. Tapin de la Thudinie, one by Ch. Ulfio de la Thudinie, and the last by Ch. Urex Bras de Fer, C.D.X. In the first litter were two dogs who became champions — Victor and Victoria — as well as the bitch Vlinder, who was owned by Mrs. Hubbard and who produced Ch. Nomura Wave ("Mindy"), who was Best in Show twice. Victor won the 1974 National Specialty and produced the 1977 and 1978 National Specialty winner, Ch. Timlor Bairgnhomme (bred, owned, and handled by Loryce Hiesel), who also won Best in Show twice. Victoria, sold to Wally and Shirley Seger, became the breed's top producing bitch for 1976 and the dam of six champions. She produced Ch. Shirwal's Yankee Doodle (owned by Gloria Molik), who became one of the breed's all-time top winners. As of March 1980, Victor, with seventeen champions, was number three on the list of top producing Bouvier studs. His dam, Silette, established herself as the top producing bitch for the breed and for all breeds in 1976, when seven dogs from her litter of eleven (by Ch. Urex Bras de Fer, C.D.X.), finished in one year.

The seven champions were: Young Husband, Yetta Lass, Yolanda, Yeates, Yve, Y'mira von Dahle, and York, C.D. With six champions as of December 1979, Yetta Lass is top brood bitch at the Deewal Kennels, with her litter sister Yve running a close second. Silette is now owned by Dr. and Mrs. Don Pruitt, who also owned her brother, American and Canadian Ch. Sigurd de la Thudinie and her son, Ch. Deewal York, C.D., as well as Ch. Deewal Thunderbuff, U.D.

Silette was the dam of Ch. Urmin de la Thudinie, imported by Peter Spiering. Urmin died in 1979.

Deewal bought from Marie Niquet of France, the 1975 Bouffles Recommended Producer, Vulcain du clos des Cytises. Having won numerous European awards, including CACIB certificates, Vulcain arrived in January 1978. His first American litter was whelped in April 1978 by Ch. Xideale du Posty Arlequin. As of January 1980, Vulcain had added his ninth champion offspring, putting him on the list of top producers.

Ch. Silette de la Thudinie was followed by Valda and Vertu de la Thudinie, who were from the kennels of Mr. Justin Chastel. Ch. Xidelae du Posty Arlequin was a Taquin granddaughter, imported from Felix Grulois. Yapo de la Thudinie (sold to Mr. and Mrs. Gene Hoenig), Nerva du Val de Rol, and Nyrop du Val de Rol, C.D., followed. Deewal's Lance de la Buthiere came from the de la Buthiere

Kennel of Mr. Desfarge (1978 National Specialty judge in Pasadena). Lance, bred to Ch. Deewal Young Husband, produced Ch. Deewal Banner de Quiche (Paquette of Canada) and Ch. Deewal Broosir de Broote (Santella of Pennsylvania).

Ch. Ivan d'an Naoned came over at one year of age with his owner, who was employed by Deewal Kennels. Deewal arranged Ivan's sale to Mr. Burgess in Texas, who wanted a "guard" dog. Ivan had suffered a broken leg, so Mr. Burgess gave up the idea of Ivan's providing protection. Claire McLean then arranged his sale to Judy Oden. Ivan has become a Group placing show dog as well as a producer of merit. Another d'an Naoned dog imported by the McLeans and co-owned by John Cooper is Nantes d'an Naoned, who finished his championship with a Group III placement under Mrs. Evers.

From Mrs. DeBlander came Zito ten Roobos, who earned his championship under the guidance of Brian Still and co-ownership with Wally and Shirley Seger.

One of the more successful show bitches to come to America via Deewal is Ch. Nelly du Clos des Jeune Plante. From the kennel of Mr. and Mrs. Gelineau, Nelly has been campaigned and promoted by Carole Gillespie, with Houston and Toddie Clark. Two more young hopefuls from the Gelineaus' kennel are at Deewal — Pepito and Puzzie du Clos des Jeune Plante.

Deewal Kennels is now located in Deale, Maryland, where Charles and Claire McLean continue to breed, to import, to train, to exhibit, and to boost Bouviers.

At the Portland Kennel Club Show on October 26, 1975, Delanda's D'artagnan, left, took Best of Breed over Ch. Terry du Posty Arlequin, center, and Delanda's Gabriel took Best of Opposite Sex.

Above: Nancy Pincus with Ch. Circee du Clos des Cerberes, Ch. Radegund du Clos des Cerberes, and Ch. Ritalee du Clos des Cerberes.

Pictured at right are Cherly Marshall, owner-handler, and Ch. Aviance du Maas.

Can. and Am. Ch. Dim de Bolshoy, owned by Gene and Margery Hoenig.

Below: Ch. Zaiko de Bolshoy with Margery Hoenig of Wingard Bouviers.

Below: Mrs. Jane Self's Jillax Chazz, Jillax l'Enjoleur Cossacx, and Ch. Jillax l'Enjoleur.

There were good Bouviers in the United States in the pioneering days of the 30's as this photo of Julius Bliss' Inga and Astra proves. Taken in 1938 by an unidentified photographer, this double portrait captures the alertness and devotion which inspires intense breed loyalty among Bouvier owners. By Ch. Bojar van Westergoo out of Lariane, Inga and Astra were litter sisters to Caprice. Bliss thought it appropriate that a member of the socially prominent Bouvier family should have a Bouvier, so he presented Caprice to Jacqueline Lee Bouvier, then living at 520 East 86th St. in New York City. Miss Bouvier, later the First Lady, was in 1942, perhaps, the first to enter a Bouvier at a Westminster show.

THE BREED'S STANDARDS

IN purebred dogs, breeders, buyers and judges require a universally agreed upon standard for guidance in forming objectives and in making selections. In the United States the formulation of such a standard is the exclusive responsibility of the group designated by the American Kennel Club as the "parent club" for the subject breed. Almost invariably the designated club is the oldest continuously active group in the breed within the AKC framework.

In the preparation of a standard the AKC will offer guidance if it is requested, but the AKC philosophy is that a standard is strictly the prerogative and responsibility of those most familiar with and most active in a breed. The AKC does examine proposed standards for conflicts with AKC procedures and requirements, for errors in grammar and for understandability. A standard becomes operative when the AKC's directors formally approve it—after publication and opportunity for objections from interested parties. AKC show judges are instructed to use only an official standard as their criteria in making placements at shows.

The AKC does not permit illustrations, whether photographic or drawn, as official parts of a standard. An endlessly repeated comment is that no artist, never having seen an example of a subject breed, could draw a recognizable picture from a standard. Be that as it may, the official standard has been the only reasonable starting point for a serious student of any breed. Understanding gained from a study of the standard can be "fleshed out" by watching good breed examples at shows, by noting which types are winning — and by attempting to understand why. One caution: making evaluations from outside the ring is much more difficult for such dense-coated breeds as the Bouvier than it would be for smooth-coated breeds where outlines are clear and musculature and skeletal formation are often sufficiently visible to form bases for conclusions. Accurate evaluations can never be made from outside a show ring because they require a physical examination of the dog — touch and sight.

Most of the canine world's governing bodies have breed standards and procedures similar to the AKC's. With few exceptions they all operate from written but unillustrated standards.

Because it is the only measuring stick of Bouvier quality at American dog shows, the standard approved by the AKC on June 10, 1975, is presented here first. Following it is the current Canadian standard for the breed. Bouvier enthusiasts everywhere are extremely fortunate, for Belgium's and France's most successful breeders met in 1972 and shaped explanations of and illustrations for the Franco-Belgium standard of 1961 which was recognized by the Federation Cynologique Internationale in 1965. For the late Florimond Verbanck, participation was his last great contribution to Bouviers.

Thus, for serious students of Bouviers, there is a viable starting point. There are, however, variations between the AKC standard and the Franco-Belgian and Canadian standards, and it must be emphasized that the AKC standard is the only standard with official status in the United States.

Oden de Ose Brulot, Reserve Winner Puppy Class, 1979.

Marty de Ose Brulot taking Winners Dog, 1979.

Official AKC Standard for the Bouvier des Flandres

The Bouvier des Flandres is a powerfully built, compact, short-coupled, rough-coated dog of notably rugged appearance. He gives the impression of great strength without any sign of heaviness or clumsiness in his overall makeup. He is agile, spirited and bold, yet his serene, well-behaved disposition denotes his steady, resolute and fearless character. His gaze is alert and brilliant, depicting his intelligence, vigor and daring. By nature he is an equable dog.

His origin is that of a cattle herder and general farmer's helper, including cart pulling. He is an ideal farm dog. His harsh coat protects him in all weather, enabling him to perform the most arduous tasks. The coat may be trimmed slightly only to accent the body line. Overtrimming which alters the natural rugged appearance is to be avoided.

He has been used as an ambulance and messenger dog. Modern times find him as a watch and guard dog as well as a family friend, guardian and protector. His physical and mental characteristics and deportment, coupled with his olfactory abilities, his intelligence and initiative enable him to also perform as a tracking dog and a guide dog for the blind.

Head—The head is impressive in scale, accentuated by beard and mustache. It is in proportion to body and build.

Skull—Well developed and flat, slightly less wide than long. When viewed from the side, the top lines of the skull and the muzzle are parallel. It is wide between the ears, with the frontal groove barely marked. The stop is more apparent than real, due to upstanding eyebrows. The proportions of length of skull to length of muzzle are 3 to 2.

Eyes—The expression is bold and alert. They neither protrude nor are sunken in the sockets. Their shape is oval with the axis on a horizontal plane, when viewed from the front. Their color is a dark nut brown. The eye rims are black without lack of pigment and the haw is barely visible. Yellow or light eyes are to be strongly penalized, along with a walleyed or staring expression.

Ears—Placed high and alert. They are rough-coated. If cropped, they are to be a triangular contour and in proportion to the size of the head. The inner corner of the ear should be in line with the outer corner of the eye. Ears that are too low or too closely set are serious faults.

Muzzle—Broad, strong, well filled out, tapering gradually toward the nose without ever becoming snipy or pointed. The cheeks are flat and lean, with the lips being dry and tight fitting. A narrow, snipy muzzle is faulty.

Nose—Large, black, well developed, round at the edges, with flared nostrils. A brown, pink or spotted nose is a serious fault.

Jaws and Teeth—The jaws are powerful and of equal length. The teeth are strong, white and healthy, with the incisors meeting in a scissors bite. Overshot or undershot bites are to be severely penalized.

Neck—The neck is strong and muscular, widening gradually into the shoulders. When viewed from the side, it is gracefully arched with upright carriage. A short, squatty neck is faulty. No dewlap.

Body or Trunk—Powerful, broad and short. The length from the point of the shoulder to the tip of the buttocks is equal to the height from the ground to the highest point of the withers. The chest is broad, with the brisket extending to the elbow in depth. A long-lined, rangy dog should be faulted.

Ribs—The ribs are deep and well sprung. The first ribs are slightly curved, the others well sprung and very sloped nearing the rear, giving proper depth to the chest. Flat ribs or slabsidedness is to be strongly penalized.

Back—Short, broad, well muscled with firm level topline. It is supple and flexible with no sign of weakness.

Flanks and Loins—Short, wide and well muscled, without weakness. The abdomen is only slightly tucked up.

Croup or Rump—The horizontal line of the back should mold unnoticeably into the curve of the rump, which is characteristically wide. A sunken or slanted croup is a serious fault.

Tail—Is to be docked, leaving 2 or 3 vertebrae. It must be set high and align normally with the spinal column. Preferably carried upright in motion. Dogs born tailless should not be penalized.

Forequarters—Strong boned, well muscled and straight.

Shoulders and Upper Arms—The shoulders are relatively long, muscular but not loaded, with good layback. The shoulder blade and humerus are approximately the same length, forming an angle slightly greater than 90 degrees when standing. Straight shoulders are faulty.

Elbows—Close to the body and parallel. Elbows which are too far out or in are faults.

Forearms—Viewed either in profile or from the front are perfectly straight, parallel to each other and perpendicular to the ground. They are well muscled and strong boned.

Wrists—Exactly in line with the forearms. Strong boned.

Pasterns—Quite short, slightly sloped forward. Dewclaws may be removed.

Feet—Both forefeet and hind feet are rounded and compact turning neither in nor out; the toes close and well arched; strong black nails; thick tough pads.

Hindquarters—Firm, well muscled with large, powerful hams. They should be parallel with the front legs when viewed from either front or rear.

Thighs—Wide and muscular. The upper thigh must be neither too straight nor too sloping. There is moderate angulation at the stifle.

Legs—Moderately long, well muscled, neither too straight nor too inclined.

Hocks — Strong, rather close to the ground. When standing and seen from the rear, they will be straight and perfectly parellel to each other and perpendicular to the ground. In motion, they must turn neither in nor out. There is a slight angulation at the hock joint. Sickle or cowhocks are serious faults.

Metatarsi — Hardy and lean, rather cylindrical and perpendicular to the ground when standing. If born with dewclaws, they are to be removed.

Coat — A tousled, double coat capable of withstanding the hardest work in the most inclement weather. The outer hairs are rough and harsh, with the undercoat being fine, soft and dense.

Topcoat — Must be harsh to the touch, dry, trimmed, if necessary, to a length of approximately 2½ inches. A coat too long or too short is a fault, as is a silky or woolly coat. It is tousled without being curly. On the skull, it is short, and on the upper part of the back, it is particularly close and harsh always, however, remaining rough.

Undercoat — A dense mass of fine, close hair, thicker in winter. Together with the topcoat, it will form a water-resistant covering. A flat coat, denoting lack of undercoat is a serious fault.

Mustache and Beard — Very thick, with the hair being shorter and rougher on the upper side of the muzzle. The upper lip, with its heavy mustache and the chin with its heavy and rough beard gives that gruff expression so characteristic of the breed.

Eyebrows — Erect hairs accentuating the shape of the eyes without ever veiling them.

Color — From fawn to black, passing through salt and pepper, gray and brindle. A small white star on the chest is allowed. Other than chocolate brown, white, or parti-color, which are to be severely penalized, no one color is to be favored.

Height — The height as measured at the withers — Dogs, from 24½ to 27½ inches; bitches, from 23½ to 26½ inches. In each sex, the ideal height is the median of the two limits, i.e., 26 inches for a dog and 25 inches for a bitch. Any dog or bitch deviating from the minimum or maximum limits mentioned shall be severely penalized.

Gait — The whole of the Bouvier des Flandres must be harmoniously proportioned to allow for a free, bold and proud gait. The reach of the forequarters must compensate for and be in balance with the driving power of the hindquarters. The back, while moving in a trot, will remain firm and flat. In general, the gait is the logical demonstration of the structure and build of the dog. It is to be noted that while moving at a fast trot, the properly built Bouvier will tend to single-track.

Temperament — As mentioned under general description and characteristics, the Bouvier is an equable dog, steady, resolute and fearless. Viciousness or shyness is undesirable.

Faults — The foregoing description is that of the ideal Bouvier des Flandres. Any deviation from this is to be penalized to the extent of the deviation.

Approved June 10, 1975

Canadian Standard for the Bouvier des Flandres

The Bouvier des Flandres is a rough-coated dog of notably rugged appearance as befitting an erstwhile cattle driver and farmers' helper of Flandres, and later an ambulance dog and messenger in World War I. He is a compact-bodied, powerfully built dog of upstanding carriage and alert, intelligent expression.

Head—The head is medium long, with the skull slightly longer than the muzzle.

Skull—Almost flat on top, moderately wide between the ears, and sloping slightly toward the muzzle. The brow is noticeably arched over the eyes. The stop is shallow, and the under-eye fill-in good.

Ears—Rough-coated, set high on the head and cropped to a triangular contour. They stand erect and are carried straight up.

Eyes—Neither protruding nor sunken, the eyes are set a trifle obliquely in the skull and not too far apart. They are of medium size and very nearly oval. Preferred color, a dark nut-brown. Black eyes, although not considered faulty, are less desirable as contributing to a somber expression. Lightcolored eyes, and staring or wild expression are faulty.

Muzzle—Wide, deep and well filled out, the width narrowing gradually towards the tip of the nose. Cheeks are clean or flat-sided, the jaws powerful, and the lips dry and tight-fitting. A narrow muzzle, suggestive of weakness, is faulty.

Teeth—Strong and white, with the canines set well apart, the teeth meet in a scissors bite.

Nose—Black and well developed the nostrils wide open. Across the top the contour is a trifle rounded as opposed to flat. Brown, pink and spotted noses are faulty.

Neck and Shoulders—The neck is well rounded, slightly arched, and carried almost upright, its thickness gradually increasing as it fits gracefully into the shoulders. Clean and dry at the throat. The shoulders are long and sloping.

Body or Tail—The brisket is deep, extending down at least to the point of the elbows, and of moderate width.

Back—Short, strong and straight.

Loins—Short, taut and slightly arched in top line, while the rump is broad and square rather than sloping. Ribs are deep and well sprung. As advantageous for breeding purposes, slightly greater length of loin is permissible in bitches.

Tail—Set high, carried up, and docked to about 10.16 cm.

Legs and Feet—The leg bones, although only moderate in girth, are made to appear heavy because of their covering with thick, rough hair.

Forelegs—Straight as viewed from the front or side, with elbows turned neither in nor out.

Hindlegs—Hindquarters are firm and well muscled, with large, powerful hams. Legs are strong and sturdy, with hocks well let down and wide apart. They are slightly angulated at stifle and hock joints. Viewed from the back they are absolutely parallel.

172

Feet — Round, compact, with toes arched and close. The nails are black, the pads thick and tough.

Coat — Rough, tousled and unkempt in appearance, the coat is capable of withstanding the hardest work in the most inclement weather.

Topcoat — Harsh, rough and wiry, and so thick that when separated by the hand the skin is hardly visible.

Undercoat — Fine and soft in texture, and thicker in winter. On the skull the hair is shorter and almost smooth. On the brows it is longer, thus forming eyebrows. Longer growth on muzzle and underjaw form moustache and beard. On the legs it is thick and rough, on the feet rather short. Soft silky or woolly topcoats are faulty.

Color — From fawn to black; pepper and salt, gray and brindle. A white star on the chest is allowed. Chocolate brown with white spots is faulty.

Height — Dogs from 59.69 cm to 69.85 cm; bitches a minimum of 57.785 cm.

SCALE OF POINTS

Coat	20
Head (eyes, ears, skull, foreface)	20
Shoulders and style	10
Hindquarters (hams and legs)	10
Back, loin, brisket, belly	15
Feet and legs	10
Symmetry, size and character	15
Total	100

Ch. Dominic's Le Duc CD, left, owner-handled by Diane Novak, is the son of Ch. Quenouille's de Bolshoy CDX, owner-handled by Judy Codd.

Owned by Mr. and Mrs. Hoffman of California, Ch. Von Hoffmans Cafe Brulot ("Guy") is the sire of two homebred champions.

Smokey de Bolshoy won Best of Breed under Judge Taylor at the Ottawa Kennel Club Show on May 7, 1977.

Franco-Belgian Standard for the Bouvier des Flandres with Explanations by the Joint Commission

Translated by Miss Edmee F. Bowles

This exposition of the standard [European] for the Bouvier des Flandres is offered to make the physical qualities of the Bouvier des Flandres better understood. It was realized through the cooperative effort of the Club du Bouvier des Flandres pour la France and the Club National Belge du Bouvier des Flandres. Serving on the joint commission which prepared it were Messers Thorp, Malaquin, Martineau and Dr. Le Lann for France. Messers Chastel and Verbanck represented Belgium. The drawings are by M. Martineau, vice-president of the French club.

First published February 1, 1972 in a booklet as a joint venture, the text and accompanying illustrations are here reproduced by kind permission. (The standard appears in light face type. The joint commission's opinions are in italic.)

174

ORIGINS: The Bouvier des Flandres, as the name indicates originated in Flandres,—both French and Belgium as there are no boundaries separating these two countries.

It is difficult to ascertain exact origins. He was produced by circumstancial breeding. It is certain that shepherds and cattle herders of Flanders needed good dogs and selected locally for their moral and physical qualities rather than bred for a predetermined type. Present Bouviers have inherited these qualities.

The Bouvier is a result of crossings amongst hardy and rustic dogs. These selections for quality produced a uniformity which attracted serious dog breeders. In 1912 they established the first Bouvier standard.

To maintain and fix the type as to purity of the breed it was necessary to eliminate all faulty recessives, both moral and physical.

APTITUDES: In the beginning the Bouvier was used to herd cattle, for draught and butter churning. Modernization has changed farm equipment. Now the Bouvier is used as guard for home or farm, for defense or police work. His great physical and moral aptitudes, his excellent nose, initiative and intelligence make him an excellent tracker, and game keeper's aid.

Because of his strength, his mass, his gruff appearance, his intelligence, fidelity to his master and attachment to all that belongs to the family with whom he lives, the Bouvier is an extraordinary guard dog. He can defend with all his energy the house, factory, garden or car. Formidable guardian and protector of children and family he is, at the same time, their friend and playmate.

GENERAL CHARACTERISTICS: Cobby, short bodied and thickset on powerful and muscular limbs; gives the impression of power, without clumsiness as a whole. The fire in his eyes denotes intelligence, energy, and audacity. He is calm, rational and prudently bold.

He is cobby in length, as contrasted with lanky. He is a blocky dog without excessive weight which would cause him to lose his agility and mobility. A Bouvier too heavy would be unfit for his work; one too light would not be a Bouvier.

The moral qualities of the Bouvier are their heritage from ancestors selected for demanding work as herders.

The Bouvier is a well balanced dog, intelligent; i.e., he is safe. He is bold, prudent, obedient to his master and very courageous in his

Hagard expression

Whistle-like muzzle

Soft coat

Light eyes, bad coat

Ram's head, vanishing forehead

Forehead too long, head too light

defense. He only bites when necessary. He is without meanness and he does not maul. His keen nose, well developed, makes him suitable as a war or police dog and also as a gamekeeper's helper.

THE HEAD: Massive, appearing more so because of his beard and mustache, it is well proportioned to his body and size. To the feel, it is finely chiseled.

The head by its shape and volume, is characteristic of the breed and has its own distinctive expression.

THE SKULL:—Well developed and flat, longer than its width. The top lines of the skull and muzzle are parallel. The proportions of the skull to the muzzle are 3 to 2.

These proportions 3 to 2 must be adhered to, as they are a characteristic of the breed. A rounded or narrow skull is a fault.

FRONTAL GROOVE: — Barely perceptible.

A deep frontal groove changes the expression of the head and gives it a common and undesirable expression.

STOP: — Barely percievable, more apparent than real because of the raised eyebrows.

The frontal-nasal angle should be between 140° and 150°. If too open it gives a receding profile which is too sharp and a common undesirable expression.

MUZZLE: — Wide, powerful, bony, straight in upper profile, diminishing toward the nose but never pointed. The muzzle is shorter than the skull — in the proportion of 2 to 3 and the circumference just below the eyes is about equal to length of head.

The proportions 2 to 3 for length of skull to muzzle, must be adhered to. So must the cubic appearance. A pointed muzzle is a fault.

NOSE — This is the continuation of the muzzle; it is slightly convex at its extremity — must be well developed, rounded at its edges — and must always be black with well opened nostrils.

Whatever the color of the coat, the nose must always be black without any spots. They are an indication of degeneracy.

CHEEKS — Flat and dry.

Flat cheeks emphasize the fine chiseled look of the head. Rounded cheeks overly suggest the fullness of the Matin.

EARS — Cropped in a triangle, they are carried well up; attached high and very mobile. It is recommended that the size and shape should match the size of the head.

At attention the ears are well up. A dog which does not carry them up is often apt to be a shy dog, or out of condition.

The standard states cropping should be in proportion to the head. In general ⅔ should be left, but this is only our counsel.

Ears badly cropped, too long or too short, change the expression of the dog. The same applies to ears carried poorly.

EYES — Bold and energetic, neither prominent nor sunken. In shape slightly oval on a horizontal plane. The color should be as dark as possible in keeping with color of the coat. Light in color or haggard in expression should be severely faulted.

The color of the eye is very important, as the tint modifies the expression. Eyes should always be dark, whatever the color of the coat —and never lighter than a hazel nut.

A light eye gives a haggard expression —a sign of degeneration. Rounded, protruding eyes are a fault. The opening of the lids of the eyes should be slightly oval but not as much as the shape of an almond, nor almost oriental.

EYELIDS—Black without a trace of deficient pigmentation; No haw should be visible.

> *When the haw shows, it changes the expression. Drooping tissues often indicate a soft and lymphatic temperament. They are often the cause of accidents by irritation. They have a potential for infection from dust, pollen and grit.*

JAWS AND TEETH—Jaws should be powerful and of equal length; the teeth strong, white and healthy. The upper incisors must meet the lower ones like the blades of a scissors or fit like a pincers. [Even bite.]

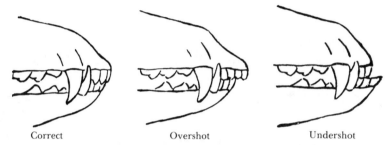

Correct   Overshot   Undershot

> *Jaws should be of equal length. If the upper jaw is longer the dog is overshot. If the lower is longer the dog is undershot. Either is a serious and degenerate fault which must be dealt with severely. In a scissors bite the inside of the upper incisors slide over the lower incisors making a minimal contact. Absence of contact here would be defined as overshot. The opposite constitutes an overshot bite. A pincer bite indicates a perfect set of jaws.*
>
> *The number of teeth is 42. Those with brownish marks, pitted or with enamel otherwise marred indicate previous decalcification. These esthetic faults should be evaluated accordingly. Some dogs have teeth covered with tartar which should be scaled off. Care should be taken to avoid scratching the enamel. With age teeth can turn yellow. This is only a sign of age and not a genetic consideration.*

NECK—The neck should be free—strong-muscled and widening into the shoulders. Its length should be slightly less than that of the head. The nape should be powerful and slightly arched. There should be no dewlap.

> *The power of a Bouvier's attack lies not only in the spring of his quarters—but in the power of his neck and jaws. The neck therefore must be powerful without being sunk into the shoulders. The head must be joined to the trunk by a continuous line*

without a sharp angle to the shoulders. The nape should be slightly arched. A good set of the neck is characteristic of a well-bred animal. A cylindrical neck, round like a stove pipe, is faulty.

WITHERS—Slightly prominent.

The withers are the points of the shoulder blades. These bony points are used to measure the height of the dog. The height at the withers is determined by dropping a perpendicular line to the floor, passing at the point of the elbow. It is indicated in centimeters.[1]

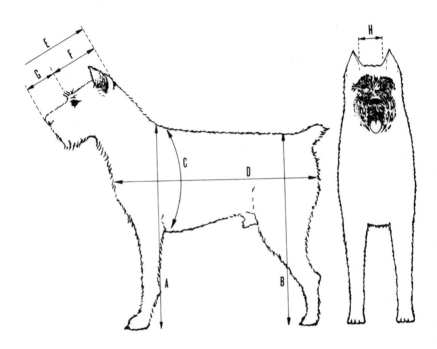

GUIDE TO TERMINOLOGY OF MEASUREMENTS

A Height measured from ground to top of withers. B Height of croup. C Thoractic perimeter (not a straight line). D Length of the torso. E Length of the head. F Length of the cranium. G Length of the muzzle. H Width of the head.

1. In almost all of the world except North America.

BODY OR TRUNK—Powerful, cobby and short. The length of the point of the shoulder to ischium should be about equal to the height at the withers. The ischium is the rear point of the rump. The chest should reach to level of elbows, and never be cylindrical, though the ribs are well sprung. The depth, i.e., the distance between the sternum and the last rib must be great— about $\frac{7}{10}$ths of the height at the withers.

The length of the trunk (or torso) is measured between two bony points which do not vary—from the points of the shoulder to the ischium.

RIBS—The first ribs are slightly curved; the others are well sprung and well inclined to the rear giving the desired depth of the chest. Flat ribs must be greatly penalized.

The Bouvier, being a powerful dog, must have bulk. This means a well developed thoracic cage with a deep, almost barrel-like chest.

Flat or ogival ribs narrow the chest by reducing its volume [including heart and lung room]. The result is a look opposite to barrel-like. [Ribs pivot inward and outward to some degree with inhalation and exhalation—so there is no arc which can be mathematically expressed.]

The depth of the chest should be such that the low point of the sternum reaches the level of the elbows. The chest should be of sufficient that the dog does not appear out at the elbows.

FLANK—The flank between the last rib and the haunch must be very short, especially in males. There is very little tuck up.

Seen from the side the sternum with the belly makes a slight curve rising into the line of the flank. The flank must be short, the belly full. The dog that shows much daylight under him like a coursing hound must be penalized.

BACK—Short, wide, muscled and firm—showing no weakness but remaining flexible.

It is essential that a Bouvier be cobby. This necessitates a short, powerful and firm back. A swayed or roached back indicates a malformation of the spine and a genetic defect.

LOIN—Short, wide and well muscled—must remain flexible but without any weakness.

This description is very clear and needs no explanation.

CROUP OR RUMP—Must follow as closely as possible the horizontal line of the back and follow [merge] smoothly into the curve of the rump. It should be wide without excess in the male, more developed [wider] in the female. A descending [steeply tilted] croup is a serious fault.

Tilted croup; hindquarters underslung; weak and frail legs; poor set of neck.

Light, lacks chest; hindquarters too long; flat thighs.

Light, poor tail set.

Swaybacked and barrel-chested.

Too long; lacks chest; swayback; neck like the flue of a stove.

Swaybacked; tilted croup; too much daylight under belly; lightly built.

Admirable cobbiness.

Standing under, descending croup.

Powerful, cobby and short.

A descending or tilted croup, one that is significantly more than the 40° illustrated in the accompanying drawing [McDowell Lyon and some other authorities have felt it should be nearer to a 30° tilt], is due to an excessive tilt of the pelvis and a grave fault.

Indeed, if the pelvis is too inclined the rear legs [and support] are too much under the body. This restricts the dog's reach in moving. With the paws placed too far forward the thrust from the rear tends to elevate the body. The up and down motion wastes energy without productivity in forward progress. The gait is fatiguing and defective. A descending croup results from either an insufficiency of the muscles in that region or a genetically caused excessive slope of the pelvic bones with an accompanying low set tail.

A croup like a mule's with a sharp spine and a lateral falling away is also a fault. A happily carried tail should not be at a right angle to the spine — but rather a continuation of the spine.

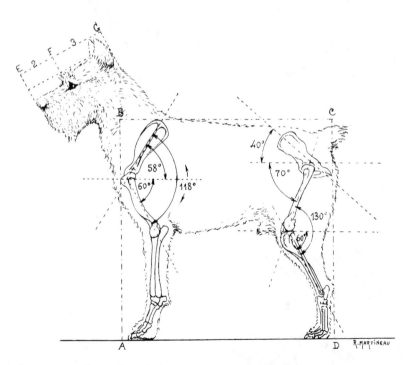

Correct proportions and angulation of the Bouvier des Flandres.

184

FRONT ASSEMBLY

FOREQUARTERS—The forequarters should have a strong bony structure, well muscled and perfectly straight.

Fiddle front.   Correct   Pigeon toed.
(Toes turn out.)   (Toes turn in.)

SHOULDERS AND FOREARMS—The shoulders are relatively long, well muscled, not loaded and moderately oblique. The humerus and shoulder blades are almost the same length.

The shoulders must be sufficiently oblique to permit free action of the elbows. The Bouvier is a trotter, the angle of the shoulder blade with horizontal should be 58°. An angle too·open would mean too straight a shoulder and would hamper forward thrust.

ELBOWS—Close to the body and parallel. Elbows out or too close are faults. In action they must remain parallel to median line of the body.

If the elbows are out and are not on a parallel plane of the median line of the body weight then sways in an oblique line.

FOREARMS—seen from profile or front they remain straight, parallel to each other and perpendicular to ground. They should be well muscled and of powerful bony structure.

The length of the forearm should be about ⅛ of the height at withers. Forearms that are concave or convex are a sign of rickets.

CARPAL (KNEE)—In plumb with the forearms, except for the accessory carpal at the back. Strong and heavy bone.

The carpal represents the wrist, which articulates the junction of the forearm with the hand, or front foot.

METACARPALS—of strong bony structure, very slightly inclined forward.

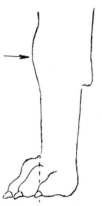

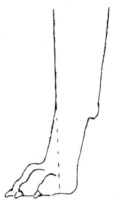

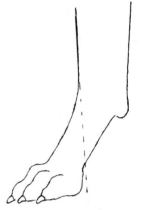

Metacarpus (pastern) too upright. Causes knee (arrow) to bulge.

Correct

Pastern too long. Paws too far forward.

> *If the metacarpals, or pasterns, are inclined too far forward it gives the appearance of leaning on the wrists; if too straight they cause a bulge at the carpals and curtail the suppleness of gait.*

FRONT PAWS — short, round and compact. The toes should be close and well arched. Nails — strong and black. Thick and hard soles.

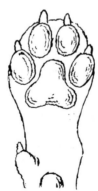

Hare foot. Too long.

Correct paw for a Bouvier.

Flat and splay-footed.

Paws that are flat and open toed are a fault.

186

POSTERIOR MEMBERS [rear legs]—Powerful and pronounced musculature is demanded. Rear legs must move in the same plane as the anterior members [front legs].

THIGHS—Wide and well muscled. The direction will be parallel to the median plane of the body. The femurs will be neither too straight nor too inclined. The buttock will be well let down with good, firm breeches. The kneecap, or patella, is situated on an imaginary line from the iliac crest to the ground.

The rump should be thick—but not like a leg of mutton. A narrow and flat rump is a fault. The slope of the femur should be about 70° to the horizontal [when the metacarpals are perpendicular to the ground].

LEGS—Moderately long, neither too straight nor too inclined.

The average inclination of the tibia should be about 60° [when the metacarpals are perpendicular to the ground] to the horizontal and the dog is posed in a "stand, stay" position. As seen from behind (see accompanying illustrations) to the tip of the hock [heel] is on a line from the ischium tip to and perpendicular to the ground when the vertebral colums is horizontal.

HOCKS—Rather close to the ground, broad, well muscled and stretched. Seen from back they will be straight and parallel in the "stand" position. In action they remain parallel.[2]

Seen from behind, the hocks, whether in stand or action, remain parallel—otherwise the dog is close or out.

METATARSI—Strong and dry, rather cylindrical; perpendicular to the ground when in position "stand". No dewclaws.

The metatarsi, or shanks, with the tarsus form the posterior shank. In "stand, stay," as seen from profile, they must be perpendicular to the ground. The correct angulation of croup, buttock, leg and shank, makes for a good rear.

POSTERIOR PAWS—Round, strong, toes close and arched. Strong, black nails and thick, hard soles.

The posterior paws must be free from dewclaws—and surely not double ones—which could only result from a random, distant and unwelcome recessive trait. Dewclaws are prone to being torn off in accidents

---

2. This requirement is in absolute opposition to a preponderance of the findings resulting from scientific investigations. It is also in direct disagreement with virtually every authority on animal locomotion. Ed.

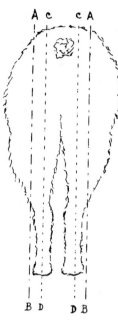

A c   c A

B D   D B

This dog's support at rest is misplaced.
The center of his pads should be directly
under the points of his pelvis (bone
underlying the rump or croup). His metacarpi,
those bones of the foot below the hock, should
be on an axis with these points. His support
should be A - B, not c - d. While his metacarpi are parallel as viewed from the rear they
are too close. Lines of force will tend to
converge when in motion and gaining speed, but
this dog at rest has precarious balance
because of his narrow base. Also,
he consumes extra energy since he must make
muscular compensations for his structural defect.
whether in motion or standing

Hocks turned in.
Cow hocked.
Line of support
not straight
requiring extra
energy just to stand.

COAT—The coat is very full. The top coat plus the dense under-coat make a perfect wrap adapted to the abrupt climatic changes characteristic of the breed's country of origin.

The Bouvier is equipped with a true mantle composed of an outer coat which sheds rain and a dense undercoat which is waterproof. This equips him to be truly resistant to inclemencies and it assures his rusticity.

COLORS—The coat of the Bouvier des Flandres is generally fawn or grey, often brindle or dark grey. Black is also allowed but is not to be favored. Light-colored coats and washed out colors are not desirable.

The standard does not allow white, yellow or salt and pepper. These are faults. Dark brindle is the ideal color. At the moment many Bouvier breedings show tendencies toward ever lighter colors on the washed out side. These are throwbacks to ancient ancestors. We have to fight this and select very dark brindles for breeding.

COAT—It must be rough to the touch, harsh and dry—neither too long nor too short (about 2½ inches), slightly tousled without ever being woolly or curly.

On the head the coat is shorter and almost shaved on the out-side of the ear, but the inside is protected by fairly long hair. On the top of the back the coat is harsh or dry; it becomes shorter on the lower legs, while still harsh. A flat coat is to be avoided since it indicates a lack of undercoat.

One of the characteristics of the breed is the coat which, while harsh to the touch all over the dog, should be dry and dull, neither too long nor too short (about 2½ inches). It should be slightly tousled without being flat or curly. It must not be woolly in spite of the dense, waterproof undercoat. Many paradoxes are hard to reconcile.

To maintain some sense of balance in these seeming conflicts the breeder will need constant adjustments. He will have to watch so the coat does not become too long and thereby too soft; or too short thereby too smooth and too close. He must obtain a dog with a harsh and slightly tousled coat as the standard requires.

UNDERCOAT—A wadding made of fine and close hairs grows under the outercoat and forms with it to provide a waterproof mantle.

The undercoat of the Bouvier can be compared to the lining of a raincoat which protects him from the weather. This is a characteristic of the breed which permits him to resist the tough climatic

Briard-type coat. Flat and too long.

Too harsh; no undercoat.

Coat wooly and too long.

Washed out color.

Coat too short and flat.

Coat rough to the touch.

A quality coat.

Dry coat.

Slightly tousled coat.

A quality coat.

changes of his native land and it is conducive to his hardiness.
The absence of undercoat is therefore a fault. It is also displeasing
because the overall result is a flat and unattractive overall appear-
ance of the coat.

MUSTACHE AND BEARD—Fully dry, shorter and harsher
on top of muzzle. The upper lip has a mustache and the chin has
a full, harsh beard which gives the gruff expression so characteristic of the breed.

The mustache and beard form the furnishings of the head giv-
ing to the Bouvier that gruff expression so characteristic of the
breed.

EYEBROWS—These are made of upstanding hair which ac-
centuate the arch of the eyebrows without ever hiding the eyes.

At the level of the stop there is a lock of hair bent forward—but
without falling on the muzzle. This would give the appearance
of a Briard and be an important fault in a Bouvier.

SKIN—Firm, without excessive laxity; visible mucous membranes are always very dark.

The skin of the Bouvier should neither be too tight nor too
loose. The pigmentation of the lips should always be very dark.
Pink exterior lips is a sign of loss of pigmentation—and a fault.

EXTERNAL SEXUAL ORGANS—well developed. In the
male the testicles must be in place.

In the males, monorchid or bilateral cryptorchidism is disqual-
ifying.

HEIGHT—Height at the withers for males is 24⅜ to 26¾
inches. Females 23¼ to 24⅝ inches. In each sex the average is
between these limits, i.e., 25½ for males and 24½ for females.

WEIGHT—Approximately 77 to 88 pounds for males; 60 to
77 pounds for females.

GAIT: The Bouvier des Flandres as a whole must be harmoniously proportioned to permit a gait free, proud and bold. The
walk and trot are habitual gaits though ambling and pacing are
also employed.

The gait of the Bouvier is very characteristic; it is that of a
determined and bold dog, i.e. free and harmonious. It shows the
functional conformation of the dog but also his temperament
and is thus, very important. The dog which shows himself shyly,
with stilted movement, head and ears low, and tail down surely
is shy and should be eliminated from a breeding program in
spite of good conformation.

The gait of the Bouvier is that of a trotter. This gait is conditioned by his conformation and the articular angles of his limbs which have to move in parallel planes and perpendicular to the ground.[3] Bad stance both front and rear, either too out or too close, are the consequences of poor conformation. Such faults result in poor gait and are therefore serious.

GRAVE FAULTS

CONFORMATION: Long in body.
EYES: Light.
EARS: Not erect.
BITE: Overshot or undershot.
RIBS: Flat, too long or overly rounded and short.
CROUP: Descending [overtilted].
COAT: Washed out colors.
HAIR: Soft, woolly, silky, too long or too short.

SERIOUS FAULTS

BUILD: Sway back.
COAT: Lack of undercoat.
HAIR: White star on chest allowed but not desireable.

DISQUALIFYING FAULTS

EYES: Wall eyed, haggard expression.
NOSE: Spotted or butterfly.
COAT: Chocolate brown—too much white.
SEXUAL ORGANS: Monorchid or bilateral cryptorchid.

The characteristics of the Bouvier des Flandres were first defined by a standard in 1912. This standard was followed by two distinct standards, one by the French Bouvier breeders, the other by the Belgium National Club of the Bouvier des Flandres.

The Club of the Bouvier des Flandres and other friends of the Bouvier in France and the Club National Belge du Bouvier des Flandres joined in 1961 to shape and jointly adopt a single standard. This is the standard here given. It was accepted by the Federation Cynologique International in 1965.

3. See footnote, page 187.

Judged by H. H. Tyler, Deewal Daphne of Battersea, left, took her first Best of Breed at six months of age in Lakeland, Florida, in 1980. She is owned by Judi A. Kramer and Robyn Waldorf.

Amulette's Seneca, right, was bred and owned by Sherry McDowell of California, and sired by Nyrop du Val de Rol CD out of Ch. Deewal Amulette.

Another Victor offspring, Can. Ch. Quiche's Bionic Bambam, is pictured below. She was owner-handled to this Best of Breed win at the Toledo Show. Bambam is out of Can. Ch. Euro's Quiche Kim.

BREEDING BOUVIERS, WHELPING AND RAISING THE LITTER
BY MARION HUBBARD

THE great hope of a conscientious breeder is that he or she will create something better of its kind than the world has ever known before. Without that motivation—and relative possibilities of its realization—there can be no reason for breeding.

The usual reasons are all invalid in the eyes of objective breeders. Here are some of them:

1. "Queenie needs sexual experience. Let her have some fun." (She'll hardly know what she has been missing until after she has experienced it.) "Every bitch should have one litter." (A pure and simple old wives' tale.)

2. "Breed Queenie and make money on the puppies." (Breeding for quality is almost always more loss than profit. And, somehow, only inferior puppies seem to result from profit breeding. Dogs are social creatures that require personal attention. They are not commodities.)

3. "I love my Queenie and I want one of her puppies." (This is the way most breeders start—and the way they get lost in a maze of undefined and unknown genetic characteristics. Frustrated, most drop out before they can make any progress. Love any dog you wish, but breed from quality with predictable genetic possibilities.)

4. "Queenie got caught so we might as well let her have the puppies." (Queenie knows and cares less about mate selection than the most careless and uninformed breeder. Get Queenie to a vet for "morning after" shots.)

5. "The experience of having Queenie's puppies born and raised in the house will be good for the children—and something of a cop-out for me in conveying sex education to my kids." (The same advantages accrue when having a quality-bred litter.)

6. "This dog game can't be so complicated that a bright and successful person like me can't figure it out in a hurry and move right to the top. Besides, I know a good dog when I'm looking at it." (Another "three month" or even "three year expert" in the making. Learn first. Pick the brains of all who might be able to help. Attend shows just to study the dogs. Read, not just about one breed of dog but about all of them. And know this. No one—but no one—can judge dogs just by looking at them. Certainly it would be impossible to do so in a dense coated breed like Bouviers. Judging must also be done with knowledgeable hands—and often a little heart.)

7. This is the predictable switch on numbers one, two and three. "Prince is lonely—in fact very sexy. I'll make him happy by getting him a female to breed with." (Bitches are breedable about ten days a year. What's Prince going to do the other 355 days after you have gotten him stirred up by letting him find out what he has been missing? If you have a male worth breeding from, owners of good bitches will come looking for him. If Prince is all that lonely and needs a pet of his own get him a cat or a turtle.)

If you are going to breed dogs you might as well do what you can to insure the venture's success. Be hard-headed and deliberate. You cannot create better than the best unless you start with the best. Study the strengths and weaknesses of the various leading kennels. Remember that genetic characteristics are not all visible. Get a known genetic inventory. Make sure your foundation stock comes from line bred winners. Don't get involved with scrambled genetics. You could spend many years and dollars getting things unscrambled.

If you feel you are not up to studying the complexities for yourself go to two or three breeders of winning stock. Make allowances because each of them will be oversold on his own dogs. At this point you will be picking a breeder as well as a puppy. Select well. The right breeder can become a most helpful mentor for you.

Note this well. The right time to buy a puppy is *not* on the day you decide to buy a puppy. *The right time to buy a puppy is on the day the right puppy becomes available to you.*

The best stock is often reserved months before the mating is made. The best stock is worth waiting for.

If you are ever going to spend money on a dog do it when you are buying your foundation bitch. That first bitch's influence will be evident in your kennel as long as you are breeding from her descendents.

One thing more: remember that temperament is the one most important characteristic in any dog. You can live with almost anything except a bad temperament. It is bad enough living with a bad temperament — breeding from it should be a punishable offense.

A knowledgeable veterinarian is important. Many well-recommended veterinarians don't like Bouviers. Ask breeders in your area for the names of good men. Find one who is interested in breeding purebred dogs in general — one who won't suggest spaying your valuable bitch at the first sign of internal problems after she has had a litter, or one who feels a certain animosity towards you because you are in a breed which requires cosmetic surgery.

You must have rapport with your vet so that when you come to him with questions on breeding your bitch or raising your litter, he will spend the time and the effort necessary to consider your specialized problems. Veterinarians with little experience in pure-bred dogs or too busy a practice will prove unworthwhile. Personal interest goes a long way toward making the difference between average medical advice and quality care.

Beware of the vet who always has an answer — even on such subjects as genetics and nutrition on which he has probably had no formal training. When you find a vet who can say: "I don't know." that is a very good indicator.

The brood bitch candidate should be in good health and free of parasites. Don't just worm your bitch as she is coming in season and feel that she is then in good health. It is necessary to consider your dog's health long in advance of the season in which you plan to breed her. Have her in moderate weight, worm-free at least six months prior to breeding and checked regularly. Keep her (distemper, hepatitis, leptospirosis) shots up to date. Our dogs have boosters every six months. Do not breed your bitch if she has skin problems. Eighteen months of age is as young as you should want to breed a bitch. Judge by age, not the number of seasons.

The selection of the stud dog should have the same deliberate judgement as was given to the bitch's acquisition. Most of the same criteria pertain. Again you won't want scrambled genetics, not, at least, until after you've acquired considerable breeding experience.

If you are inexperienced you had better trust the public record rather than your own judgement. Insist that the sire be a winner of some note or, even better, a producer of notable winners.

Don't be dazzled by a pedigree full of champions. In itself the title (except under the Federation Cynologique Internationale) can have a limited meaning. "Bests of breeds" in a minority breed such as Bouviers could mean the dog has had only himself to defeat. Champions have been made in many breeds, including Bouviers, by competing only against kennelmates—or even littermates. The table of "Bouviers defeated" has more meaning. So do group placements. The "Bouviers defeated" table does, however, require some explanation. Say there are enough bitches showing in the classes to comprise a "major" toward a championship—but only one dog in the classes. That dog becomes "winners dog" almost automatically. He has an opportunity to also gain a major of the same number of points if he defeats the "winners bitch" for "best of winners." It is the custom of some judges to spread the points around. It doesn't take anything really significant away from the bitch but it gives treasured credit to the dog. It has also made it easier for the dog to become a champion. *Examine the quality of a prospective stud's victories.*

Ask the owners of the stud candidates if you can go over them. Train your hands as well as your eyes. The owners will be glad to point out the dogs' best qualities. It's up to you (or someone helping you) to determine the faults.

It would be helpful to have a qualified person go over your bitch and fault her. Be objective! Try to select a mate that will compliment her and perhaps help her weaker points.

Don't just breed to a dog who lives in the next town or the current most-winning dog. Raising a good litter of puppies is just as costly as raising a poor litter—and the time involved can seem endless. You should make every effort to improve each new generation.

In considering a stud dog it would be wise to look at his get. Ask for a copy of his pedigree. Know whether you would be line breeding or out-crossing. When evaluating a stud's get give weight to the qualities of the bitch that whelped his puppies. What did she add, or subtract, from the litter's quality? Do puppies or young adults sired by the stud have the same faults or weak points you see in your own bitch? If so, seek another male.

A list of some of the more common failings in Bouviers follows, not necessarily in order of seriousness: Weak hindquarters, long backs, light eyes, straight shoulders, no spring of ribs, too much white on the chest, lack of furnishings and flat coat, undershot and overshot bites, too much undercoat in comparison to top coat, no neck, oversized and undersized dogs, dogs with small heads in proportion to their bodies or are otherwise out of balance, loosely-knit dogs that shamble, clumsy, thick-set dogs that are coarse and without grace and style.

After you've selected the stud, thoroughly discuss your agreement with his owner. Then reduce the agreement to a written and signed contract with copies for each. Neither the courts nor the AKC will recognize anything except a written contract. And, there *are* many misunderstandings and disagreements in such relationships.

It is the stud owner's responsibility to handle the actual mating. You may be asked to steady your bitch or hold her head but the owner of the male conducts the affair.

If the stud is inexperienced you probably shouldn't have considered him and certainly not for a maiden bitch. But if you've committed yourself it is reasonable to ask his owner to have the dog's sperm checked for count and motility. You won't want to wait a month or more watching for signs of pregnancy, or to miss a breeding season, because the stud lacks sufficient of what is vital. The same holds for aging studs. This practice has another benefit. Ejaculate stored in a male's body diminishes with time. That's one reason why second or third day repeats of matings are common practice. Another is to insure that viable sperm will be available when actual ovulation takes place.

The *average* term for a canine pregnancy is 63 days. Your pre-natal care of the puppies begins almost at once. Keep your bitch on a normal diet for the first month even though she may be asking for more food. *Do not fatten her up.* Supplement her feedings with a good pre-natal vitamin as Natabec (Park-Davis) daily during pregnancy. Extra protein food is recommended. I use a half-ounce of liver daily. At about a month into gestation your bitch will lose interest in food for several days. This is a good indication that she is in whelp. Her appetite will come back quickly and *do* feed her well at this time.

You may find you want to put her on three meals daily to give her sufficient food. As the whelps grow it will become increasingly difficult for her to consume sufficient food in two large meals. Ask your veterinarian about proper quantities for your bitch. Trotting exercise is very good for your pregnant Bouvier. Cut or hand strip the coat on your bitch two to three weeks prior to whelping. Remove the coat from around her teats and cut it very short in the vaginal area.

Organize your whelping room well in advance of the event. A good quiet room with outside access is best. Remember that your bitch will want to go outside to relieve herself frequently and that you won't want her tracking through the house, at least for the first few days after whelping. Try to select quarters, in any case, where neighborhood children will not be walking through and where you can maintain an even temperature. If the dam and her puppies seem in good condition I do not maintain too warm a room. I prefer 60°–65° Do not permit young children to approach closely or to handle the whelps. Measles can be a disaster for your puppies. Besides, intruders worry a bitch and she might react forcefully.

The whelping box should be constructed several weeks before the puppies arrive so your bitch can become accustomed to her new quarters. It may be built of ¾″ plywood or 1 x 8 inch stock. The latter is easier to saw with simple tools but not as durable. Our boxes are 4 x 8 feet. This allows the bitch adequate room to move about. And, as the puppies develop, they will crawl away from the dam to relieve themselves. Dogs are naturally clean. If the puppies are kept clean and have sufficient space they will quickly learn to move away from their living quarters before defecating.

The box should have a "pig rail" about four to five inches above the floor. This keeps the bitch from getting flush against the sides and allows space for the puppies to crawl behind the bitch without becoming stuck or smothered against the sides of the box. A two inch by four inch board turned on edge and bolted to the sides and ends of the box serves well.

A plastic covered foam mattress, one to two inches thick (made by you) makes a good floor. The resilient surface acts to protect the puppies if the dam accidentally steps on them; it is more comfortable for your bitch; it is easily wiped clean. We cover the mattress with toweling sewn to a five foot by 10 foot size. The rough surface is absorbent and provides good footing for the whelps. The covers are changed as necessary to keep the box clean.

The whelping box should have a door cut into its side just above the pig rail. This should be hinged and have slide bolt fasteners at the top. The door will permit the dam to come and go during the first weeks. Later, when the puppies are about three weeks old, you can close the door to keep them from climbing out. By that time the dam will be with the pups only to wash them and nurse them.

The materials and equipment needed for normal puppy whelping are minimal. Have on hand paper toweling, newspaper for the box prior to and during whelping (put the mattress into the box *after* whelping), a large plastic trash can with liners, a wicker basket in which to place the whelps after birth so that the dam won't step on them while whelping and cleaning her next puppy and a heat lamp to keep the newborn whelps warm. Do not place the lamp close enough to the newborn puppies to burn their skin. Be prepared with towels you won't mind staining. Use these to rub the whelps dry. A blunt-nose scissors for trimming umbilical cords may be necessary. Use a disinfectant, such as Lysol, to wipe the mattress clean. A rectal thermometer can be helpful, as will a scale, notebook and clock if you are keeping records. Esbilac and premature baby bottles should also be available for supplemental feeding.

We never let our bitches whelp unattended, and we have never found the temperature drop suggested by all the books written on whelping to be very relevant. Some bitches' temperatures do drop several days prior to whelping but we have had others go all day with a normal temperature and then late in the evening start labor. Before we could check her temperature the first puppy would arrive.

During whelping try to keep the bitch as clean as possible. Some try to eat the afterbirth. We allow the dam to eat several if she desires, but dispose of the majority. *Do* keep count of the afterbirths—all should be expelled.

It is most important that the sac be broken and the puppy's mouth lifted clear of membranes and fluids with breathing started as soon as possible. Do not allow the dam to drag the whelp about by the umbilical cord. If necessary, press the remaining blood down the cord toward the whelp. Sever the cord by grasping it firmly between thumb and forefinger of one hand about an inch from the navel. With your other hand take a similar hold another inch away from the pup. Pull with the hand furthest away until the cord breaks. Do not pull the cord away in such a manner that you put pressure on the navel. That will cause an umbilical hernia. Wipe each pup briskly with a towel simulating the mother's licking them to stimulate their systems.

You may want to offer your bitch some milk and brandy during a long whelping. Sponge off and dry the dam's hindquarters after she is finished.

After your bitch is through whelping, it is necessary to take her to the veterinarian for a pituitrin shot, anti-biotics, and to be checked for possible retention of afterbirths or unborn whelps. If you have doubts about her puppies put them in a wicker wash basket lined with toweling. Cover them well and take them along. Pups with birth defects such as cleft palates, open abdomens, and crooked jaws can be dealt with by the vet if you haven't the moxie to do it yourself. Pups should have their dewclaws removed and their tails docked at three to five days of age. I advise making arrangements with the vet for these services before the actual whelping. You won't have time to shop for a vet later. Go by appointment. You won't be sitting with your pups in a waiting-room full of sick dogs.

Following whelping, your bitch will probably only want chicken broth, bouillon, or milk. Her water bowl should be kept full at all times. A liquid or semi-soft diet for 48 hours following whelping is a good idea. Protein makes milk; maintain a high protein diet with things like eggs, cheese, and meat. Continue the vitamins. You may find that it is necessary to feed the dam every 4–5 hours, depending on the size of the litter and her physical condition. Do not supplement feed the whelps for the first 48 hours unless necessary. The bitch's milk during the first hours passes temporary immunity to the pups for all those diseases to which the bitch has a resistance. Esbilac was mentioned earlier as advisable to have on hand. This commercial product is a synthetic bitch's milk. It is a fine supplement for the nursing dam and it might be needed at any time to help out the weaker puppies—or all of them if the bitch's milk fails. We like to bottle feed the puppies once daily. We use Esbilac and doll bottles but there is another way with a catheter tube your vet can demonstrate for you. The puppies are more readily weaned as a result of hand feeding and they are handled daily which is very important to their emotional development.

At about three weeks of age start training the puppies to eat from a dish. A convenient and easily digested mixture is a combination of Esbilac and prescription ID diet purchased from your vet. The ID diet may be run through a blender—thinned out with water or Esbilac. Use just a small quantity of the canned food to start. We train each puppy to lap—either on the floor or in our laps. This keeps their coats from becoming clogged with sticky food. As the puppies become more proficient at eating put them all on the floor to eat from a shallow baking pan outside the whelping box. Raise the pan height by using short pieces of two by four laid on their edges. A combination of wash cloth and dam helps clean them up following the meal. Our puppies are raised on Esbilac and the ID diet to between five and six weeks of age. Then they are gradually switched to a quality dry meal, and powdered skim milk and beef. Do not change the puppies' diet abruptly or diarrhea will result. Use a minimum of powdered vitamins in the food. We like Prenatal Theralin.

Between three and four weeks of age the puppies will start outgrowing the whelping box. Either double the size of their living quarters with one area for activity and one for sleep, or move them to a larger facility. Our pups are put in a whelping room with a concrete floor and outside door. They can come and go as soon as they can walk. A raised platform covered with toweling serves as a bed. Be careful not to keep pups on a slippery floor as paw and hip problems may result.

The following schedule is very convenient for Bouvier puppy care.

3–5 days:	Tails docked, dewclaws removed.
3 weeks;	Worm with piperazine adipate.
3–4 weeks:	Wean puppies away from dam.
5 weeks:	Worm again.
6 weeks:	First DHL vaccine shot.
7 weeks:	Ears cropped.
8 weeks:	Sutures out.
9 weeks:	Second DHL shot and either worm again or check stools.
12 weeks to	
3 months:	Third DHL shot.

The Bouvier is basically a guard dog and some puppies exhibit guarding tendencies earlier than others. Do start giving the puppies a great deal of attention from three weeks on. Play with them, handle them, talk to them. A radio in the whelping room with talk shows on is one good method of helping to socialize them. They should be encouraged to go outside as soon as they have their feet under them. If the weather isn't severe let them out, rain or shine. By the time the puppies have a second DHL shot, we like to have our friends drop by to play with them and expose the litter to new faces and new situations. Do not keep them cloistered away.

You should consider the problem of ear-cropping before your bitch whelps. Start looking for a veterinarian who will crop the puppies' ears. Ask Bouvier breeders who live near you for names of competent men. It is worth driving some distance if you feel that you will have better ear crops. Perhaps your own vet is willing to try. If so, you must be prepared to instruct him as to shape and method. If you use someone who comes well-recommended, look at the ears on puppies or adults he has done. Do compare these with the shape on the Belgian imports—always excellent. The ear should be triangular and not too tall. *Be sure to stipulate no bell shape.* The length of the ear is measured to the outer corner of the eye, when cropping a young puppy. The ears should be sutured, and allowed to hang free. They heal more rapidly this way and it is easier to get them to stand erect later. Do not tape them down over the skull. This method puts a crease in the cartilage which is very difficult to overcome later on. The sutures are removed a week after the operation. The ears should be allowed to heal completely before any taping is considered. Hydrogen peroxide, applied twice daily, is excellent to promote healing. After the ears are healed massage helps a great deal to encourage the ears to stand. So does an exercise manipulating the ears backward and forward on the head so the puppy gains control of those ear muscles which pull the ears backward and parallel with the neck.

Masking tape works very well if you need to tape the ears in an upright position. Buy the ¾″ width. It adheres well to the ears and comes off readily. If you have a particularly difficult set of ears with heavy cartilage ask your veterinarian for some ether to soften the adhesive on cloth tape and then adhere this to the ears.

The coat should be kept short on the ears and skull if you are taping ears. The coat should be cut short on the ears in any case as it makes it easier for the ears to assume correct carriage without additional weight. As the permanent teeth come in, you will notice that the ears tend to drop. This situation is only temporary and will correct itself.

At about three months of age, you will begin to see major changes in your puppies. If you have been undecided about which puppies to keep it is wise to wait until after these changes to make final decisions. You may want to ask another breeder his opinion. Or ask a professional handler or judge who knows working dogs.

South African Ch. Summer Hill's Ulema, left, owned by Mr. and Mrs. Schmidts, Port Elizabeth, South Africa.

Also owned by the Schmidts is the Bouvier at right, South African Ch. Summer Hill's Aidan.

"A moment of reflection": Owner Diane Schanz with her Puppy Sweepstakes winner, Gamby's N' Zack's Beauregard, after the judging in October 1978. The judge was Mrs. Marion Hubbard.

Deewal Dark Shadows, right, is shown taking her first win as a puppy at the January 20, 1980, Pontiac Show. She is owned by Rick and Diane Gwschender, and completed her American and Canadian championships at sixteen months of age. Dark Shadows was sired by Ch. Vulcain du Clos des Cytises and from Ch. Deewal Blue Astra.

GROOMING YOUR BOUVIER
BY LIL MEES

THE Bouvier's double coat enables him to adapt to the most drastic types of weather, and one finds that he can easily adapt to all climates. Wet, cold, foggy weather so typical of his homeland is no hardship for our friend; neither is snow nor hot sun. However long exposures to the sun will brown and tinge the coat. The orangeness or brownness one sometimes sees in the beard is not from sunburn but is usually from food and water staining.

Shedding by Bouviers can be kept minimal. A stiff brushing once or twice a week, getting vigorously down into the dead hairs will forestall most of the noticeable shedding.

For grooming use a table the dog can easily jump up on and one that will be easy for you to work around. Bouviers normally enjoy the attention of grooming, brushing, combing and trimming.

It is not necessary to bathe a Bouvier often—only when he becomes "dirty" to the touch. His rough, tousled coat tends to repel water, dirt and grime.

Most owners find their Bouviers enjoy a bath occasionally. In the summer a good rinsing down with the hose and a good pet shampoo will keep your Bouvier clean and sweet-smelling. Most Bouviers enjoy water and are excellent swimmers.

For more than mere maintainence grooming an owner should go

Bouvier grooming is a step by step procedure when Lil Mees' instructions are followed in conjunction with the outline drawing, above.

over his dog in the manner described in the remainder of this chapter at least once every four weeks.

Basic grooming requires that once a week you brush your dog with a slicker brush and comb out with a coarse comb. Cut his nails. Clean his teeth with a tooth scaler followed by scrubbing with baking soda on a damp wash cloth or toothbrush: and clean his *outer* ears thoroughly by rubbing them with a cotton ball dampened in alcohol. To trim, start out with a completely brushed and combed dog.

1. Trim hair on the ears very short on the outside and down to the leather on the amputated part. This may be done with a scissors or a #10 blade on electric clippers. With tweezers pull out all the hair on the

A slicker brush is used to unsnarl the facial furnishings. Care should be taken not to scratch the ears or eyes. Grooming photos by Howard Kling.

inside of the ear, especially the long hairs in the canal. Trim close with the scissors at the lower part of the ear just above the jawbone.

2. Cut the hair on top of the skull from the occiput to the eyebrows and down to the temples to a length of about one-half inch. This can be done with a thinning scissors or a #7 blade.

3. Eyebrows should be trimmed back to about one inch long with thinning scissors and a trimming knife. Avoid a sharp effect. Hair between the eyes should not be removed or trimmed across (as with a terrier). Allow it to come down over the muzzle, trimming at the nostrils.

In trimming hair along the edges of the ears care must be taken not to nip the ear. Use a strong light and rest fidgety dogs.

209

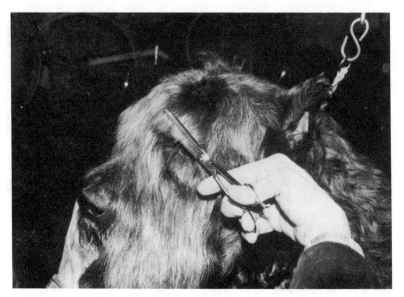

Thinning shears are used to shorten the hair over the eyes. This permits the Bouvier to see better and his expression to be seen better. Some groomers prefer to leave this hair a bit longer than is illustrated. Eyebrows can be hand plucked but the difference gained in appearance isn't worth the discomfort to the dog.

4. Brush and comb the beard thoroughly, trimming excessive length only. With a trimming knife thin out cheek hairs. Avoid a 'chipmunk' look, blending and working the cheek hairs into a heavy beard.

5. Beginning at the jawbone, trim the throat closely, slightly tapering the hair until it is about $1\frac{1}{2}$ inches long as it approaches the breastbone. Hair below the body at the lower part of the brisket (where the front legs join the body) should be about 2–$2\frac{1}{2}$ inches long. On the sides of the neck the hair should be blended to a roundness and left about two inches long.

6. Blend hair from the occiput into the neck with a trimming knife. Trim the neck evenly down into the back.

7. Trim the back evenly leaving the coat about 2–$2\frac{1}{2}$ inches long. Level the topline right back to the tail.

8. Trim hair on the shoulders evenly down to the front legs.

9. Hair on the front legs should be carefully combed out. Trimming

(preferably with a duplex razor-type knife) should be slight to give a straight line effect, especially on the back of the legs. Sometimes the front and sides of the legs must also be trimmed of excess shaggy hairs to give the desired effect. Cut hair from between toes with a *blunt-nosed* scissors. Shape the paws to roundness with a thinning scissors.

10. The tail should be clipped quite close. The coat on either side of the tail and immediately below should be trimmed sufficiently close to give a sharp outline. This can be done with straight and thinning scissors, or with a #10 blade on the tail and a #4 blade on the rump.

11. Trim the stern of shaggy hairs. Round the rear and blend from short hairs under the tail to a heavier growth at the hocks.

12. Trim and blend from the back to the middle of the thigh. Leave the hair longer and heavier as you work down on the legs.

The stripping knife illustrated in use here is made in Belgium. Its blade is adjustable. There are several variations of this instrument on the market. This one is favored because of its handiness in shortening hair on the top of the head and on the ears. Readers who wish to locate the market for this knife may write to Mrs. Mees in care of the publisher.

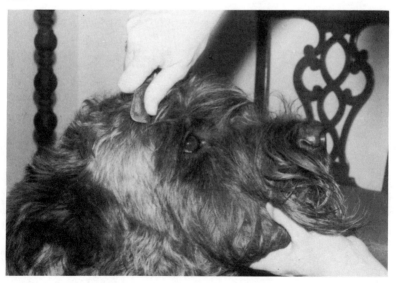

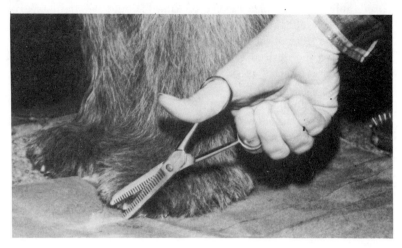

Thinning shears are used to trim the hair around the paws so as to make them appear neat and compact. A plain scissors can be used if the points are carefully directed downward.

A dog is usually more comfortable lying down. It is both thoughtful and productive to let him rest while doing those parts of his coat which permit a reclining or sitting position. Remember that a dog's judgements about people are largely based upon tactile response. He can decide if he likes you by your touch because it tells him a great deal about you.

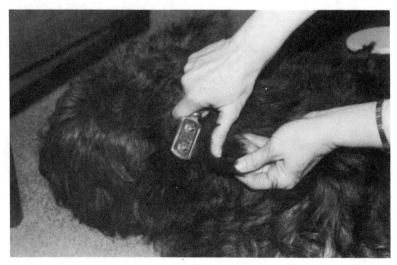

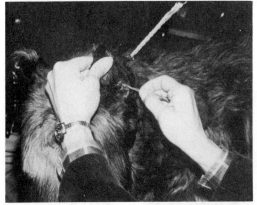

Because the ears of cropped Bouviers are open to air circulation they are less subject to infection. But they are more inclined to get dirty than in flap-eared dogs. The outer ear *only* can be cleaned with a blunt-end tweezer, cotton and alcohol.

Here's a side view of a Bouvier's head groomed for a proud walk—or the show ring.

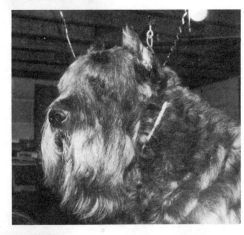

Grooming finished, Bouvier and groomer celebrate with a handshake.

It's a better relationship all around when a child takes a hand in the care of his dog. Even a very young child can use the combing brush for daily or weekly maintenance. Photo by Walter Chandoha.

The whole idea of grooming is to emphasize Bouvier character and to make the dog more comfortable, cleaner and more welcome in the home. This is Mrs. Carrie Adell's Del-Poppy du Clos des Cerberes.

13. With a trimming knife, lightly even out shaggy hairs from the middle of the thigh to the hock.

14. Trim the backline of the hocks evenly with a scissors and round out the hocks. Cut the hair from between toes and round out the paws.

15. Trim the torso, blending from the shorter hair on the back to a fuller coat at the sides.

16. Trim the underline to show a slight tuck-up from the elbows to the loin. Even out the chest hairs to blend.

Stripping. Periodically some stripping is necessary to remove excess undercoat and allow the outercoat to come through. Keep this problem in check. Do it *once a month!*

1. Brush the torso thoroughly with a slicker brush and comb out with a coarse comb.

2. Back-brush with a pin brush and back-comb with a coarse comb.

3. Back-comb again with a fine comb.

4. Re-brush with the slicker, going only with the grain.

The alternative to monthly stripping is an annual takedown with a stripping knife—a very painful and tedious task.

Ch. Vacher's Alpha Centauri Schutzhund I, TD, CD, TT, OFA 315-T, is owned by Jim and Kathy Engel of Centauri Kennels; he was sired by Ch. Lutteur du Val de Rol out of Ch. Yataghan du Clos des Cerberes.

Pictured above, a training session at Bolshoy Kennels.

Three West Coast Bouviers who have made their mark in the breed and in obedience are, from left to right, Palmar's Cyprian UD and Ch. Madrone Ledge Tamboryn CDX, both owned and trained by Tom and Florence Sanches, and Ch. La'Roches L'Imance Ours Noir CD, who is owned and trained by Judy Higgins.

THE BOUVIER IN OBEDIENCE

THOSE of us who live in complete isolation from other people and their property can please ourselves about whether or not we are going to teach our dogs to be good citizens. Bouviers are big enough, brave enough, and powerful enough to become threats to people and proprty unless they are trained and subjected to reasonable discipline. Fortunately, answers to a potentially difficult problem are at hand.

Dog training is available to anyone. If classes are not offered nearby, any of three or four good books will offer expert guidance.

Under the AKC scheme of things for pure-bred dogs, there are various levels of obedience training, with titles awarded to dogs proving their competence at each level. "Companion Dog" training covers the basics all dogs need to be good canine citizens: coming, sitting, staying, lying down and stopping on command, heeling on and off the leash, and staying in a standing position. Once completed, this training makes a dog a safer, more welcome neighbor. It removes owner fears about getting pulled over by a dog with a tow-pony attitude; it keeps dogs from dashing into streets where they can get killed or cause serious accidents by startling drivers. Consider, also, that a reasonably disciplined dog is a happier dog because he doesn't have to make all of his own decisions — he can feel secure in following the instructions of his "pack leader."

For those who find they especially enjoy training and the competition available at most dog shows, there are formal competitions for

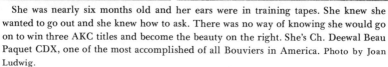

She was nearly six months old and her ears were in training tapes. She knew she wanted to go out and she knew how to ask. There was no way of knowing she would go on to win three AKC titles and become the beauty on the right. She's Ch. Deewal Beau Paquet CDX, one of the most accomplished of all Bouviers in America. Photo by Joan Ludwig.

Gentleman Jim Gent's Andre became the second Bouvier in AKC history, and the first male, to earn a Utility Dog title. He is owned by W. Novis Smith of Exton, Pa.

the additional titles of "Companion Dog Excellent," "Utility Dog," and "Tracking Dog." Almost any Bouvier has the potentiality of achieving all of these titles with the proper training and sufficient opportunities to prove himself in obedience trials.

Obedience competition is quite different from that found in nearby conformation rings. The obedience *handler* is participating to a much greater degree. When things are going right, there is thrilling teamwork between handler and dog. Also, dog and handler have three immediate objectives, the most important of which is attainable even if they defeat no other dogs.

First there is the qualifying score to be made. Done three times (only once in Tracking), it brings the appropriate obedience degree to the dog. (For members of the American Bouvier des Flandres Club there is a club medal for each obedience title won, just as there is for a conformation championship.)

The next objective of obedience competitors is a high score. Even if it does not bring them a prize, it is exciting to see how close to a perfect score of 200 a handler and his dog can get. The third objective is the possibility of getting into the ribbons and prizes.

Effective July 1, 1977, the AKC approved the awarding of an additional title, Obedience Trial Champion (O.T. Ch.). To be eligible for this title, a dog must have earned the Utility Dog title and then must earn one hundred championship points in certain types of competition, placing first three times under different judges.

In late 1979, the AKC approved the test for the T.D.X. title, to become effective March 1, 1980. Eligibility for this title is limited to dogs that have already earned the Tracking Dog title.

The number of Bouviers with obedience titles has increased more than 100% since the first edition of this book was published. By 1974, sixty-one dogs had recorded seventy-one titles. The first thirty-four titles took sixteen years. Then in four additional years thirty-four more Bouviers earned titles. Now, after six more years, 103 additional Bouviers have earned titles.

Records published in *Pure-Bred Dogs — American Kennel Gazette* through the September 1980 issue show that Bouviers with the C.D. title totaled 222. Of these, forty had the championship title before completing the obedience title. Bouviers with the C.D.X. title totaled 22, and those with the T.D. title totaled eight. Only six Bouviers had earned the U.D. title, and none had earned the O.T. Ch. title or the T.D.X.

Her titles, correctly stated are: OT Deewal Merveille UD. She was the AKC's first Bouvier Utility Dog and the second in the records of the Canadian Kennel Club to win the OT degree, roughly the equivalent of a UD. She has won a total of six titles in the U.S. and Canada. She is owned by Mr. and Mrs. F. A. Holmes. Below she does the broad jump.

Ch. Hanover's Chienne D'ore, CD was sired by Urex, below. Both are show and obedience winners.

Ruffkell's Beau Ombre CDX is one of six Bouviers that have won that AKC title. He's owned by Tim and Loryce Heisel of Nanuet, N.Y.

Like Chienne D'ore, above, Ch. Urex Bras de Fer CD belongs to Dr. Clifford and Joyce Bodarky who both enjoy shows and obedience trials.

Ajax of Rivendell CD, left, owned by Tom Boyd and handled by Sandy Boyd, won a four point major at the Oakland Kennel Club Show, March 25, 1979, under exhibitor-breeder-judge Mr. Ralph Goldman.

The late Mr. Jack Godsol, below, is shown with two of Dr. Don Pruitt's Bouviers. On the right is Ch. Deewal Thunderbuff UD, and on the left is Deewal Ian Argus CD. Ch. Deewal Thunderbuff is one of the most accomplished Bouviers in the history of the breed, having earned both an American and a Canadian CDX.

It is interesting to note that there has not been a Bouvier Tracking Dog that also won a championship in the show ring, but two Tracking Dogs, Fantome du Clos des Cerberes and Ufala des Preux Vuilbaards, also earned the C.D. title.

Vacher's Alpha Centauri, bred by Janice and Eugene Hudak, is noted for being the youngest Bouvier ever to earn a T.D. title — and possibly the youngest of any breed. The first champion male Bouvier to earn the U.D. is Ch. Bras de Fer Ursus (12-76), and the first champion bitch Bouvier to earn the U.D. is Ch. Deewal Thunderbuff, owned by Don and Connie Pruitt.

Thunderbuff was the Pruitts' first Bouvier, and when she had completed her championship with Clint Harris as handler and had made several Best of Breed wins, the Pruitts proudly felt she had achieved all they could hope for. As her inbred potential began to surface, however, it was apparent that Buffy was meant to be a working dog. Her Schutzhund and obedience work came easily to her, and she earned her C.D. with a 194 average and some high-in-trial awards along the way. Buffy was also introduced to tracking and enjoyed it enough to be certified for a tracking trial.

In Open work the independence of her background began to play more of a role in her training. Sure of herself, Buffy apparently felt that she could work as well without the handler's instructions, and that repeating some of the exercises was unnecessary. Sometimes it seemed that only the motel stays and the alternate applause and laughter from the crowd made the effort worth her while. Her patience with the Pruitts prevailed, however, and she eventually awarded them with a C.D.X. title.

Buffy made it clear then that it was time for some sort of change of pace, and even though she was well into her Utility training, her owners decided that at six years of age, if Buffy was ever to be bred, the time had arrived. Ch. Sigurd de la Thudinie was chosen for the match, and Buffy, in her new role as mother, did all that was expected of her. She conveniently kept the litter small (two males and two females), but what was lacking in quantity was made up for in quality. Both males have completed their championships, and Thunderbuff's Butler, owned and handled by Anita James, has taken several Group placements and has finished in Canada. The females are well on their way, too.

With her family grown and out on their own, Buffy reluctantly turned her attention back to Utility work. In spite of her inherent stubbornness, she now understood that it was a challenge that needed to be met and mastered; besides, she had tried everything she knew, including feigned blindness, to get out of it. After many months of backyard scores of 200 and just as many muffed trials, Buffy finally made up her mind and completed her Utility title, with Kyle James as handler, to become the first Bouvier bitch to add the U.D. title to a breed championship.

Aldo, owned, trained, and handled by Robert C. Moore of Leamington, Ontario, was the first dog to earn the AKC's Tracking Dog title. He holds two Canadian tracking titles, Tracking Dog and Tracking Dog Excellent. With all of his titles, it is fortunate that he has a short name. Since he is a Canadian dog, his Canadian titles are listed first: Aldo, C.D.X., T.D.X., U.S. C.D.X. and T.D.

Moore states he has trained other breeds, including German Shepherds and Doberman Pinschers, but that he prefers to work with Bouviers "because once they learn, it is not necessary to constantly rehearse them. I just run them through once before we go into the ring and they've got it. I was able to train Aldo for the tracking in five weeks. I started because I was being told Bouviers couldn't take the training and I wanted to prove something. Aldo was only two when he completed his titles. I put another Bouvier, Euro's Heidi, through a Canadian C.D., but a buyer came along and took her. I've replaced her with a puppy out of Aldo's dam. I've trained some other breeds for other people, but I prefer the Bouviers. And, they're so darned good with the kids!"

Aldo was bred by a neighbor of Moore's, Henry van de Bovekamp of Ruthven, Ontario, from Troll van de Woolderwei, a Dutch-bred dog out of Villandria's Argena, that made her AKC C.D. in 1970.

Deewal Merveille, (Hardy l'Ideal de Charleroi — Deewal Katona), also won six titles for and with her owners, Mr. and Mrs. Frank Holmes of Livonia, Michigan. She was the first American U.D. Bouvier, and the second Bouvier to win the equivalent in a Canadian title (the O.T.), and prerequisite AKC and CKC obedience degrees. She was, of course, also the first AKC Bouvier to win a C.D.X. and the first to win both the Canadian and U.S. titles. The Holmeses also trained and handled Deewal Fredrica to American and Canadian C.D.s.

Gentleman Jim Gent's Andre was the second American U.D.

Bouvier. He qualified in 1970 for W. Novis Smith of Exton, Pennsylvania. Merveille had won her AKC U.D. at Akron, Ohio, in 1967, and her O.T. at Oakville, Ontario, in 1965 when she was only three.

Bouviers have achieved so much as police, military, and guide dogs, and as protector dogs in the United States, that their proponents seem not to be fully exploiting their potentialities in obedience competition. In Europe Bouviers have been used in a great variety of services. They are a favorite of the obedience enthusiasts there — and they are here with those who have trained them.

Many obedience people feel show enthusiasts who haven't tried obedience competition don't know how much more enjoyment they could find in dog shows.

The handsome face, left, belongs to Toro de Bolshoy, who was sired by Ch. Max de Bolshoy; his dam was Olah de Bolshoy.

The Tanq of Pal-Mar, Schutzhund II, AD, CD, TD, TT, is the first Bouvier (American bred or import) in the United States to have earned these Schutzhund degrees, the Endurance Degree, and Companion Dog, Tracking Dog, and Temperament Test titles.

The bronze matrix statue, left, sculpted by Dorothy DeSilva of New Jersey, is a rare piece. Only two statues were cast; one is owned by Virginia Martus of New Jersey, and the other by Deewal Kennels, Reg.

BOUVIER DES FLANDRES

CH CHANTERIE VICAIRE

This bronze statue of Ch. Chanterie Vicaire is done by June Hazzah and was commissioned and owned by Dr. and Mrs. Horowitz.

THE BOUVIER IN ART
BY MURRAY HOROWITZ, M.D.

THE Bouvier des Flandres as he presently appears in generally predictable form is so recent a development that exact representations of him can be encountered only in rather recent art expressions. However his identifiable ancestors are sometimes found in a variety of media. Of course the danger here is that the wish to see Bouvier characteristics depicted on the canvas of an old master can foster false belief.

An example might be the fine etching of two dogs by Jan Fyt, 1642. The heads are not unlike the Bouvier's, blocky and rather short muzzled. The bodies are also blocky and strongly built. There are resemblances. But, as a bit of Bouvier history this cannot be called anything more than a "could be." It is better to appreciate such a work for its merit and not try to read significance into it.

There are Bouvier types and transitional ancestors of the breed readily recognizable in occasional artistic expressions of the latter half of the nineteenth century. The etching by Leon Hermann which is reproduced in an earlier chapter is one example. Bronzes by "the Animaliers" with their explicit detail place no strain upon the imagination of those who are looking for undeniable Bouvier characteristics. One of these is illustrated on the next page.

Of course there is always a remote possibility that a definite Bouvier type will be discovered in a very early piece. Certainly even the minor finds each offer some new understanding of the evolution of the Flanders work dogs into our modern Bouvier.

One of the greatest of "The Animaliers," Pierre Jules Mêne (1810-1877), titled his grouping (opposite top) "Dogs Burrowing." The dog in the center has unmistakable Bouvier characteristics. At bottom opposite is a close-up from a different angle of Mêne's signed bronze sculpture. Above are two bronze Bouvier types. They once decorated an 18th-century clock—which accounts for the fact the dog on the right was sculpted with only a part of its right rear leg. There is no documentation on the silver plated plaque below. Again the dogs are undeniable Bouvier types. All are from the collection of Murray and Shirley Horowitz.

The three ceramic Bouviers above were executed by Shirley Horowitz. The plaque of two Bouviers, carved by Ray Marshall, is also in the collection of Murray and Shirley Horowitz.

The etching of two presumably Flemish dogs is by Jan Fyt, 1642. There are some head and body characteristics seen in the modern Bouvier but there is a danger of reading too much into early artistic representations. The carved dog at left is just two inches high and of European origin. The ceramic Bouviers, below, are without documentation. Above pieces from the editor's collection, those below from the Horowitz collection.

Taken at the Pasadena K.C. Show, October 1978. Pictured from left to right are: Mr. Bob Stevens, Show Chairman; Mr. George DesFarge, Judge; Mr. Bert Ennis, President of the American Bouvier des Flandres Club; Mrs. William Suazo; Mrs. Pat Ennis; and Mr. William Suazo, Vice President of the American Club.

CAMPAIGNING THE BOUVIER
BY CHET COLLIER

THOSE of us who believe the Bouvier is the world's finest kind of dog like to see it winning over the other breeds. While it is useful to us to compete within our breed we need the respect of those who do not yet fully appreciate Bouviers. The surest routes to this respect are wins in the group rings—and in the best in show rings.

The interbreed wins only rarely come to dogs that are shown intermittently. Candidates for group wins should be shown week after week on the better circuits so they can both build and maintain momentum. This means competing in 80 to 125 shows a year.

There are some matters which must be considered before undertaking such a campaign. You must first of all have a good dog. This may appear to be stating the obvious but there are people who believe a handler can win with a mediocre dog if carefully campaigned. A handler can add only so much. At the top of the competition every other dog has a good handler and any advantage which might accrue to one over the others is negligible. The person who sets his mind to campaigning a dog will find the cost of the best available animal to be his smallest single expense item.

Take your time. If necessary wait for the right dog. Be businesslike and analytical. Emotional evaluations will almost certainly result in defeat and disappointment.

Next to consider is the choice of a handler. A few owners have developed the skill to compete with the best professionals. Not all of us have the talent or the time to develop it. Nor do many of us have the time for, or the stomach for, constant travel. A few owners enjoy following the show circuits and that is fine for them. They know the best professional handlers could do the job at least equally well and at a fraction of the cost. The professional can carry 12 to 20 dogs as compared to one or two for the circuit-riding amateur.

Like most owners who are out after the group wins or better, I have no choice. My business commitments require that I either utilize a handler or give up the idea of campaigning.

Handling is a very tough and exacting profession. It goes far beyond what is seen in the ring. Not only must the good handler be adept at presenting a dog to judges, he must also have the know-how to keep the dog in top condition (weight, coat, general health, etc.) and, importantly, keep the dog happy and enjoying the showing.

The good handler likes what he does. It is more than just a job. True, he earns his living showing dogs but the good handler thrives on the competition in the show rings. Every time he puts a lead on a dog and parades it for a judge it is with enthusiasm.

It is a plus if a handler has had previous success with your breed. He should at minimum be well experienced with the more nearly similar breeds. He should have the requisite facilities and enjoy the respect of fellow handlers, exhibitors and judges. I prefer a handler who shows sufficiently in my area that I can watch my dog in competition regularly.

The exhibitor who campaigns a dog must have infinite patience. You can't win every time or when you want to. Just as baseball players and golfers have their good and bad streaks, so do dogs. There will be times when you think you will never again win but suddenly everything comes together and it seems your dog can't lose. The exhibitor must learn to live with the highs and lows and take them in stride.

Some people feel that if you are going to campaign a dog it helps to advertise him in the various dog magazines. At one time I thought it was necessary to do this but experience has indicated such advertising is primarily an ego exercise. It does not help winning to the extent that some imagine. The best advertising comes free. If you have

Left to right: Judge Charles Hamilton, Roy Holloway with Taquin du Posty Arlequin, and George Edge with Tania du Posty Arlequin (Taquin's litter sister).

a good dog presented in good condition members of the dog game
will talk about him. You'll find word of mouth is the best advertising
possible. Put the money that would go into "see my wonderful dog"
advertising into the breeding or purchasing of a good dog. In the long
run you will be happier.

A Shirwal Yankee Doodle litter, bred and owned by Gloria Molik, Los Angeles.

Kelly McDonough, 3, hugs Rommel, the Bouvier who saved Kelly's life by alerting his parents when the child fell into a six-foot-deep well. Rommel was owned by Terry and Arlene Sheeran.

Can. and Am. Ch. Sigurd de la Thudinie and his litter sister, Ch. Silette de la Thudinie, both owned by Dr. Don and Connie Pruitt of Indiana, sit with an appearance of protection and loyalty beside Lonn Wood.

ON THE CHARACTER OF THE BOUVIER DES FLANDRES
BY JUSTIN CHASTEL, DE LA THUDINIE KENNELS, THUIN, BELGIUM

THE true nature of the Bouvier des Flandres combined with the selfless utilitarian goals of his breeders has given him a very high and balanced character.

These past years we have confirmed with satisfaction that breeders were ready to give to the Bouvier des Flandres a vigor and a certain perseverance, an individuality which was lacking in the past.

All trainers know it is more agreeable and more feasible to achieve with an alert dog than it is with a lazy dog.

We can then consider the character of the Bouvier is satisfying and that there is nothing to envy in any other breed. We can develop examples and proofs endlessly. After the war of 1914-1918 when amateurs began to become seriously interested in the Bouvier there was in this breed a certain percentage of really ferocious and unmanageable dogs. In my country in most farming areas Bouviers were then kept on chains. At this time the breed held a ferocious reputation.

Since then judicious breeding has eliminated dangerous characteristics. At present the calm and stability of the Bouvier always enchants those who have enough luck to own one of these dogs.

This said, we must carefully guard against losing this heritage and not let it be compromised by insufficiently instructed breeders. In breeding dogs characteristics are quickly set. In only a few generations one can see not only the positive qualities appearing but also the faults. It is, good then, to be forewarned on each matter of character before mistakes are made.

Those in clubs should insist on useful work as a test of Bouvier character.

The Bouvier is nothing of a dandy. Its charm resides in great part in its character. Witness the almost human look through shaggy eyebrows! If it lost this quality what would it have left?

For breeders of Bouviers success will never be complete. There will always be, here and there, individuals of less than true Bouvier character. Regardless of how beautiful or otherwise attractive, such individuals should not be bred from.

All ought to perceive the correct character of the Bouvier des Flandres and look on it as a heritage on which we have no right to infringe, a trust which is ours to enjoy and to pass on unaltered.

Breeders and judges must never forget this obligation.

Ch. Pouky Jones on "lunch break" between cart rides at a Cub Scout Fair. "Pouky" is owned by Elsie A. Guseila.

BOUVIERS IN THE SERVICE OF MAN

THE Bouvier's name is in part a misnomer. The frugal farmers of Flanders evolved him as a utility dog with a specialty. Herding cattle may have been the primary function of the Bouvier and his predecessors but, like farm dogs everywhere, they were expected to contribute by the performance of a wide variety of rural chores.

We have already seen how in their native Flanders Bouviers served as watch and guard dogs, as family companions, as herders of sheep and other livestock in addition to cattle, as destroyers of vermin and even as sometime partners in hunting small game. As cart dogs they have hauled people and produce, dairy and baked goods, traveling tinkers and mobile butcher shops—in fact anything that could be put on wheels and drawn by up to four-dog teams. And it went beyond that. They were even used to power grist mills and to tow canal boats.

In war Bouviers and Bouvier types have served the Belgian military as sentry and Red Cross dogs and even as haulers of machine guns and the wounded. They have been used by Belgian police as patrol and attack dogs. And it will be remembered that the first Bouvier exhibition was restricted to dogs in the service of customs officers— and that their specialty in this service was the capture of smuggler dogs, many of *them* Bouviers, carrying contraband over the border.

The Bouvier's sense of responsibility and property, his concentration and his anxiety to please, his intelligence, his courage and his strength have fitted him well for a great variety of services beyond his nominal role as a herder of cattle.

We have Miss Edmee Bowles' account of how her Bouviers scented out a cache of fifth column ammunition and of how they would give an alert at the approach of German planes before the military warning system knew of the danger. She told of the several times Belco saved her mother and herself during the near-anarchistic stampede of refugees before the advancing Nazis, of how a World War I veteran credited a Bouvier for refusing to leave him for dead on a battlefield. And she told of how Belco, using split second judgement, used himself as a living anchor to save her from a fall down a mountainside.

Louis and Virginia de Rochemont told how their first Bouvier bitch arrived understanding only French but quickly and effectively learned she was being depended upon to warn immediately at the first indication their small son was starting into insulin shock. On a lighter note they also recalled that a Bouvier had played a role in the movie, Outward Bound.

Another Bouvier on the American scene early drew a cart advertising a dog food.

During World War II Bouviers had a greater percentage, by far, of their number serving in the U.S. military than any other breed. Their employment as sentry dogs was chiefly in the Coast Guard's coastal patrol.

The deeper one researches into Bouvier history the more one comes to believe that the tasks the Bouvier hasn't yet accomplished are the ones he hasn't yet been asked to attempt.

Here are some observations on the Bouvier repeatedly encountered in Bouvier research:

1. Under training there seems to be a delay between instruction and response. It is almost as if the Bouvier feels it is necessary to contemplate the advisability of the task assigned him before deciding to accept and execute. Using an idiom of the day, he "gets himself together" before he starts.

2. Once a Bouvier accepts a task as a proper thing for him to do he never challenges it again; he complies quickly and he does not forget.

3. Bouviers are inclined to stick close to home and what they recognize as their responsibilities.

4. The older dogs instruct the young in Bouvier duties.

...ouviers acting as "guiding eyes." All show their tremendous alertness.

5. Because of a strong paternal drive, or whatever, Bouviers tolerate what they seem to recognize as unknowing abuse from children.

6. Like self-appointed foster parents Bouviers will guard and protect their small human charges from anything they deem to be a threat.

7. Most Bouviers exhibit a delicate judgement in responding to threats. If the intimidation of their presence will suffice most will go no further. Louis de Rochemont says his son never lost a playground fight. His Bouvier would gently and firmly grasp any opponent by the seat of his pants and haul the lad out of the fray. A fireman in uniform who approached the de Rochemont home to sell tickets was knocked down and pinned to the ground — but not hurt. Still we know Bouviers can be trained to launch crunching attacks upon command.

The few Bouviers that have had full opportunities to gain the ultimate obedience titles have done very well. The Canadian Bouvier, Aldo, was trained to gain the highest of all tracking titles in just five weeks — and tracking is the specialty of scent hounds, not Bouviers.

In the United States Bouviers serve humans in a variety of roles and we might well examine some of them closely.

The Bouvier as a Guard Dog

In most parts of America crimes of violence have increased sharply in recent years and the dog buying public is more and more focusing on "protection dogs." In fact, many people who would not be otherwise interested in dog ownership have been buying dogs of the larger, more rugged breeds. These do not make good Bouvier owners because people who don't value a dog's companionship beyond what the dog can do for them seldom make successful owners or trainers. A few such "investors" discover the joys of a dog's devotion after the fact but most are incapable of relating to a dog on a mutually happy basis.

There was a controversial article in *Sports Illustrated* magazine based upon an interview with one American breeder. It portrayed the Bouvier as very nearly the ultimate in a guard dog. A pre-existing polarization between Bouvier breeders in North America was exposed by the article's publication. The majority, including most who are interested in conformation competition, felt a gentle-natured breed had been maligned. The minority at the other end felt dog shows would sissify a rugged dog with strong character and great utilitarian

242

A Guiding Eyes Bouvier and its sightless master grow accustomed to each other on city streets, while a school trainer follows close behind.

potentialities. Under competitive conditions in both the United States and Canada each of the extremes is free to pursue its own direction. Under the Federation Cynologique Internationale guard and attack training is a prerequisite to Bouvier success in the show ring. FCI competitions have conclusively demonstrated the Bouvier can be simultaneously outstanding as a show dog and as an utilitarian dog.

It has also been demonstrated in the United States (where competitions are not interlocked) that continuous breeding in divergent directions over several decades can produce two breeds with a single name and a common ancestry. It has been so with bench and field English Setters and with bench and field Pointers, and with bench and field Beagles, etc. It might be well, therefore, if all Bouvier parties were to reread, and carefully, the counsel of M. Justin Chastel in the chapter immediately preceeding.

In the United States Bouviers have served, and are serving, in police K-9 Corps and with a number of private security agencies. Because service organizations usually fall well short of being high bidders they haven't been acquiring many Bouviers during the period of the breed's ascending popularity. Therefore most Bouviers doing guard duty on this continent are home-protecting family dogs without specialized training.

The Bouvier as a Cattle Dog

The Bouvier arrived in North America a little late to find employment as a drover's dog. A number of excellent breeds had seniority, there was hot new competition arriving from Australia, small farms were disappearing and even the cowboy was finding himself displaced, in part, by helicopters. It is well that the Bouvier has his own charms and other aptitudes.

The Bouvier's classic technique is to move at a fast trot in a semi-circle behind his master while focusing on the herd. He is constantly ready to run at any straying beast. He isn't a heeler nipping at his charges. (Heelers get kicked in the head a lot and usually have short careers.) The Bouvier throws body blocks at the fore-end of a cow when necessary—and it is only necessary until that cow has learned to quickly respond to his directions. His method is more akin to that of a springing lion than to a hamstringing wolf.

One Bouvier fancier, Mrs. Christy Comer of Ventura, Calif. utilizes

Above, a Bouvier leaps through a flaming barrier for a Canadian Police officer. Below, a Bouvier serves with a sergeant in the Delray Beach, Fla. Police. (Photo by Stan Sheets)

Above, Bouviers serve as guard dogs in Detroit. The plaque below needs no further testimonial to the ability of Bouviers to serve mankind.

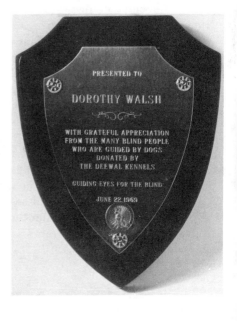

PRESENTED TO

DOROTHY WALSH

WITH GRATEFUL APPRECIATION
FROM THE MANY BLIND PEOPLE
WHO ARE GUIDED BY DOGS
DONATED BY
THE DEEWAL KENNELS

GUIDING EYES FOR THE BLIND

JUNE 22, 1969

the herding talents of her Bouviers. Her Madrone Ledge Blaise was just a pup when she helped "push" two drop calves and their nurse cows in for milking. Blaise, essentially self-taught, became quite proficient in handling dairy cattle. Mrs. Comer's Deewal Brutus, a big fellow, was able to drive a large bull into its paddock.

Herding training is an on-the-job proposition and the best instructor is usually a skilled older dog. It is hardly the sort of thing any dog can be expected to pick up during a Sunday afternoon on Uncle Frank's farm. That could present some dangers to dog, cattle and property.

Perhaps, someday there will be field trials for herding dogs just as there are for sheepdogs. They would give Bouvier owners incentive to train their dogs and develop ancient talents. There is great joy in watching a dog discover and respond to the instincts of his ancestors. For the dog it is exaltation and adrenalin time. For both handler and dog there is a camaraderie far beyond anything either might experience in any other mutual activity.

The Bouvier and the Blind

Most people have a need to be needed and appreciated. *Some* dogs have those same needs. *Most* Bouviers do. And that is the one biggest reason for their outstanding record as successes in guiding the blind.

It is necessary that a guide dog fully understand the importance of, and respond with dedication to, his duties. Needed is a solid, rather stolid, canine citizen with a strong sense of responsibility and the intelligence to make sound independent judgements.

A further listing of the attributes requisite in a guide dog almost accumulate into a description of a Bouvier. He must be patient, unflappable, brave, capable of adjusting easily to a variety of situations and have the capacity to concentrate upon an assigned task for extended periods of time—then become nearly invisible until called upon again.

Guide dogs must be of a robust, hardy breed, 20 to 26 inches at the shoulder when fully grown. Their coats must be easy to keep clean and to otherwise maintain. The individual dog must be healthy, free of hip dysplasia and without any serious breed blemishes or faults. The guide dog can be neither timid nor aggressive. A pedigree is not necessary and the preferred sex is female.

Most of the dogs in this service have either been bred by the school or donated by their breeders. If donated, they cannot be more than two years old and they must have been well socialized to people. Both donated and school-raised puppies are placed with 4-H youngsters for careful care and socialization until they are about ten months old and ready to begin their training programs.

Although there have been outstanding guide dogs of many breeds, those breeds generally preferred, in alphabetical order, are: Alaskan Malamute, Bouvier des Flandres, Doberman Pinscher, German Shepherd, Golden Retriever, Labrador Retriever, and mongrels.

Guiding Eyes for the Blind in Yorktown Heights, N.Y., has had extensive experience with Bouviers. That is because Dorothy Walsh, over a period of years, took great satisfaction in donating Bouviers for the Guiding Eyes' program. Today, Guiding Eyes breeds most of the dogs it uses. The training is expensive and

From left to right, Cheriė Stump's Brussels, Elsie Guseila's Deacon Jones, and Terri Bennett's Tina give cart rides at a Cub Scout Fair.

Duc, top Belgian attack dog, demonstrates his prowess at a training session.

The Camden, N.J. Police Department has made excellent use of the Bouvier, both in the K-9 Division and for promotion of an anti-jaywalking campaign.

a puppy is ten months old before its training can begin. Therefore each dog rejected after its training begins represents a loss in both time and money. By developing its own strains of Labradors and Golden Retrievers the school hopes to constantly reduce the incidence of rejections and simultaneously intensify those genetic character-istics it finds most desirable. The breeding program is producing both consistency and high acceptability. Nevertheless, Bouviers are especially welcome at Guiding Eyes because they have been star pupils and extremely effective after their graduation. Only one of the first 39 had to be rejected (for hip dysplasia).

Bouviers have one important advantage over Labs, Boxers and Goldens. It is deterrent quality. Unfortunately, there are some who prefer to steal from the blind. A blind person traveling about a city needs a guide dog that *looks* like a capable protector and that can, if necessary, *be* an effective protector.

At the invitation of Geoffrey Lock, director of Guiding Eyes, the author spent a day there. It was an impressive and rewarding experi-ence.

A Bouvier, Deewal Charm, just one year old, had been assigned to her new master a week earlier and I had an opportunity to watch them learning to work and live together.

Our entourage set out to test the streets of the city of Peekskill, N.Y. Charm's master was in his early thirties, an upright, quick stepping chap with obvious confidence in Charm and in himself. Their in-structor, a young lady, followed a couple of paces to the rear. Fifty or more feet further back Mr. Lock, a photographer and I followed. Our first responsibility was not to interfere.

Each time the team approached a dangerous obstacle I was tempted to voice a warning—but there was no need. The first was an open cellar door in the middle of the sidewalk. Charm picked a path between the hazzard and the curb. Next came three exuberant and noisy small boys racing down the sidewalk on their bikes. Charm paused and stood her ground until they passed. On command she resumed. Next there was a street to cross. They stopped at the curb. The man stepped forward until he could feel the curb with his feet. Expertly judging the traffic flow by sound, he commanded "forward" and they crossed safely. At another intersection Charm refused the "forward." There was a right-turning car. When the street was safe she proceeded.

Next they encountered a man using an electric saw. Lumber and sawhorses were arranged like a labyrinth. The carpenter looked up, saw the blind man and Charm approach—and went right on with his work. I thought he was crass and unfeeling. Mr. Lock must have read my thoughts. He explained that the people of Peekskill were used to such situations and encouraged by the school to just go on with their business.

Charm and the young man next proceeded up a hill. The sidewalk was composed of uneven blocks, presumably to make it negotiable in slippery weather. Soon their progress was slowed by two elderly ladies inching their way up. To pass them Charm would either have to take to the street or cross a lawn. She evaluated the situation neatly and took the lawn route—with some delicate timing.

The temptations of the next hazzard can only be fully appreciated by dog-wise people. A hound noticed their approach and trotted out to the sidewalk. As the blind man and Charm approached he stiffened and bristled. Charm ignored him completely, striding right past him. There was one more busy intersection to negotiate. Then we all returned to the school.

Charm's new master had to describe his almost-solo to the other students gathered. Each bragged on his or her dog and I am sure each had reason to do so.

Mr. Lock told me his is the only school which undertakes to help the blind who have a second major handicap. He told of a deaf girl who has written back: "Rego hears for me now." A young man with cerebral palsy discovered his Guiding Eye dog not only guided his footsteps but steadied them. And, doesn't that suggest a new area of service by dogs such as Bouviers to people who have difficulty moving or maintaining their balance?

No Guiding Eye Bouvier has ever failed on the job. None has ever had to come back for a refresher course or any other reason—except one.

Arga, a spayed bitch was teamed with an American Indian youth. Together they went to a South Dakota reservation to live. Peter Iron Mountain and the big daughter of Ch. Argus de la Thudinie had been first in their graduation class at Guiding Eye. On the reservation they lived happily for several years. Peter Iron Mountain, no longer helpless, enjoyed a new respect in his community. Pranksters who had teased him before learned to respect Arga.

Peter Iron Mountain's mother wrote the school explaining why she was returning Arga. Peter had gone joy riding in a fast car with other youths. He was killed in a crash. At first Arga waited by the door for his return. She refused food. Later, as was her custom, she lay by his bed with her head across his old shoes. At night she began lifting her head to the skies and howling — almost wolflike. Still she wouldn't eat. Fearing Arga might die too, the grieving mother shipped her back to Guiding Eyes. Arga was thin, weakened, and still mourning when she arrived in Yorktown.

By then Arga was too old to be assigned to a new student. Lock refused to entertain thoughts of putting her to sleep. He called Mrs. Walsh and asked if she could help. Fortunately, the mistress of Deewal knew just the right home for Arga. A friend, the artist and illustrator Kurt Wiese, had a great love for dogs — and room for another at his rural studio-home in Frenchtown, New Jersey. Perhaps it was the complete change of environment, or the tender, loving care. More likely it was both, but Arga lived there happily. She stayed close to Wiese though — just in case he had need of a guiding eye.

Bouviers Bubba, Ghent, Brussels, and Beau at a 1979 City Wayne Cart Pull.

Ch. Xavier de Marquis is the youngest Bouvier to finish his championship. He earned his title September 7, 1974, at the age of seven months, eleven days, with five three point majors and one point. Xavier was sired by Ch. Raby du Posty Arlequin out of Ch. Asta du Clos des Cerberes.

BOUVIER RECORDS AND STATISTICS.

Ours is a young enthusiasm. It is less than fifty years since the first Bouvier was registered with The American Kennel Club and since the first was exhibited at an American show. It is less than twenty-five years since Bouviers became known to more than a handful of breed boosters in North America.

While we continue to be dependent upon importations for the improvement of our strains, it is encouraging to note that American-bred Bouviers are more and more winning their share of the shows and trials. Now, while our history is more ahead of us than behind us, it is well to record here the achievements of Bouvier pioneers of today and earlier: importers, breeders, exhibitors, trainers—and their Bouviers. These records will provide us with a measuring stick of our progress. The common goal of American Bouvier des Flandres Club members is the constant improvement of our dogs. Each *new* record will be an indicator that we are progressing—that we are producing better and better Bouviers.

It would have been helpful to record here every feat and accomplishment that the Bouvier has attained in this world, but such a monumental undertaking defies attacking by even the most ardent statistician. We are most grateful for the records kept in the past by Mr. Carl B. May, Jr., and for the work done recently by Diane Novak of Watchbear Bouviers in Arizona. Also, a special thanks to

253

Loryce Heisel, Secretary of the American Bouvier des Flandres Club, for her contributions. Without the records maintained by The American Kennel Club and published in *Pure-Bred Dogs—American Kennel Gazette,* there would be, of course, no records; for it is only through the AKC that breeders and owners are able to strive for titles, degrees, and awards. There are, however, other statistics recorded by organizations that are gaining repute rapidly, so it is with the hope of encouraging owners to participate in their programs that we also publish the list of Bouviers certified by the Orthopedic Foundation for Animals, Inc.

We hope to be able to include in future editions much more pertaining to Bouviers in Canada and their accomplishments, so we hope that a statistician is hard at work there.

American Bouvier Des Flandres Club
Specialty Winners

1965:   Kennel Club of Philadelphia
       BOB   Ch. Konard du Rotiane
       BOS   Ch. Giaconda du Clos des Cerberes
1966:   Kennel Club of Philadelphia
       BOB   Ch. Job de la Thudinie
       BOS   Ch. Deewal la Belle de Belgique
1967:   Kennel Club of Philadelphia
       BOB   Ch. Deewal Lorenzo
       BOS   Ch. Aurega du Clos des Cerberes
1968:   Kennel Club of Philadelphia
       BOB   Ch. Naris du Posty Arlequin
       BOS   Ch. Odelette du Posty Arlequin
1969:   Kennel Club of Philadelphia
       BOB   Ch. Odelette du Posty Arlequin
       BOS   Ch. Blandford's Raoel
1970:   Sand and Sea Kennel Club, New Jersey
       BOB   Ch. Prudhon des Preux Vuilbaard
       BOS   Ch. Deewal Altesse
1970:   Kennel Club of Philadelphia
       BOB   Ch. Picolette du Posty Arlequin
       BOS   Ch. Naris du Posty Arlequin
1971:   Westchester Kennel Club
       BOB   Ch. Jasper du Clos des Cerberes
       BOS   Ch. Sia du Posty Arlequin

1971: Kennel Club of Philadelphia
BOB   Ch. Madrone Ledge Socrates
BOS   Ch. Tamara Bras de Fer
1972: Somerset Hills Kennel Club
BOB   Ch. Tamara Bras de Fer
BOS   Ch. Quiar de la Thudinie
1973: Harrisburg Kennel Club
BOB   Ch. Tamara Bras de Fer
BOS   Ch. Sir Jumbo du Clos des Cerberes
1974: Detroit Kennel Club
BOB   Ch. Deewal Victor
BOS   Ch. Dominique du Clos des Cerberes
1975: Somerset Hills Kennel Club
BOB Ch. Chanterie Vicaire
BOS Ch. Brigitta du Plateau
1976: Devon Kennel Club
BOB Ch. Taquin de Posty Arlequin
BOS Ch. Vlaanderens I'm Kelli Too
1977: Cabrini College First Independent Specialty
BOB Ch. Timlors Bairgnhomme
BOS Ch. Hanovers Elsa Yandanne
1978: Pasadena Kennel Club
BOB Ch. Timlors Bairgnhomme
BOS Heve de Bolshoy
1979: Detroit Kennel Club
BOB Ch. Hollandia's Evil of Adele
BOS Ch. Vlaanderen's Emilie 1 Etoile
1980: Windsor Locks, Connecticut, Second
Independent Specialty
BOB Ch. Adele's Alexander
BOS Ch. Kutah Ouden Dalerdyk

These uncropped South African Bouviers are at a dog show in South Africa.

BOUVIER FIRSTS AND RECORDS TO BE BROKEN

First Bouvier registered with the AKC: Hardix, 1931

First Bouvier exhibited in the U.S.A.: Laddie, owned by P. O'Brien of Old Westbury, N.Y. Bred by G. McCullough (Hardix-Diane de Montreuil) at Westminster KC, N.Y.C., 1931.

First to win a group placement: Ch. Marius du Clos des Cerberes, AKC A-744749

First bitch to win a group placement: Si Jolie du Clos des Cerberes

First to attain an AKC championship: Ch. Bojar van Westergoo, June 10, 1939

First bitch to attain an AKC championship: Ch. Lisa AKC A224994, 1943

First to win a working group first placement: Ch. Coquin de la Thudinie

First to win best in show: Ch. Argus de la Thudinie

First bitch to win best in show: Ch. Picolette du Posty Arlequin

First to win more than one best in show: Ch. Naris du Posty Arlequin

First American-bred AKC champion: Ch. Marius du Clos Cerberes

First best of breed at an American Bouvier des Flandres Club specialty: Ch. Konrad du Rotiane

First American-bred to win best in show: Ch. Madrone Ledge Socrate

First American-bred to win a working group first placement: Ch. Deewal Lorenzo

256

First American-bred bitch to win a working group first:	Ch. Tamara Bras de Fer
First littermates to win AKC championships:	Ch. Ciskoldo, Ch. Riasta and Ch. Ellydria
First breeder of record:	Julius Bliss
First to qualify for an AKC obedience degree:	Astra-Yerta W98090, 1954
First to qualify for the obedience degree, "companion dog excellent:"	Deewal Merveille UD, Can. OT
First to qualify for the obedience degree, "utility dog:"	Deewal Merveille UD, Can. OT
First to qualify for the obedience degree, "tracking dog:"	Aldo CDX, TD, Can. CDX and TDX
First to attain an AKC championship on the west coast:	Ch. Ciskoldo
First bitch to attain an AKC championship on the west coast:	Ch. Riasta
First champion to qualify for an obedience degree:	Ch. LaBette de la Cucarde CD
First west coast champion to qualify for an obedience degree:	Ch. Deewal Beau Paquet CDX
First AKC champion to qualify for the obedience degree, "companion dog excellent:"	Ch. D'Artagnan le Duc de Maidan CDX
First to place in the working group on the west coast:	Ch. Deewal Benjamen
First American-bred to win best in show in Canada:	Ch. Blandford's Basko
First handler-breeder-judge:	Mrs. Patricia Marcmann
First male, second to earn AKC obedience title, "utility dog:"	Gentleman Jim Gent's Andre UD

First to win both AKC and Mexican titles: Ch. and Mex. Ch. Zorina du Clos des Cerberes

First to win AKC, Canadian and Mexican championships: Ch., Can. and Mex. Ch. Redfox Liberty Bell

First Bermudian, Mexican and AKC champion: Ch., Ber. and Mex. Ch. Konard du Rotiane

First to qualify for the obedience degree "companion dog" in the U.S., Canada and Bermuda: Ch. Redfox Smokie, CD, Can. and Ber. CD

First to win championships in both the U.S. and Canada: Ch. and Can. Ch. Deewal Argusue CD

Largest litter whelped and reported—18 puppies, 3 stillborn, August 1962: Ch. Kaline du Posty Arlequin (to Ch. Erlo de la Thudinie)

Oldest to attain an AKC championship—9 years, 5 months, 15 days: Ch. Argus de la Thudinie

First to win a best in show in Mexico: Ch. and Mex. Ch. Wiljamarks Barney de Jorlee

Youngest to win best in show: Ch. Deewal Candidate of Qupei (20 months, 16 days)

First champion bitch to qualify for the obedience degree "utility dog": Ch. Deewal Thunderbuff UD

Youngest to attain an AKC championship: Ch. Xavier du Marquis (7 months, 11 days)

Youngest to attain AKC and Canadian championships: Ch. Maijeune D'artagnan

First to win the working group in the Pacific Northwest: Ch. Delanda's Garcon Brave

First to win best in show in the Pacific Northwest: Ch. Delanda's Jacques Raoul CDX

First owner-handler to make best in show win: Niron Conrad (Ch. Maijeune's D'artagnan)

First breeder-owner-handler to make best in show win: Loryce Hiesel (Ch. Timlor Bairgnhomme)

Top producing bitch in the history of the breed: Ch. Silette de la Thudinie (12 champion get)

Top producing stud dog in the history of the breed: Ch. Prudhon des Preux Vuilbaards (26 champion get)

All-time top winner with most impressive record for group and best in show wins: Ch. Taquin du Posty Arlequin (40 BIS)

Most impressive bitch record: Ch. Bo Peep des Ours (4 BIS, 18 Group I's, 35 placements, over 100 BOBs)

Most impressive record for an American-bred: Ch. Beaucrest Ruffian (12 BIS in 9 months of campaigning — February—September 1980)

Most impressive litter earning titles in the history of the breed:

Ch. Silette de la Thudinie X Am. and Can. Ch. Urex Bras de Fer CDX—11 pups whelped: 7 champions, 2 CDs, 1 group winner, 1 group placer. Bred by Charles and Claire McLean (Deewal)

Second most impressive litter earning titles in the history of the breed:

Ch. Odelette du Posty Arlequin X Ch. Quiar de la Thudinie—10 whelped: 5 champions, 2 CDs, 1 CDX. Bred by Ray and Marion Hubbard (Madrone Ledge)

TOP TWENTY-FIVE BOUVIERS DES FLANDRES, AKC
COMPETITIONS, THROUGH APRIL 1980
(Rating by the number of Bouviers defeated)

	Best of Breeds	Bouviers defeated
1. Ch. Taquin du Posty Arlequin	293	1,445
2. Ch. Maijeune's D'artagnan	119	1,245
3. Ch. Timlor Bairgnhomme	152	808
4. Ch. Shirwal Yankee Doodle	121	711
5. Ch. Duxbury House's Ulrich	101	607
6. Ch. Hollandia's Evil	44	505
7. Ch. Ivan D'an Naoned CD	84	461
8. Ch. Uriah Bras de Fer	104	460
9. Ch. Chanterie Vicaire	90	398
10. Ch. M. Bonnafont de Silverado	49	357
11. Ch. Raby du Posty Arlequin	145	354
12. Ch. U Oliver des Preux Vuilbaards	88	330
13. Ch. Naris du Posty Arlequin	179	322
14. Ch. Prudhon des Preux Vuilbaards	93	281
15. Ch. Sir Jumbo du Clos des Cerberes	54	276
16. Ch. Konard du Rotiane	65	273
17. Ch. Deewal Lorenzo	66	258
18. Ch. Tamara Bras de Fer	52	248
19. Ch. Hion de la Thudinie	75	241
20. Ch. Deewal Benjamen	108	224
21. Ch. Argus de la Thudinie	66	216
22. Ch. Delanda's Jacques Raoul CDX	46	207
23. Ch. Bo Peep des Ours	67	206
24. Ch. Nomura Wave	73	199
25. Ch. Picolette du Posty Arlequin	82	199

Dr. and Mrs. Erik Houttuin's Flander Field Bouviers are very prominent throughout the United States.

Top AKC Show Winning Bouviers By Year

Name	Breeder	Owner	Bouv Def.	BOB	Group Placements				BIS
					I	II	III	IV	
		1965							
1. Ch. Konard du Potiene	Adams	Neylon	129	27	1	3	2	4	1
2. Ch. Deewal Lorenzo	Deewal	Currie	95	31	1	1	1	3	
3. Ch. De Ney's Grosse Knabe	Neylon	Thiele	35	9	1			1	
4. Ch. Job de la Thudinie	Chastel	Deewal	19	4				1	
		1966							
Ch. Konard du Rotiane	R. Adams	Neylon	92	25	1	3	3	4	
Ch. Deewal Lorenzo	Deewal	Currie	49	19	1	1	2	2	
Ch. Job de la Thudinie	Chastel	Deewal	41	4					
Ch. Redfox Lariat CD	Markham	Markham	26	12					
Ch. Deewal Beauregard	Deewal	Marcus	19	4					
Ch. Boris v.d. Ouden Dijk	Van Vorst	Miller	12	8					
Ch. Schandor du Clos des Cerberes	Bowles	Bowles	10	1					
Frisia's Tawney Miss	Prinsen	Morin	7	2					
Ch. Redfox Clonmel	Markham	Markham	7	3					
Ch. Deewal Desiree	Deewal	Hallerman	7	2					
Madrone Ledge Masker	Hubbard	Hubbard	6	3					
Ch. Deewal Yvette	Deewal	Deewal	5	1					
Ch. Marc de la Thudinie	Chastel	Abady	5	2					
		1967							
Ch. Deewal Lorenzo	Deewal	Currie	81	13	1	1		2	
Ch. Job de la Thudinie	Chastel	Deewal	49	11			2	1	

Ch. Boris v.d. Ouden Dijk CD	von Vorst	Miller	42	10					2
Ch. Tristan du Clos des Cerberes	Bowles	Cook	40	7					
Ch. Redfox Lariat CD	Markham	Markham	24	13					
Ch. Marc de la Thudinie	Chastel	Abady	19	3					
Ch. Konard du Rotiane	Adams	Neylon	16	2					
Deewal Tristan	Deewal	Deewal	14	4					
Deewal Daniel	Deewal		13	2					
Ch. Nic de Ney	Neylon		12	2					
Ch. Schandor du Clos des Cerberes	Bowles	Bowles	11	2					
Ch. Deewal Beauregard	Deewal	Marcus	11	2					
Ch. Picard des Preux Vuilbaards	Abady	Menken	8	3					
Ch. Deewal Grand Prix	Horowitz	Horowitz	8	3					

1968

Ch. Naris du Posty Arlequin	Grulois	Collier	91	33	7	4	4	4	
Ch. Boris v.d. Ouden Dijk CD	Von Vorst	Miller	87	23	1	1		4	
Ch. Marc de la Thudinie	Chastel	Abady	72	22	4	4	1	3	
Ch. Odelette du Posty Arlequin	Grulois	Hubbard	41	12			1	3	1
Ch. Prudhon des Preux Vuilbaard	Abady	Mees	41	12	1			2	
Ch. Zorina du Clos des Cerberes	Bowles	Rutherford	29	16					
Ch. Job de la Thudinie	Chastel	Deewal	21	15			1	3	
Ch. Bibarcy's Job's Daughter	Deewal	Pedersen	27	5		1	1		
Ch. Bibarcy's Gendarme	Pedersen	Pedersen	27	4					
Ch. Genius Teddy Boo Bear	Beckwith	Parker	16	4					

Name	Breeder	Owner	Bouv Def.	BOB	Group Placements				BIS
					I	II	III	IV	
		1969							
Ch. Naris du Posty Arlequin	Grulois	Collier	148	78	11	21	12	4	2
Ch. Prudhon des Preux Vuilbaard	Abady	Mees	74	33	4	3	2	4	
Ch. Raoul des Preux Vuilbaard	Abady	Chernoff	15	6			1	1	
Ch. Odelette du Posty Arlequin	Grulois	Hubbard	62	3					
Ch. Qarlo Segundo De Ney	Neylon	Neylon	14	2		1		1	
Ch. Picolette du Posty Arlequin	Grulois	Hubbard					1		
Ch. Quiar de la Thudinie	Chestel	Deewal	14	5				3	
Ch. Tgauchsin Machque	Deewal	Lepic					1		
		1970							
Ch. Prudhon des Preux Vuilbaards	Abady	Mees	24	94	3	4	4	1	
Ch. Picolette du Posty Arlequin	Grulois	Hubbard	38	88	3	5	4	1	
Ch. Naris du Posty Arlequin	Grulois	Collier	68	87	18	8	9	10	7
Ch. Deewal Benjamen	Deewal	Deewal	46	76			1	4	
Ch. Bibarcy's Soldat de Plomb	Pedersen	Pedersen	11	46					
Ch. Banquo du Clos des Cerberes	Bowles	Rutherford	16	16					
Ch. Tgauchsin Machque	Deewal	Lepic	20	28					
Ch. Quiar de la Thudinie	Chastel	Deewal	6	27					
Ch. Redfox Smokie CD	Markham	Markham	9	24					
Ch. Blandford's Basko	Miller	Miller	3	18					
Ch. Blandford's Nicholas	Miller	Herec	6	18					
		1971							
Ch. Picolette du Posty Arlequin	Grulois	Hubbard	43	107	2	3	5	6	1
Ch. Deewal Benjamen	Deewal	Deewal	36	98		3	1	1	
Ch. Raby du Posty Arlequin	Grulois	Collier	51	82	6	3	10	6	1

Ch. Prudhon des Preux Vuilbaards	Abady	Mees	24	59	2	2	2	3	3
Ch. Madrone Ledge Socrate	Hubbard	Hubbard	19	57	1		2	2	2
Ch. Tamara Bras de Fer	Mees	Mees	15	41					
Ch. Quiar de la Thudinie	Chastel	Deewal	3	31					
Ch. Madrone Ledge Tamboryn	Hubbard	Weaver	10	30					
Ch. Bougie de Fau Allure	Rosenberg	Herec	6	28					
Ch. Bibarcy's Soldat de Plomb	Pedersen	Pedersen	20	21					
Ch. Sasa des Preux Vuilbaards	Abady		11	28					
1972									
Ch. Tamara Bras de Fer	Mees	Mees	122	24		3	1		
Ch. Raby du Posty Arlequin	Grulois	Collier	92	39	6	6	4	5	
Ch. Bibarcy's Soldat de Plomb	Pedersen	Pedersen	64	62	20	14	11	5	
Ch. Madrone Ledge Socrate	Hubbard	Hubbard	54	29		3	1	3	
Ch. Hanover's Alon	Bodarky	Bodarky	47	11					
Ch. Jasper du Clos des Cerberes	Bowles	Bowles	42	4					
Ch. Trajan des Preux Vuilbaards	Abady	Medefessor	42	11					
Ch. Deewal Benjamen	Deewal	Deewal	32	13		1			
Ch. Terry du Posty Arlequin	Grulois	DeLanda	20	3					
Ch. Prudhon des Preux Vuilbaards	Abady	Mees	19	2			1		
Ch. Ruffkell's Delight	Goldman	Levy					1		
Ch. Taquin du Posty Arlequin	Grulois	Collier				3	1	2	
Ch. Quiar de la Thudinie	Chastel	Deewal	1			1		6	1

Name	Breeder	Owner	Bouv Def.	BOB	Group Placements				BIS
					I	II	III	IV	
		1973 (No records kept for number defeated & BOB)							
Ch. Taquin du Posty Arlequin	Grulois	Collier			9	14	8	6	2
Ch. Uriah Bras de Fer	Mees	Wyatt			2	5	3	4	
Ch. Bibarcy's Soldat de Plomb	Pedersen	Pedersen			4	6	3	2	1
Ch. Tamara Bras de Fer	Mees	Mees			1	2	2	1	
Ch. U Oliver des Preux Vuilbaards	Abady	Horowitz			0	0	3	1	
Ch. Raby du Posty Arlequin	Grulois	Dvornik & Vols			0	1	1	0	
Ch. Duxbury House Ulrich	Smith	Spencer & Mees			0	0	0	1	
		1974 (No records kept for group wins)							
Ch. Taquin du Posty Arlequin	Grulois	Collier	334	72					
Ch. U Oliver des Preux Vuilbaards	Abady	Horowitz	223	59					
Ch. Raby du Posty Arlequin	Grulois	Collier	159	45					
Ch. Uriah Bras de Fer	Mees	Wyatt	158	45					
Ch. Deewal Victor	Chastel	McLean	85	21					
Ch. Valois des Preux Vuilbaards	Abady	Milanovits	60	27					
Ch. Duxbury House Ulrich	Smith	Copeland	67	22					
Ch. Hanovers Charleroi	Bodarky	Bodarky	43						
Ch. Sir Jumbo du Clos des Cerberes	Bowles	Kornheiser	42	12					
Ch. Blandfords Basil	Bowles	Miller	39	8					
Ch. Dominique du Clos des Cerberes	Bowles	Suazo							
Ch. Madrone Ledge Valerie	Hubbard	May							
		1975							
Ch. Taquin du Posty Arlequin	Grulois	Collier	367	81	43	16	2	2	12
Ch. Chanterie Vicaire	Arnold	Horowitz	249	53	4	8	9	5	
Ch. Uriah Bras de Fer	Mees	Wyatt	190	27	0	5	1	3	

Ch. Duxbury House Ulrich	Mees	Copeland	126	28	2	1	2	1	
Ch. Xavier de Marquis	Dvornik	Dvornik	102	27	0	0	1	1	
Ch. Torro van Dafzicht	Semmler	Horlings	101	28	0	0	1	2	
Ch. Sir Jumbo du Clos des Cerberes	Bowles	Kornheiser	95	15	1	1	1	1	
Ch. Wallou des Preux Vuilbaards	Abady	Milanovits	65	32	1	0	0	0	
Ch. Terry du Posty Arlequin	Grulois	Landa	56	12	0	0	0	0	
Ch. Deewal Victor	Chastel	McLean	56	16	0	0	1	1	
Ch. Hollandia Evil of Adele	Westra	Vander Muren			1	0	0	0	
Gravine de Bolshoy	DeRycke	DeRycke			0	0	0	2	
Ch. Whizbang de la Tour	Ennis	Ennis			0	0	0	1	
1976									
Ch. Taquin du Posty Arlequin	Grulois	Collier	343	68	34	11	5	4	18
Ch. Duxbury House Ulrich	Mees	Copeland	326	39	0	1	0	3	
Ch. Chanterie Vicaire	Arnold	Horowitz	149	37	3	4	5	1	
Ch. Urus de la Buthiere	Desfarge	Tornai	106	31	0	1	1	1	
Ch. Denards Davey	Chouinard	Chouinard	99	8					
Ch. L'Esprit Fier Xeres	Wyatt	Wyatt	66	15					
Ch. Ulfio de la Thudinie	Chastel	Getty	64	9					
Ch. Pouky Jones CDX	D. Guseila	E. Guseila	52	5					
Ch. Agenta Jabbar	Bostian	G. Robertson	50	1					
Ch. Hollandia Evil of Adele	Westra	Vander Muren	46	8	0	0	0	1	
Ch. Ivan d'an Naoned CD	Bouriaud	Odom	46	10	0	0	1	0	
Ch. Whizbang de la Tour	Ennis	Ennis			0	0	1	1	
Ch. Maijeunes Babiliard	May	Horowitz			0	0	2	0	
Ch. Nomura Wave	Cox	Horowitz			0	0	0	1	
Ch. Jumbour Ygor	Kornheiser	Kornheiser			0	0	1	0	
Ch. Deewal York	McLean	Pruitt			0	0	1	0	

Name	Breeder	Owner	Bouv Def.	BOB	Group Placements				BIS
					I	II	III	IV	
Ch. Timlor Bairgnhomme	Heisel	Heisel			0	0	0	1	
		1977 (No records kept for group wins)							
Ch. Hollandia Evil of Adele	Westra	Vander Muren	326	33					
Ch. Timlor Bairgnhomme	Heisel	Heisel	239	34					
Ch. Ivan d'an Naoned CD	Bouriaud	Odom	226	36					
Ch. Deewal Young Husband	McLean	McLean	168	30					
Ch. Shirwal Yankee Doodle	Seger & McLean	Molik	143	24					
Ch. Maijeune Babiliard	May	Horowitz	142	43					
Ch. Nomura Wave	Cox	Horowitz	129	44					
Ch. Roc de la Montagne	Laska	Kohn	93	13					
Ch. Duxbury House Ulrich	Smith	Copeland	88	12					
Ch. Yogi de Broussaileux	Watt	O'Brien	78	8					
		1978							
Ch. Maijeune D'artagnan	May	Conrad	699	55	9	11	9	1	1
Ch. Timlor Bairgnhomme	Heisel	Heisel	433	78	3	7	4	7	
Ch. Shirwal Yankee Doodle	Seger & McLean	Molik	392	67	1	1	4	2	
Ch. M. Bonnafont de Silverado	Greer & Moon	Dilsaver	141	22	0	0	2	0	
Ch. Yrk du Posty Arlequin	Grulois	Seger	136	22	1	1	0	2	
Ch. Delanda's Garcon Brave	Landa	Landa	102	14	1	0	0	0	
Ch. Ivan d'an Naoned CD	Bouriaud	Odom	92	19	0	0	1	1	
Ch. Bo Peep des Ours	Wray	Horowitz	82	16	0	0	1	0	
Ch. Wittebrug Thor of Oakridge	Christenson	Anderson	80	4	0	2	1	0	
Ch. Nomura Wave	Cox	Horowitz	67	25	3	0	2	6	2
Ch. Maijeune Destinee	May	May			0	1	0	0	
Ch. Wabouve des Preux Vuilbaards	Abady	Milanovits			0	0	1	0	
Ch. Whizbang de la Tour	Ennis	Ennis			0	0	0	2	

268

			475	56	16	10	8	3	5

1979

Dog									
Ch. Maijeune D'artagnan	May	Conrad	475	56	16	10	8	3	5
Ch. M. Bonnafont de Silverado	Greer & Moon	Dilsaver	216	27	0	1	1	0	2
Ch. Shirwal Yankee Doodle	Seger & McLean	Molik	116	30	1	1	1	3	
Ch. Delanda's Jacques Raoul CDX	Landa	Criss	158	35	4	2	2	4	
Ch. Hollandia Evil of Adele	Westra	Vander Muren	124	1	0	0	0	1	
Ch. Bo Peep des Ours	Wray	Horowitz	124	51	5	8	5	4	
Ch. Timlor Bairgnhomme	Heisel	Heisel	121	35	6	2	2	2	
Ch. Kutah Ouden Dalerdyk	Greer & Moon	Phippin	115	14	0	0	0	1	
Ch. Beaucrest Ruffian	Schiller	Schiller	110	28	2	0	1	3	
Ch. Nelly du Clos des Jeunes Plante	Gelineau	McLean & Gillespie	102	51	2	1	2	2	
Ch. Foxfire Able Luke	Guy	Span & Buxton			5	5	5	3	

1980

Dog									
Ch. Maijeune D'artagnan	May	Conrad	274	32	3	9	1	3	
Ch. Beaucrest Ruffian	Schiller	Schiller	254	88	38	17	2	6	13
Ch. Wiljamark Barney de Jorlee	Hasson	Davis	240	26	2	1	2	3	
Ch. Kutah Ouden Dalerdyk	Greer & Moon	Phippin	233	18			2	1	
Ch. Deewal Candidate of Quepei	Deewal	Kramer & Waldorf	233	73	13	9	11	4	3
Ch. Foxfire's Able Luke	Guy	Spann & Buxton	219	83	17	14	9	8	3
Ch. Sharduk du Clos des Cerberes II CD	Bowles & Jacobsohn	Novak & Schuurman	202	25			2	2	
Ch. Delanda's Jacquel Raoul CDX	Landa	Criss	106	20	15		3	1	
Ch. Bo Peep des Ours	Wray	Horowitz	97	56	9	9	7	2	3
Ch. Maijeune Mr. Gottfried	May	Conrad	95	4					
Ch. Adele's Alexander	Vander Muren	Miller	90	2					

269

TOP PRODUCING STUD DOGS
(Based on records available through September 1980)

	Champions Produced		
	Males	Females	Total
Ch. Prudhon des Preux Vuilbaards	10	16	26
Ch. Deewal Victor	11	9	20
Ch. Uriah Bras de Fer	10	10	20
Ch. Quiar de la Thudinie	8	9	17
Ch. Urex Bras de Fer CDX	7	10	17
Ch. Jasper du Clos des Cerberes	4	11	15
Ch. Job de la Thudinie	8	4	12
Ch. Rhombus des Preux Vuilbaards	6	6	12
Ch. Lutteur du Val de Rol	6	4	10
Ch. Sigurd de la Thudinie	6	4	10
Ch. Noceur de la Thudinie	6	3	9
Ch. Vulcain du Clos des Cytises	6	3	9

TOP PRODUCING BITCHES
(Based on records available through September 1980)

	Champions Produced		
	Males	Females	Total
Ch. Silette de la Thudinie	6	6	12
Ch. Odelette du Posty Arlequin	3	6	9
Ch. Bibarcy's Job's Daughter	4	4	8
Ch. Casey Jones	4	4	8
Regine de la Thudinie	3	5	8
Ch. Bianca du Clos des Cerberes	3	3	6
Ch. Deewal Victoria	2	4	6
Ch. Deewal Yetta Lass	3	3	6
Oriane des Preux Vuilbaards	2	4	6
Penny the Pooh	6	0	6
Ch. Remado's Katleen	4	2	6
Tania du Posty Arlequin	1	5	6
Ch. Wendy de la Tour	4	2	6

Belgian Challenge Trophy Winners

The Club National Belge du Bouvier des Flandres has donated the Belgian Challenge Trophy, but it cannot be awarded in the ring because the conditions for winning it do not conform with AKC rules. However, this hand-wrought, chased pewter tray, approximately twenty-four inches in diameter, may be awarded outside the ring if the following stipulations are met:

1. That it be offered only at the National Specialty each year.

2. That for permanent possession it be won either three times in succession or a total of five times by an American-bred dog or bitch who wins Best of Breed, and who was bred and owned by the same person, and owned by that person at the time of the winning. The dog need not be the same dog for all winnings, but the owner-breeder must be.

Bouviers who have won the Belgian Challenge Trophy to date are:

1971, Ch. Madrone Ledge Socrates
1972, Ch. Tamara Bras de Fer
1973, Ch. Tamara Bras de Fer
1977, Ch. Timlors Bairgnhomme
1978, Ch. Timlors Bairgnhomme

Dorothy Walsh Challenge Trophy Winners

The American Bouvier des Flandres Club offers for competition at its shows only, the Dorothy Walsh Challenge Trophy (a silver plated punch bowl) for Best of Winners. For permanent possession, it must be won three times by the same owner, but not necessarily with the same dog. A silver plated replica trophy is presented to commemorate each win.

Winners to date are:

1971, Duxbury House Ulrich
1972, Terri Bras de Fer
1973, Ullya des Preux Vuilbaards
1974, Hanover's Chienne d'Ore, CD
1975, Bronsville Darren
1976, Timlor Bhaleleigh
1977, Nuit Amour du Beaucrest
1978, Heve de Bolshoy
1979, Dareventure Tigger Jones
1980, Flander Field Weardo

Ch. Acoma's Festival of Lights (11/80)
Ajax de la Thudinie (7/78)
Ajax of Riverndell (9/78)
Akbar of Mission Bell (7/77)
Aldo TD (Can. CDX-TDX)
Alexi du Clos des Cerberes (4/79)
Alfred Chien de Bouvier (8/77)
Andelane's Casana
Anna du Clos des Cerberes (11/76)
Anna du Tour de force
Ch. April Roma (2/79)
Astra-Yerta (54)
Athena de Lagonissi (71)
Audubon Mesiur de Bolshoy
Ch. Babouche Rude de Tornai
Ch. Barbichette Sur Qui Compter (9/79)
Baron de Chien Vila (11/79)
Beau Andre de Green Henge (71)
Beau Garth of Asgard (70)
Beaugeste (5/79)
Beau's Gentle Ben (70)
Beta le Monstre de la Foret (7/79)
Betelgeuse of the Big Bird (3/79)

Betsy of Mission Bell (7/74)
Bibarcy's Boldface Boover (9/78)
Ch. Bibarcy's Fashionette (11/74)
Bibarcy's Robert Jericu (9/79)
Bibarcy's Spook (73)
Ch. Bibarcy's Unemployed (9/74)
Bibarcy's Wotan (4/76)
Bijou de Belgique (80)
Blandford's Ursula (10/75)
Bluerox Titan (7/80)
Ch. Boris v.d. Ouden Dijk (66)
Bouvchon Cassiopea (80)
Bras de Fer Undine (3/74)
Ch. Bras de Fer Ursus
Ch. Bric du Clos des Cerberes
Cale Monroe Falcroft (3/77)
Cameo du Clos des Cerberes (10/79)
Caprice Fou a la Tete (3/80)
Cassie du Clos des Cerberes
Causey's Po-An Bojock Supreme (7/79)
Chelsa of Acoma (11/80)
Cherie du Bois Joli (9/78)
Cher Paraduclos des Cerberes

Ch. Czar du Clos des Cerberes (2/80)
Crookhaus Foxy Lady (12/77)
Cubcake Sur Qui Compter (12/80)
Dareventure's Bubba Jones (8/79)
Ch. Dareventure's Darcy Jones (6/78)
Dareventure's Deacon Jones (6/78)
Ch. Dareventure's Delta Dawn (11/79)
Dareventure's Monsieur Etain (12/78)
Dareventure's Tom Jones (9/80)
Ch. D'Artagnan le Duc Maidan (66)
Ch. Deewal Argusue (64)
Ch. Deewal Beau Paquet (71)
Ch. Deewal Beauregard (66)
Ch. Deewal Beulah II (66)
Ch. Deewal Blitzen (3/73)
Deewal Cajurey Tutankhamen (8/80)
Ch. Deewal Calant de Charlaire (69)
Ch. Deewal Chaco of Mariposa (80)
Deewal Dominic Gibralta
Deewal Entre Nous (65)
Deewal Fredrica (71)
Deewal Gabriel d'Artois (66)
Deewal Ian-Argus (10/76)
Deewal Indian Hills (8/77)
Deewal Ironside (10/75)
Deewal Jobey Junior (70)
Deewal Luc Triomphe de Carole (71)
Deewal Manifique (67)
Deewal Maurice du Plateau (68)
Deewal Merveille (Can. OT)
Deewal Owyhee Brogan (69)
Deewal's du Val Adrian (7/75)
Deewal Shane Du (68)
Deewal Therodore Romasto (79)
Deewal Thunderbuff
Deewal Yeoman de la Moille (8/76)
Deewal York (8/79)
Deewal Zera (4/79)
Dejoy Kalon (5/78)
Ch. Dejoy Kedar (80)
Dejoy Kelda (8/78)
Dejoy Kieron (5/78)
Dejoy Marc (7/80)
Dejoy Nic (10/79)
Delanda's Arestaeus
Delanda's Benjamin Rainier (10/72)
Delanda's Daphnis (11/78)
Delanda's Jacques Raoul

Delanda's Jan'ette Racquel
De Margo du Clos des Cerberes (80)
Ch. De Ney's Argus Marteau D'or (65)
Dexter de Leroy of Dale (7/74)
Diablo of Detroit (6/76)
Ch. Dominic's LeDuc (3/78)
Ebony Misty Star (80)
Ed's Triumph of Marlborough (9/77)
Ch. Electa du Clos des Cerberes (70)
Era la Reine Noire TD (11/78)
Ethan Allen Falcroft
Fantome du Clos des Cerberes TD (1/74)
Ch. Faustine de Saint Roch (3/78)
Fearless du Clos des Cerberes (1/79)
Flander Field's Xanka (1/79)
Flanette d'Pranhky (66)
Francois du Bois Joli (9/78)
Frisia's Maximillian (7/77)
Ch. Gailliette du Plateau (1/77)
Gandalf's Mystic Shadowfax (6/80)
Gentleman Jim Gents Andre (72)
Grand Ours du Plateau (5/77)
Grenadier Alida O'River Oakes
Greta von Liebshen (1/77)
Greycliff's Kimo TD (73)

Guerrire Obscurite des Ghent (69)
Hagenah's Bruno (6/74)
Hanover's Anor (6/72)
Hanover's Chienne D'or (73)
Ch. Hanover's Elsa Yandanne (4/78)
Harlan's Little Bridget (80)
Holda (56)
Inisglen Beau-Chien Emily
Ch. Ivan D'an Naoned (77)
Jason Boefje de la Thudinie (4/77)
Ch. Jay Pico v.d. Pony Hoeve (1/79)
JD's Ozzie (1/78)
Je T'Adore (71)
Ch. Jez Zaa Bell (70)
Joey the Rascal of Haal (69)
Jolie Animee de Merveille (7/79)
Joy-A-Len's Holla Hendrika (12/78)
Jumbouv Rok Clos des Cerberes
Kerry Dant's Katrinka (12/75)
King Cortzon Floyd (6/76)
Ch. Koala du Clos des Cerberes (12/76)
Ch. Kristinik's Baron Von Baldur (12/76)
Ch. La Bete de la Cocarde (58)
Lady Elizabeth of Laird (4/79)
Ch. Laroche's L'imance Ours Noir (2/77)

Le Chien Valeureux Lance (80)
Le Chien Valeureux Tyrus (5/80)
L'Esprit Fier's Lady Bov
L'Etoille Quotidienne Bennet (69)
Ch. Lisa
Liska du Clos des Cerberes (6/72)
Madame Simone de Bolshoy (12/74)
Ch. Madrone Ledge Abigail (10/80)
Madrone Ledge Augustus (7/78)
Madrone Ledge Bold (1/80)
Ch. Madrone Ledge Tamboryn
Ch. Madrone Ledge Taussant (10/76)
Ch. Madrone Ledge Tosca (7/72)
Ch. Madrone Ledge Vanilla (11/77)
Magnum Royce From Oakridge (11/78)
Maidan's Cavalier Tigre (67)
Maidan's Truffelyn (67)
Maijeune's Gamin La Gailose
Maijeune's Izekeal (4/80)
Marcel Max Du Bois Joli (4/80)
Ch. Mariposa Afternoon Delight (9/78)
Ch. Mariposa Miracle Mouchete (9/79)
Maxwell's Boomer Bates TD (8/79)
Mercedes Ben (12/79)
Ch. Merveille des Rocheuses (2/79)

Mission Bell Kajara (7/74)
Ms Leggs (10/76)
Murphie du Clos des Cerberes (6/78)
Nero LeDuc de Bies (10/79)
Nikiya la Bayadere (4/76)
Noelle du Plateau (3/78)
Norton's Ten Pen (10/79)
Nyrop du Val de Rol (2/79)
Orion du Clos des Cerberes (5/74)
Osa Miel (7/77)
Pal-Mar's Cyprian
Pandora des York (67)
Peche (12/76)
Piwackett of Janard (7/77)
Ch. Pouky Jones
Praia du Val de Rol (80)
Quantasori Vuilbaard de Ney (68)
Ch. Quenouille de Bolshoy
Redfox Aimee (8/75)
Redfox Bit O'Bina (2/77)
Ch. Redfox David (1/76)
Ch. Redfox Lariat
Redfox Silver Snuggles
Ch. Redfox Smokie
Ch. Redfox Velvet Lassie

Ch. Robertson's Ali
Robertson's Charlie (7/80)
Roxanne's Beau
Roxanne's Carlo Rex A'dele
Ruffkell's Beau Ombre
Ruffkell's Inka Dinka Do (80)
St. Michaels Bon Ami Rocheuses (12/80)
Sassi de la Pooh
Shadylady's Tasha O'Frisia (6/77)
Shah Jahan of Riverdell (5/78)
Ch. Sharduk du Clos des Cereberes II (8/78)
Ch. Shirwal Yves Takarevau (9/80)
Shiva (9/74)
Sia du Posty Arlequin (71)
Silta II (58)
Sir Jason du Clos des Cerberes (4/79)
Ch. Sonja du Clos des Cerberes (1/80)
Tasha Bras de Fer (72)
Tasja of Argena (72)
The Tanq of Pal Mar TD (7/75)
Ch. Timlor D'Artagnan (2/77)
Ch. Timlor Bhaleleigh (11/79)
Titus du Pti Blond (72)
Tocane de Bolshoy (5/76)

Tonnerre du Plateau (8/80)
Toska de la Duyn Ranch (11/77)
Toye Mattox (12/80)
Ch. Trajan des Preux Vuilbaards (11/74)
True Love's Fantasy (12/80)
True of Windy Hill (7/78)
Ufala des Preux Vuilbaards (10/76)
Ch. Urex Bras de Fer (73)
Usbe des Preux Vuilbaards (7/73)
Ch. Vacher's Alpha Centauri TD (10/80)
Vachienne De Lindamere (9/80)
Villandrias Argena (70)
Vin's Max de lo Vin Car (6/77)
Vintage Montlouis (9/77)
Vlaanderen's Eliza Zing (9/78)
Vlaanderen's Enchantress (2/79)
V Sasha des Preux Vuilbaards (11/74)
Wabula de Llenbruc
Witteburg Athena of Oakridge (10/79)
Zabeth (73)

Companion Dogs Excellent

Aldo TD (Can. CDX-TDX) (71)
Andelane's Casana (3/77)
Anna du Tour de force (10/76)
Ch. Babouche Rude de Tornai (12/77)
Ch. Bras de Fer Ursus
Cassie du Clos des Cerberes (7/75)
Crookhaus Foxy Lady
Ch. D'Artagnan le Duc de Maiden (66)
Ch. Deewal Beau Paquet (71)
Deewal Merveille (Can. CDX)
Ch. Deewal Thunderbuff (9/76)
Ch. Delanda's Jacques Raoul (3/77)
Ch. Delanda's Jan'ette Racquel
Flander Field's Xanka

Gentleman Jim Gent's Andre
Greycliff's Kimo
Holda (56)
Joy-A-Lens Holla Hendrika (80)
Jumbouv Rok Clos des Cerberes (4/78)
Lady Elizabeth of Laird (11/80)
L'Esprit Fier's Lady Bov (76)
Ch. Madrone Ledge Tamboryn (1/75)
Pal Mar's Cyprian
Ch. Pouky Jones
Ch. Quenouille de Bolshoy (11/76)
Ruffkell's Beau Ombre (72)
Ch. Urex Bras de Fer (72)
Wabula de Llenbruc (10/76)

Utility Dogs

Ch. Bras de Fer Ursus (12/76)
Deewal Merveille (Can. OT) (67)
Ch. Deewal Thunderbuff

Gentleman Jim Gent's Andre (72)
Greycliff's Kimo TD
Pal Mar's Cyprian

Tracking Dogs

Aldo CDX (Can. CDX-TDX)
Era La Reine Noire CD (1/76)
Fantome du Clos des Cerberes CD
Greycliff's Kimo UD

The Tanq of Pal Mar
Ufala des Preux Vuilbaards CD (2/79)
Vacher's Alpha Centauri (2/79)
Zonia de la Moille (2/78)

COMPLETE LIST OF AMERICAN KENNEL CLUB BOUVIER DES FLANDRES CHAMPIONS 1939 to 1980

(B) following name of dog indicates bred in Belgium; (C) bred in Canada; (F) bred in France; and (N) bred in The Netherlands.

Year	AKC Champion	Sire	Dam
1939	Bojar Van Westergoo (N)	Kamboro (N)	Alexandrina Olga van Marberg (N)
1943	Lisa	Ch. Bojar van Westergoo (N)	Coba uit het Zuiderlicht (N)
1949	Marius du Clos des Cerberes	Belco	Ch. Lisa
1952	Ciskoldo	Basko Alieda v.d. Zaanhoeve (N)	Silta (N)
	Riasta	Basko Alieda v.d. Zaanhoeve (N)	Silta (N)
1953	Bonapart v Darling Astrid (N)	Altor (N)	Elisa Alieda v.d. Zaanhoeve (N)
	Ellydria	Basko Alieda v.d. Zaanhoeve (N)	Silta (N)
1956	Coquin de la Thudinie (B)	Ygor des Coudreaux (F)	Zola de la Thudinie (B)
	Katrien du Clos des Cerberes	Ch. Marius du Clos des Cerberes	Ch. Ellydria
1957	Bel Echo du Clos des Cerberes	Ch. Marius du Clos des Cerberes	Ch. Ellydria
	Zorra du Clos des Cerberes	Bel Ami du Clos des Cerberes	Elfrida du Clos des Cerberes
1958	Deewal Toronto	Ch. Bonapart v Darling Astrid (N)	Ch. Deewal Zita
1959	Argus de la Thudinie (B)	Volpi de la Vallee de l'Escaillon (B)	Ucaba (B)
	Deewal Bianca	Bel Ami du Clos des Cerberes	Yhelot
	Deewal Zita	Bel Ami du Clos des Cerberes	Yhelot
	Draga de la Thudinie (B)	Ch. Argus de la Thudinie (B)	Canaille de la Thudinie (B)
	Erlo de la Thudinie (B)	Ch. Argus de la Thudinie (B)	Zolla de la Thudinie (B)
	Labete de la Cocarde CD	Ch. Coquin de la Thudinie (B)	Ch. Draga de la Thudinie (B)

1960	Deewal Argusette	Ch. Argus de la Thudinie (B)	Ch. Fausette l'Ideal de Charleroi (B)
	Deewal Nicole	Etoile des Coudreaux (F)	Trixie
	Fausette l'Ideal de Charleroi (B)	Bonzo l'Ideal de Charleroi (B)	Asta l'Ideal de Charleroi (B)
	Rostan du Clos des Cerberes	Bel Ami du Clos des Cerberes	Si Jolie du Clos des Cerberes
1961	Caramel Truffe	Ch. Coquin de la Thudinie (B)	Ch. Draga de la Thudinie (B)
	Chef de Truffe	Ch. Coquin de la Thudinie (B)	Ch. Draga de la Thudinie (B)
	Deewal Argusue CD	Ch. Argus de la Thudinie (B)	Ch. Fausette l'Ideal de Charleroi (B)
	Deewal Estioc Mon Ami Pierrot	Ch. Argus de la Thudinie (B)	Ch. Deewal Nicole
1962	Briska du Clos des Cerberes	Bel Ami du Clos des Cerberes	Si Jolie du Clos des Cerberes
	Dante of Grey Mer	Hardy l'Ideal de Charleroi (B)	Ch. Fausette l'Ideal de Charleroi (B)
	Deewal Arguson CD	Ch. Argus de la Thudinie (B)	Ch. Fausette l'Ideal de Charleroi (B)
	Deewal Bonne Amie	Ch. Argus de la Thudinie (B)	Ch. Deewal Nicole
	Deewal Taikoun	Ch. Caramel Truffe	Deewal Argus Lass
	Hion de la Thudinie (B)	Cendrillo de l'Ile Monsin (B)	Demoiselle de la Thudinie (B)
1963	Electra du Clos des Cerberes CD	Ch. Rostan du Clos des Cerberes	Grenadier Alida O'River Oakes
	Gentleman Jim Gent	Ch. Caramel Truffe	Deewal Deone
	Irca de la Thudinie (B)	Hardy l'Ideal de Charleroi (B)	Demoiselle de la Thudinie (B)
	Kaline du Posty Arlequin (B)	Ch. Hion de la Thudinie (B)	Iota du Posty Arlequin (B)
	Tristan du Clos des Cerberes	Ch. Chef de Truffe	Sapho du Clos des Cerberes
1964	Deewal Georgiana	Hardy l'Ideal de Charleroi (B)	Ch. Deewal Argusette
	Deewal Hardiesse	Ch. Deewal Arguson CD	Compeer Paulette
	Deewal Lorenzo	Hardy l'Ideal de Charleroi (B)	Ch. Deewal Argusette
	Giaconda du Clos des Cerberes	Ch. Chef de Truffe	Sapho du Clos des Cerberes
	Job de la Thudinie (B)	Ch. Hion de la Thudinie (B)	Hulotte de la Thudinie (B)

Year	AKC Champion	Sire	Dam
	Konard du Rotiane (B)	Bonzo l'Ideal de Charleroi (B)	Hosca l'Ideal de Charleroi (B)
1965	Deewal Claudette	Hardy l'Ideal de Charleroi (B)	Ch. Deewal Argusue
	Deewal Grand Prix	Hardy l'Ideal de Charleroi (B)	Ch. Deewal Argusue
	Deewal La Belle de Belgique	Ch. Deewal Arguson	Ch. Deewal Nicole
	Deewal Lady Argus	Hardy l'Ideal de Charleroi (B)	Ch. Deewal Argusette
	Del Poppy du Clos des Cerberes	Ch. Chef de Truffe	Ch. Remados Katleen (B)
	DeNey's Grosser Knabe	Ch. Hion de la Thudinie (B)	Ch. Remados Jasmine (B)
	Eliane du Clos des Cerberes	Ch. Chef de Truffe	Ch. Remados Katleen (B)
	Krespie de la Thudinie (B)	Ch. Job de la Thudinie (B)	Iatte de la Thudinie (B)
	Prince v. Young	Duke Von Young	Arendine
	Redfox Clonmel	Ch. Rostan du Clos des Cerberes	Ch. Deewal Bonne Amie
	Redfox Lariat CD	Ch. Rostan du Clos des Cerberes	Ch. Deewal Bonne Amie
	Remado's Jasmine (B)	Ike de Belgique (B)	Irisa de l'Ile Monsin (B)
	Remado's Katleen (B)	Ike de Belgique (B)	Irisa de l'Ile Monsin (B)
	Walden's Etranger	Grenadier Alfego de la Vons	Kara du Posty Arlequin (B)
1966	D'Artagnan le Duc de Maidan CDX	Ch. Chef de Truffe	Ch. Briska du Clos des Cerberes
	Deewal Beauregard CD	Ch. Job de la Thudinie (B)	Compeer Paulette
	Deewal Hion	Ch. Hion de la Thudinie (B)	Ch. Deewal Georgiana
	Deewal Yvette	Ch. Job de la Thudinie (B)	Compeer Paulette
	Schandor du Clos des Cerberes	Ch. Chef de Truffe	Ch. Remado's Katleen (B)
	Telstar du Clos des Cerberes	Ch. Rostan du Clos des Cerberes	Ch. Remado's Katleen (B)
	Thor du Clos des Cerberes	Ch. Rostan du Clos des Cerberes	Ch. Remado's Katleen (B)
1967	Aurega du Clos des Cerberes	Ch. Telstar du Clos des Cerberes	Deewal Marzie Lamb
	Boris van de Ouden Dijk CD (N)	Arnoroh (N)	Herta Carla v.d. Ouden Dijk (N)
	Deewal Beulah II CD	Hardy l'Ideal de Charleroi (B)	Ch. Deewal Argusue CD
	Deewal Desiree	Ch. Hion de la Thudinie (B)	Ch. Deewal Georgiana

		Ch. Deewal Georgiana
	Ch. Hion de la Thudinie	Ch. Deewal Hardiesse
Deewal Nomura	Ch. Deewal Grand Prix	Ch. Remado's Jasmine (B)
Deewal Samantha	Ch. Hion de la Thudinie (B)	Frisia's Hertha II (N)
De Ney's Argus Marteau D'Or CD	Ch. Deewal Arguson CD	Ch. Giaconda du Clos des Cerberes
Gretal of Frisia	Ch. Konard du Rotiane (B)	Lolo du Posty Arlequin (B)
Nic de Ney	Lais du Posty Arlequin (B)	Ch. Giaconda du Clos des Cerberes
Nota du Posty Arlequin (B)	Ch. Konard du Rotiane (B)	Ch. Nota du Posty Arlequin (B)
Perrette du Maidan de Ney	Ch. Marc de la Thudinie (B)	Ch. Deewal Bonne Amie
Picard des Preux Vuilbaards	Ch. Rostan du Clos des Cerberes	
Redfox Velvet Lassie CD		
1968	Ch. Deewal Demon Ripp	Ch. Bibarcy's Job's Daughter
Bibarcy's Casanova	Ch. Deewal Demon Ripp	Ch. Bibarcy's Job's Daughter
Bibarcy's Gendarme	Ch. Job de la Thudinie (B)	Ch. Deewal Argusette
Bibarcy's Job's Daughter	Ch. Deewal Demon Ripp	Ch. Bibarcy's Job's Daughter
Bibarcy's Petite Patrice	Ch. Deewal Lorenzo	Ch. Irca de la Thudinie (B)
Deewal Altesse	Ch. Job de la Thudinie (B)	Ch. Deewal Beulah II CD
Genius Teddy Boo Bear	Ch. Chef de Truffe	Ch. Remado's Katleen (B)
Iseult du Clos des Cerberes	Ch. Job de la Thudinie (B)	Remado's Kitty (B)
Marc de la Thudinie (B)	Ch. Marc de la Thudinie (B)	Johane du Posty Arlequin (B)
Naris du Posty Arlequin (B)	Moka de la Thudinie (B)	Liska du Posty Arlequin (B)
Odelette du Posty Arlequin (B)	Olaf de la Thudinie (B)	Linouche du Posty Arlequin (B)
Pebbles du Posty Arlequin (B)	Olaf de la Thudinie (B)	Linouche du Posty Arlequin (B)
Pepita du Posty Arlequin (B)	Ch. Marc de la Thudinie (B)	Ch. Nota du Posty Arlequin (B)
Prudhon des Preux Vuilbaards	Ch. Chef de Truffe	Ch. Remado's Katleen (B)
Zorina du Clos des Cerberes		
1969	Ch. Deewal Demon Ripp	Ch. Bibarcy's Job's Daughter
Bibarcy's Casandra	Ch. Boris v.d. Ouden Dijk CD (N)	Penny the Pooh
Blandford's Nicholas	Ch. Boris v.d. Ouden Dijk CD (N)	Penny the Pooh
Blandford's Raoel	Grenadier Alfrego de la Vons	Coquette de la Thudinie (B)
Grenadier Coquette of Walden	Ch. Konard du Rotiane (B)	Ch. Giaconda du Clos des Cerberes
Maidan's Alvin		

Year	AKC Champion	Sire	Dam
	Ninette de la Thudinie (B)	Lais du Posty Arlequin (B)	Hermine de la Thudinie (B)
	Noceur de la Thudinie (B)	Lais du Posty Arlequin (B)	Lolo du Posty Arlequin (B)
	Pallas du Clos des Cerberes	Ch. Schandor du Clos des Cerberes	Ch. Eliane du Clos des Cerberes
	Pica des Preux Vuilbaards	Ch. Marc de la Thudinie (B)	Ch. Nota du Posty Arlequin (B)
	Qarlo Segundo de Ney	Ch. Konard du Rotiane (B)	Ch. Remado's Jasmine (B)
	Quiar de la Thudinie (B)	Ch. Naris du Posty Arlequin (B)	Nia de la Thudinie (B)
	Quina de la Thudinie (B)	Ch. Naris du Posty Arlequin (B)	Nia de la Thudinie (B)
	Raoul des Preux Vuilbaards	Ch. Noceur de la Thudinie (B)	Mouche du Posty Arlequin (B)
	Redfox Smokie CD	Ch. Redfox Clonmel	Ch. Deewal Bonne Amie
	Sarita du Clos des Cerberes	Ch. Picard des Preux Vuilbaards	Ch. Eliane du Clos des Cerberes
1970	Altair du Clos des Cerberes	Ch. Schandor du Clos des Cerberes	Ch. Aurega du Clos des Cerberes
	Bibarcy's Soldat de Plomb	Ch. Deewal Homer (B)	Ch. Bibarcy's Job's Daughter
	Blandford's Basko	Ch. Boris v.d. Ouden Dijk CD (N)	Penny the Pooh
	Deewal Benjamen	Ch. Job de la Thudinie (B)	Ch. Deewal Altesse
	Deewal Lucette	Ch. Deewal Demon Ripp	Ch. Deewal Yvette
	Madrone Ledge Renni	Ch. Naris du Posty Arlequin (B)	Madrone Ledge Masker
	Picolette du Posty Arlequin (B)	Ch. Naris du Posty Arlequin B)	Ch. Odelette du Posty Arlequin (B)
	Ronnie des Preux Vuilbaards	Ch. Marc de la Thudinie (B)	Onega des Preux Vuilbaards
	Rostansa du Clos des Cerberes	Ch. Schandor du Clos des Cerberes	Ch. Aurega du Clos des Cerberes
	Rouette des Preux Vuilbaards	Ch. Marc de la Thudinie (B)	Onega des Preux Vuilbaards
	Tamara Bras de Fer	Ch. Prudhon des Preux Vuilbaards	Oriane des Preux Vuilbaards
1971	Asgard Bravado	Ch. Pebbles du Posty Arlequin (B)	Ch. Deewal la Belle de Belgique
	Babette de Saint Roch	Ch. Redfox Smokie CD	Blandford's Bianca
	Babka de Saint Roch	Ch. Redfox Smokie CD	Blandford's Bianca
	Banquo du Clos des Cerberes	Ch. Schandor du Clos des Cerberes	Gaea du Clos des Cerberes
	Bibarcy's Fashionette CD	Ch. Deewal Demon Ripp	Ch. Bibarcy's Job's Daughter
	Bibarcy's Solitaire	Ch. Deewal Ringo	Bibarcy's Guinevere

Bibarcy's Songuese	Ch. Deewal Homer (B)	Ch. Bibarcy's Job's Daughter
Bibarcy's Tambour de Ville	Ch. Pebbles du Posty Arlequin (B)	Ch. Bibarcy's Casandra
Bibarcy's Tourterelle	Ch. Pebbles du Posty Arlequin (B)	Ch. Bibarcy's Casandra
Blandford's Bolto	Ch. Boris v.d. Ouden Dijk CD (N)	Penny the Pooh
Bougie de Fer Allure	Ch. Prudhon des Preux Vuilbaards	Ranni Bras de Fer
Deewal Homer (B)	Kous de la Thudinie (B)	Perette de la Thudinie (B)
Deewal Ringo	Ch. Job de la Thudinie (B)	Ch. Deewal Altesse
De Landa's Nemo	Frisia's Bob (C)	Nanay du Clos des Cerberes
Glad-Stans' Barabbas	Ch. Banquo du Clos des Cerberes	Ch. Zorina du Clos des Cerberes
Glad-Stans Maria	Ch. Banquo du Clos des Cerberes	Ch. Zorina du Clos des Cerberes
Hilprize Kelli Sandra	Ch. Job de la Thudinie (B)	Ch. Deewal Hardisse
Jasper du Clos des Cerberes	Brabo du Clos des Cerberes	Ch. Altair du Clos des Cerberes
Madrone Ledge Socrate	Ch. Naris du Posty Arlequin (B)	Pepita du Posty Arlequin (B)
Madrone Ledge Tamboryn CDX	Ch. Quiar de la Thudinie (B)	Ch. Odelette du Posty Arlequin (B)
Madrone Ledge Troll	Ch. Quiar de la Thudinie (B)	Ch. Odelette du Posty Arlequin (B)
Ola du Clos des Cerberes	Ch. Marc de la Thudinie (B)	Ch. Eliane du Clos des Cerberes
Pouky de l'Ile Monsin (B)	Omsky de l'Ile Monsin (B)	Kata de l'Ile Monsin (B)
Raby du Posty Arlequin (B)	Ch. Quiar de la Thudinie (B)	Lolo du Posty Arlequin (B)
Redfox Liberty Bell	Ch. Picard des Preux Vuilbaards	Ch. Redfox Velvet Lassie CD
Ripeau Bras de Fer	Ch. Prudhon des Preux Vuilbaards	Oriane des Preux Vuilbaards
Sadine du Posty Arlequin (B)	Rasquin de la Thudinie (B)	Rumba du Posty Arlequin (B)
Sasa des Preux Vuilbaards	Ch. Noceur de la Thudinie (B)	Racha des Preux Vuilbaards
Scherif des Preux Vuilbaards	Ch. Noceur de la Thudinie (B)	Racha des Preux Vuilbaards
Sibon des Preux Vuilbaards	Ch. Noceur de la Thudinie (B)	Onega des Preux Vuilbaards
Terry du Posty Arlequin (B)	Ch. Job de la Thudinie (B)	Ch. Deewal Altesse
Tgauchin Machque	Rico de la Thudinie (B)	Praline du Posty Arlequin (B)
1972		
Blandford's Rudo	Ch. Boris v.d. Ouden Dijk CD (N)	Penny the Pooh
Deewal Beau Paquet CDX	Ch. Job de la Thudinie (B)	Ch. Deewal Argusue CD
Deewal Thor	Ch. Quiar de la Thudinie (B)	Deewal Johanna

Year	AKC Champion	Sire	Dam
	Duxbury House's Ulrich	Ch. Prudhon des Preux Vuilbaards	Ch. Ronni des Preux Vuilbaards
	Hanover's Alon	Ch. Prudhon des Preux Vuilbaards	Ch. Sarita du Clos des Cerberes
	Hanover's Ardanne	Ch. Prudhon des Preux Vuilbaards	Ch. Sarita du Clos des Cerberes
	Jez Zaa Bell CD	Deewal Brutus	Madrone Ledge Blaise
	Madrone Ledge Terpodian	Ch. Quiar de la Thudinie (B)	Ch. Odelette du Posty Arlequin (B)
	Madrone Ledge Tosca CD	Ch. Quiar de la Thudinie (B)	Ch. Odelette du Posty Arlequin (B)
	Nikos Kazantzakis	Ch. Deewal Homer (B)	Ch. Bibarcy's Job's Daughter
	Ruffkell's Delight	Flanette Ruff	Ch. Hilprize Kelli Sandra
	Sir Jumbo du Clos des Cerberes	Brabo du Clos des Cerberes	Ch. Eliane du Clos des Cerberes
	Taquin du Posty Arlequin (B)	Rico de la Thudinie (B)	Praline du Posty Arlequin (B)
	Terri Bras de Fer	Ch. Prudhon des Preux Vuilbaards	Oriane des Preux Vuilbaards
	Thias des Preux Vuilbaards	Rhombus des Preux Vuilbaards	Regine de la Thudinie (B)
	Trajan des Preux Vuilbaards CD	Rhombus des Preux Vuilbaards	Regine de la Thudinie (B)
	Urex Bras de Fer CDX	Ch. Prudhon des Preux Vuilbaards	Ranni Bras de Fer
1973	Andelane's Simone	Picolo de la Thudinie (B)	Cambo's Yvette
	Bianca du Clos des Cerberes	Ch. Jasper du Clos des Cerberes	Ch. Pallas du Clos des Cerberes
	Bibarcy's Symphonie	Ch. Deewal Ringo	Bibarcy's Angelique
	Blandford's Audrie	Ch. Boris v.d. Ouden Dijk CD (N)	Leida Herta v.d. Ouden Dijk (N)
	Blandford's Toby	Ch. Blandford's Raoel	Miss Boleyn
	Bodres Baron of Greycliff (C)	Ch. Blandford's Rudo	Greycliff's Tina (C)
	Cal-Grons Baldur Noup van Dafzicht (N)	Noup de la Thudinie (B)	Yulca van Dafzicht (N)
	Chanterie Redfox Venti	Ch. Prudhon des Preux Vuilbaards	Ch. Ripeau Bras de Fer
	Chanterie Vicaire	Ch. Prudhon des Preux Vuilbaards	Ch. Ripeau Bras de Fer
	Charlemagne de Harris	Ch. Deewal Thor	Ch. Madrone Ledge Tamboryn CDX
	Deewal Calant de Charlaire CD	Ch. Job de la Thudinie	Ch. Deewal Argusette
	Deewal Thunderbuff UD	Ch. Quiar de la Thudinie	Flanette Jemina
	Deewal Victor (B)	Tapin de la Thudinie (B)	Ch. Silette de la Thudinie (B)
	Dom'nique du Clos des Cerberes	Ch. Roland du Clos des Cerberes	Ch. Altair du Clos des Cerberes

Hanover's Beatrix — Ch. Jasper du Clos des Cerberes — Ch. Hanover's Ardan.
Hanover's Belle Amie — Ch. Jasper du Clos des Cerberes — Ch. Hanover's Ardanne
Laska's April Mist — Ch. Madrone Ledge Terpodian — Jacqueline K
Madrone Ledge Valmur — Ch. Madrone Ledge Socrate — Ch. Madrone Ledge Renni
Madrone Ledge Venus — Ch. Madrone Ledge Socrate — Madrone Ledge Tigrette
Madrone Ledge Viking — Ch. Prudhon des Preux Vuilbaards — Ch. Odelette du Posty Arlequin (B)
Redfox Whisp of Smoke — Ch. Redfox Smokie CD — Sia du Posty Arlequin (B)
Roland du Clos des Cerberes — Ch. Telstar du Clos des Cerberes — Ch. Pallas du Clos des Cerberes
Silette de la Thudinie (B) — Rico de la Thudinie (B) — Quelly de la Thudinie (B)
Taurus du Clos des Cerberes — Brabo du Clos des Cerberes — Ch. Ola du Clos des Cerberes
Timlor Vitalite — Ch. Quiar de la Thudinie (B) — Ch. Hilprize Kelli Sandra
U Oliver des Preux Vuilbaards — Ch. Noceur de la Thudinie (B) — Taquine des Preux Vuilbaards
Ullya des Preux Vuilbaards — Ch. Noceur de la Thudinie (B) — Regine de la Thudinie (B)
Ur des Preux Vuilbaards — Rhombus des Preux Vuilbaards — Taquine des Preux Vuilbaards
Uraine des Preux Vuilbaards — Rhombus des Preux Vuilbaards — Rachea des Preux Vuilbaards
Uriah Bras de Fer — Ch. Prudhon des Preux Vuilbaards — Ranni Bras de Fer
Valois des Preux Vuilbaards — Ch. Noceur de la Thudinie (B) — Taquine des Preux Vuilbaards

1974
Angeta Jabbar — Picolo de la Thudinie (B) — Cambo's Argusette
Aries du Clos des Cerberes — Ch. Jasper du Clos des Cerberes — Ch. Pallas du Clos des Cerberes
Asta du Clos des Cerberes — Ch. Hanover's Alon — Ch. Ola du Clos des Cerberes
Bibarcy's Ulterior Motive — Ch. Bibarcy's Tambour de Ville — Ch. Sadine du Posty Arlequin
Bibarcy's Unemployed CD — Ch. Bibarcy's Tambour de Ville — Ch. Sadine du Posty Arlequin
Bibarcy's Vision Naire — Ch. Bibarcy's Tambour de Ville — Ch. Bibarcy's Songeuse
Blandford's Basil — Ch. Blandford's Raoul — Ch. Aurega du Clos des Cerberes
Blandford's Julia Van — Ch. Blandford's Raoul — Andrea de Ver
Bras de Fer Ursa — Ch. Prudhon des Preux Vuilbaards — Oriane des Preux Vuilbaards
Bras de Fer Ursine — Ch. Prudhon des Preux Vuilbaards — Oriane des Preux Vuilbaards
Chariton Joie De Vivre — Ch. Madrone Ledge Terpodian — Jacqueline K
Faustine de Saint Roch CD — Ch. Madrone Ledge Viking — Ch. Babette de Saint Roch

Year	AKC Champion	Sire	Dam
	George du Clos des Cerberes	Ch. Roland du Clos des Cerberes	Ch. Altair du Clos des Cerberes
	Hanover's Chienne D'Ore CD	Ch. Urex Bras de Fer CDX	Ch. Sarita du Clos des Cerberes
	Jo Mo Kenyetta	Gabriel de la Terres	Ax la Chapelle
	Le Boof de Chardonnay	Anaris du Pontier	Grenadier Lady Annissa
	L'Esprit Fier's Antoinette	Ch. Prudhon des Preux Vuilbaards	Ranni Bras de Fer
	Lillies Veette	Rhombus des Preux Vuilbaards	Ricca des Preux Vuilbaards
	Madrone Ledge Taussant CD	Ch. Quiar de la Thudinie (B)	Ch. Odelette du Posty Arlequin (B)
	Madrone Ledge Valerie	Ch. Prudhon des Preux Vuilbaards	Ch. Odelette du Posty Arlequin (B)
	Madrone Ledge Vanilla CD	Ch. Madrone Ledge Socrate	Ch. Madrone Ledge Renni
	Nomura Victoria	Ch. Prudhon des Preux Vuilbaards	Deewal Kobe
	Pal-mars Hasson Valient	Ch. Deewal Thor	Ch. Madrone Ledge Tamboryn CDX
	Rians La De Da	Deewal Owyhee Brogan CD	Lady Luv
	Roland de Pago (C)	Roland Ouden Dijk (N)	Hutta de Bolshoy (C)
	Ruffkell's Impressive	Ch. Prudhon des Preux Vuilbaards	Ch. Ruffkell's Delight
	Sergean des Preux Vuilbaards	Ch. Noceur de la Thudinie (B)	Racha des Preux Vuilbaards
	Tapeurs de la Thudinie (B)	Ringo de la Thudinie (B)	Nina de la Thudinie (B)
	Tatia du Posty Arlequin (B)	Nicko du Posty Arlequin (B)	Rivette du Posty Arlequin (B)
	Titine du Posty Arlequin (B)	Nicko du Posty Arlequin (B)	Lorita du Posty Arlequin (B)
	Toro Van Dafzicht (N)	Bica v.d. Rozenheerd (N)	Astra Noup v. Dafzicht (N)
	Ulfio de la Thudinie (B)	Tapin de la Thudinie (B)	Sola de la Thudinie (B)
	Vandermint of Greycliff (C)	Ch. Blandford's Rudo	Shagg-Essa
	Vangogh des Preux Vuilbaards	Rhombus des Preux Vuilbaards	Riba des Preux Vuilbaards
	Veto de la Thudinie (B)	Uberty de la Thudinie (B)	Sagette de la Thudinie (B)
	Vlaanderen's I'm Kelli Too	Ch. Prudhon des Preux Vuilbaards	Ch. Hilprize Kelli Sandra
	Wacquel Relch du Meier	Ch. Bibarcy's Soldat de Plomb	Ch. Sadine du Posty Arlequin (B)
	Wendy de la Tour	Ch. Madrone Ledge Viking	Ch. Madrone Ledge Renni
	Xavier de Marquis	Ch. Raby du Posty Arlequin (B)	Ch. Asta du Clos des Cerberes
	Yancy du Clos des Cerberes	Ch. Jasper du Clos des Cerberes	Ch. Pallas du Clos des Cerberes
1975	Aspenglen's Blandford Shaika	Ch. Blandford's Fionne of Norloch	Miss Boleyn

Barbu Hardi Guerrier
Bibarcy's Samson of Acoma
Bibarcy's Winemaker
Blandford's Hercule
Blandford's Sielegina
Bras de Fer Ursus UD
Brigitta du Plateau
Brookwood Bonanza
Casey Jones
Chariton Wacoumba
Charlerois Xon Misty Morn
Czarous du Clos des Cerberes
Damas Soraja du Oais Bas v Dafzicht (N)
Dar
Dax du Clos des Cerberes
Deewal Colette L'Ours
Deewal Icon D'Argent Nuit
Deewal Isabella
Deewal Victoria
Delanda's Black Orchid
Delanda's Ida Del Oeste
Delanda's Oly
Elsa's Christina Roma
Gaillard du Plateau
Gailliette du Plateau CD
Hobo de Bolshoy
Jaffna's Antares Centurion
Jillene du Clos des Cerberes
Joy-a-len's Beatrix Beauty (C)
Kirk of Troy

Ch. Quiar de la Thudinie (B)
Ch. Bibarcy's Soldat de Plomb
Ch. Bibarcy's Soldat de Plomb
Ch. Boris v.d. Ouden Dijk CD (N)
Ch. Blandford's Fionne of Norloch (C)
Ch. Prudhon des Preux Vuilbaards
Ch. Quiar de la Thudinie
Beau Ami de Mein
Picolo de la Thudinie (B)
Rhombus des Preux Vuilbaards
Unbloc des Preux Vuilbaards
Ch. Roland du Clos des Cerberes
Quarsy de l'Ile Monsin (B)
Ch. Trajan des Preux Vuilbaards
Ch. Schandor du Clos des Cerberes
Ch. Quiar de la Thudinie (B)
Ch. Ulfio de la Thudinie (B)
Ch. Ulfio de la Thudinie (B)
Tapin de la Thudinie (B)
Ch. Terry du Posty Arlequin (B)
Ch. Delanda's Nemo
Ch. Terry du Posty Arlequin (B)
Ch. Deewal Homer (B)
Ch. Deewal Homer (B)
Ch. Deewal Homer (B)
Ch. Sigurd de la Thudinie (B)
Ch. Glad-Stan's Barabbas
Ch. Telstar du Clos des Cerberes
Greycliff's Bo-Hans of Frisia (C)
Troy v.d. Woolderwei (N)

Ch. Bibarcy's Symphonie
Ch. Bibarcy's Tourterelle
Ch. Bibarcy's Tourterelle
Penny the Pooh
Miss Boleyn
Oriane des Preux Vuilbaards
Ch. Hilprize Kelli Sandra
Banjo Bear
Cambo's Argusette
Regine de la Thudinie (B)
Ch. Uraine des Preux Vuilbaards
Ch. Altair du Clos des Cerberes
Benda Noup van Dafzicht (N)
Ch. Bibarcy's Solitaire
Ch. Aurega du Clos des Cerberes
Deewal Johanna
Ch. Silette de la Thudinie (B)
Ch. Silette de la Thudinie (B)
Ch. Silette de la Thudinie (B)
Redfox Flaxie
Redfox Flaxie
Ch. Titine du Posty Arlequin (B)
Deewal Elsa
Deewal Elsa
Deewal Elsa
Roxanne's Peanuts (B)
Glad-Stans Contessa
Ch. Pallas du Clos des Cerberes
Hollandia Josephine (C)
Vallandria's Ouderox Tammy (C)

Year	AKC Champion	Sire	Dam
	Kristiniks Baron von Baldur CD	Ch. Cal-Grons Baldour Noup van Dafzicht	Mission Bell's Jezah
	Madrone Ledge Vonnie	Ch. Prudhon des Preux Vuilbaards	Ch. Odelette du Posty Arlequin (B)
	Madrone Ledge Wenduine	Ch. Madrone Ledge Viking	Madrone Ledge Tigrette
	Maijeune's Alouette	Ch. Prudhon des Preux Vuilbaards	Ch. Madrone Ledge Venus
	Ms Juno du Clos des Cerberes (B)	Sim de Bronchain (B)	Tania du Posty Arlequin (B)
	Nomura Kane No Tomodachi	Ch. Madrone Ledge Viking	Deewal Kobe
	Nomura Wave	Ch. Madrone Ledge Viking	Deewal Vlinder
	Pouky Jones CDX	Ch. Pouky de l'Ile Monsin (B)	Ch. Casey Jones
	Quenouille de Bolshoy CDX (C)	Ch. Sigurd de la Thudinie (B)	Razzia des Herbages Normands (C)
	Redfox Tubby Two	Ch. Redfox Smoky CD	Redfox Quina Tubbina
	Ruffkell's Inspiration	Ch. Prudhon des Preux Vuilbaards	Ch. Ruffkell's Delight
	Ruffkell's Intrepid	Ch. Prudhon des Preux Vuilbaards	Ch. Ruffkell's Delight
	Ruffkell's Invincible	Ch. Picard des Preux Vuilbaards	Ch. Ruffkell's Delight
	Sylvan de la Taupiniere	Rhombus des Preux Vuilbaards	Tatie des Preux Vuilbaards
	Toro de Bolshoy (C)	Ch. Sigurd de la Thudinie (B)	Themice
	Ura des Preux Vuilbaards	Ch. Noceur de la Thudinie (B)	Regine de la Thudinie (B)
	Urmin de la Thudinie (B)	Tapin de la Thudinie (B)	Ch. Silette de la Thudinie (B)
	Vif des Preux Vuilbaards	Task des Preux Vuilbaards	Regine de la Thudinie (B)
	Voodoo des Preux Vuilbaards	Unbloc des Preux Vuilbaards	Rachea des Preux Vuilbaards
	Wallou des Preux Vuilbaards	Rhombus des Preux Vuilbaards	Regine de la Thudinie (B)
	Whizbang de la Tour	Ch. Madrone Ledge Viking	Ch. Madrone Ledge Renni
	Woden du Clos des Cerberes	Ch. Jasper du Clos des Cerberes	Ch. Ola du Clos des Cerberes
	Xalgernon de Marquis	Ch. Raby du Posty Arlequin (B)	Ch. Asta du Clos des Cerberes
	Xarika de Marquis	Ch. Raby du Posty Arlequin (B)	Ch. Asta du Clos des Cerberes
	Xico Ten Roobos (B)	Rico de la Thudinie (B)	Tomerana de la Thudinie (B)
	Xuta de la Thudinie (B)	Tapin de la Thudinie (B)	Tanajca de la Thudinie (B)
1976	A La Chance	Deewal Ithan	Leddy's Medvec Bright
	Alchemain's Kasey of Bolshoy	Ch. Uriah Bras de Fer	Alchemain's Nora

Arita Vedette v. Dafzicht (N) — Poetra v. Dafzicht (N) — Vedette v.d. Maceclers (B)
Babouche Rude de Tornai CDX — Ch. Deewal Vic-son de Tornai — Julia de la Buthiere (F)
Bibarcy's Veinard — Ch. Quiar de la Thudinie (B) — Ch. Bibarcy's Petite Patrice
Bibarcy's Yankee Peddler — Ch. Deewal Victor (B) — Ch. Bibarcy's Casandra
Bibarcy's Yerma — Ch. Deewal Victor (B) — Ch. Bibarcy's Casandra
Bolshoy's Tricha of Sanrick (C) — Max de Bolshoy (C) — Gravine de Bolshoy (C)
Bronson (C) — Toffy (C) — Black Lady (C)
Cosmo Jac de Chehalem — Ch. Hobo de Bolshoy (C) — Wendy Sooty of Iroquois (C)
Croix de Guerre Xavier — Ch. L'Esprit Fier's Wilhelm — Blandford's Ursula CD
Croix de Guerre Xena — Ch. L'Esprit Fier's Wilhelm — Blandford's Ursula CD
Dakota Snows van Koppelpoort — Ch. Blandford's Toby — Samantha v.d. Susannapolder (N)
Damar's Appley — Ch. Torro van Dafzicht (N) — Tora (N)
Deewal Yeates — Ch. Urex Bras de Fer CDX — Ch. Silette de la Thudinie (B)
Deewal Yetta Lass — Ch. Urex Bras de Fer CDX — Ch. Silette de la Thudinie (B)
Deewal Y'Mira van Daele — Ch. Urex Bras de Fer CDX — Ch. Silette de la Thudinie (B)
Deewal Yolanda — Ch. Urex Bras de Fer CDX — Ch. Silette de la Thudinie (B)
Deewal York CD — Ch. Urex Bras de Fer CDX — Ch. Silette de la Thudinie (B)
Deewal Young Husband — Ch. Urex Bras de Fer CDX — Ch. Silette de la Thudinie (B)
Deewal Yve — Ch. Urex Bras de Fer CDX — Ch. Silette de la Thudinie (B)
Delanda's Gabriel de Lysien — Ch. Terry du Posty Arlequin (B) — Ch. Moza du Clos des Cerberes
Denard's Davey — Ch. Hollandia's Evil of Adele (C) — Ch. Europs Lucky Sonya Denard (C)
Ex de Saint Roch — Ch. Blandford's Basko — Ch. Babette de Saint Roch
Greycliff's Moses (C) — Ch. Blandford's Rudo — Greycliff's Ming (C)
Hilltop's Le Grand Ours — Deewal Noah — Zabeth CD
Hilltop's Noir Gredin — Deewal Noah — Zabeth CD
Hollandia's Evil of Adele — Cambo's Thorton de la Thudinie — Siska de la Thudinie (B)
Ivan D'an Naoned CD — Quarl du Clos des Jeunes Plante (F) — Sarah de Lann Breinz (F)
Jenbedon's Tuff Tully — Ch. Blandford's Toby — Samantha v.d. Susannapolder (N)
Joost du Plateau — Ch. Quiar de la Thudinie (B) — Deewal Johanna
Jumbouv's Ygor — Ch. Sir Jumbo du Clos des Cerberes — Ch. Ms. Juno du Clos des Cerberes (B)

Year	AKC Champion	Sire	Dam
	L'Esprit Fier's Mystique	Ch. Uriah Bras de Fer	Ch. Bianca du Clos des Cerberes
	L'Esprit Fier's Wilhelm	Ch. Uriah Bras de Fer	Ch. Bianca du Clos des Cerberes
	L'Esprit Fier's Xebec	Ch. L'Esprit Fier's Wilhelm	Ch. L'Esprit Fier's Antoinette
	L'Esprit Fier's Xeres	Ch. L'Esprit Fier's Wilhelm	Ch. Bianca du Clos des Cerberes
	Majeune's Bouttoniere	Ch. Uris Bras de Fer	Ch. Madrone Ledge Venus
	Marquis du Plateau	Ch. Madrone Ledge Viking	Ch. Madrone Ledge Tosca CD
	Nicholas Ouder Dalerdyk	Quintas Astra v.d. Dijk (N)	Delilah Bell
	Niro of Bolshoy (C)	Ch. Sigurd de la Thudinie (B)	Themice (C)
	Pal-mars Caesar Maximillian	Ch. Madrone Ledge Socrate	Pal-mars Victory
	Pal-mars Coup de Grace	Ch. Deewal Thor	Ch. Madrone Ledge Tamboryn CDX
	Ramcac Vic the Brave	Samson le Poilee de Ney	Hanover's Anor CD
	Redfox David CD	Ch. Redfox Smokey CD	Redfox Quina Tubbina
	Redfox Jessamy Juno	Ch. Redfox Smokey CD	Ch. Chanterie Redfox Venti
	Rienzi du Clos des Cerberes (B)	Sim de Bronchain (B)	Tania du Posty Arlequin (B)
	Roc de la Montagne	Ch. Sylvan de la Taupiniere	Ch. Laska's April Mist
	Shirwal Yankee Doodle	Ch. Uriah Bras de Fer	Ch. Deewal Victoria
	Shirwal Yorrick	Ch. Uriah Bras de Fer	Ch. Deewal Victoria
	Sigurd de la Thudinie (B)	Rico de la Thudinie (B)	Quelly de la Thudinie (B)
	Timor D'artagnan CD	Troubadour du Plateau	Ch. Timlor Vitalite
	Uris Bras de Fer	Ch. Prudhon des Preux Vuilbaards	Ranni Bras de Fer
	Urus de la Buthiere (F)	Rais de la Thudinie (B)	Sarah de la Buthiere (F)
	Winnie des Preux Vuilbaards	Unbloc des Preux Vuilbaards	Ubette des Preux Vuilbaards
	Wrene des Preux Vuilbaards	Unbloc des Preux Vuilbaards	Raska des Preux Vuilbaards
	Xcheque de la Grande Maison	Ch. Vif des Preux Vuilbaards	Verite des Preux Vuilbaards
	Xideale du Posty Arlequin (B)	Vulcain du Posty Arlequin (B)	Udella du Posty Arlequin (B)
	Xuxy Rabel du Meier	Ch. Raby du Posty Arlequin (B)	Ch. Hanover's Belle Amie
	Yataghan du Clos des Cerberes	Ch. Yancy du Clos des Cerberes	Ch. Radegund du Clos des Cerberes
	Ygran de la Thudinie (B)	Ullou de la Thudinie (B)	Via de la Thudinie (B)
	Yogi de Broussailleux	Ch. Uriah Bras de Fer	Andelane's Asprevue

Zina	Deewal Norah	Zabeth CD
1977		
Adele's Attilla (C)	Euro's Marco (C)	Denard's Evil Jewel (C)
Alexis Zevealia	Ch. Deewal Victor (B)	Sunnybrook Deewal Winifred
Andrameda of Acoma	Ch. Bibarcy's Samson of Acoma	Ch. Bibarcy's Vengeresse
Baudelaire of Oakridge	Ch. Trajan des Preux Vuilbaards	Ch. Wacquel Relch du Meier
Beauchin du Plateau	Troubadour du Plateau	Deewal Johanna
Bibarcy's Adonis	Ch. Bibarcy's Yankee Peddler	Ch. Sadine du Posty Arlequin (B)
Bibarcy's Mr. Bo Jangles	Ch. Bibarcy's Tambour de Ville	Bibarcy's Velour de Coten
Bibarcy's Nicole	Ch. Bibarcy's Soldat de Plomb	Ch. Sadine du Posty Arlequin (B)
Bibarcy's Renee	Ch. Bibarcy's Yankee Peddler	Ch. Bibarcy's Ulterior Motive
Bibarcy's Vengeresse	Ch. Quiar de la Thudinie (B)	Ch. Bibarcy's Petite Patrice
Bibarcy's Witch of the West	Ch. Bibarcy's Soldat de Plomb	Ch. Bibarcy's Tourterelle
Blandford's Bartholemew	Ch. Xirocco Rabel du Meier	Blandford's Molly
Bokkiri-de-la Turner	Augavi-de-la Turner	Velu Famille de la Turner
Bronsville's Glen (C)	Iwan (C)	Bronsville's Ely (C)
Croix de Guerre Xerif	Ch. L'Esprit Fier's Wilhelm	Blandford's Ursula CD
Deewal Alexander August	Ch. Jenbedon's Tuff Tully	Bibarcy's Veilleuse
Deewal Blitzen CD	Ch. Quiar de la Thudinie (B)	Deewal Johanna
Deewal Vic-son de Tornai	Ch. Deewal Victor (B)	Valda de la Thudinie (B)
Deewal Zarah	Ch. Deewal Victor (B)	Freitheit's Weisel Den Helder
Delanda's Garcon Brave	Ch. Ruffkell's Invincible	Delanda's Reena del Oeste
Delanda's Jacques Raoul CDX	Ch. Ruffkell's Invincible	Urana des Preux Vuilbaards
Delanda's Jan'ette Racquel CDX	Ch. Ruffkell's Invincible	Delanda's Indian Maiden
Desiree of Oakridge	Ch. Trajan des Preux Vuilbaards	Ch. Wacquel Relch du Meier
Dominic's Le Duc CD	Ch. Deewal Victor (B)	Ch. Quenouille de Bolshoy CDX (C)
Euro's Lucky Sonya Denard (C)	Cambo's Thorton de la Thudinie	Quite de la Vallee du Lay (B)
Gimra du Clos des Cerberes	Ch. Jasper du Clos des Cerberes	Xurie de la Thudinie (B)
Goof of Flanderfield (C)	Ch. Sigurd de la Thudinie (B)	Fina de Bolshoy (C)
Hanover's Elsa Yandanne CD	Ch. Yancy du Clos des Cerberes	Ch. Hanover's Ardanne

291

Year	AKC Champion	Sire	Dam
	Janard's Hondo	Ch. Blandford's Rudo	Ch. Vandermint of Greycliff (C)
	Jumbouv's Azha Clos des Cerberes	Ch. Jasper du Clos des Cerberes	Xurie de la Thudinie (B)
	Jumbouv's Y Athena	Ch. Sir Jumbo du Clos des Cerberr	Ch. Aries du Clos des Cerberes
	Koala du Clos des Cerberes CD	Ch. Yancy du Clos des Cerberes	Ch. Istar du Clos des Cerberes
	La Roch's L'Imance Ours Noir CD	Ch. Sylvan de la Taupiniere	L'Esprit Fier's Saucie
	L'Esprit Fier's Xabesque	Ch. Uriah Bras de Fer	Ch. Bianca du Clos des Cerberes
	L'Esprit Fier's Xenia	Ch. L'Esprit Fier's Wilhelm	Ch. L'Esprit Antoinette
	L'Esprit Fier's XInt	Ch. Uriah Bras de Fer	Ch. Bianca du Clos des Cerberes
	L'Esprit Fier's Yule	Ch. Uriah Bras de Fer	L'Esprit Fier's Windy
	Lutteur du Val de Rol (F)	Ch. Vulcain du Clos des Cytises (F)	Tamise du Val de Rol (F)
	Madrone Ledge Highregard Zoe	Ch. Nomura Wave	Madrone Ledge Winterset
	Madrone Ledge Zolla	Ch. Nomura Wave	Madrone Ledge Winterset
	Maijeune's Babiliard	Ch. Uris Bras de Fer	Ch. Madrone Ledge Venus
	Maijeune's Calinerie	Ch. Nomura Wave	Ch. Madrone Ledge Valerie
	Maijeune's D'artagnan	Ch. Ulfio de la Thudinie	Ch Maijeune's Alluette
	Mighty Maxwell Morgan	Deewal Ithan	Leddy's Medvec Bright
	Morchen de Garnett	Varick du Clos des Cerberes	Norina du Clos des Cerberes
	New Dawn Tobias de Tornai	Ch. Deewal Vic-son de Tornai	Deewal Invincible de Tornai
	Pedrohm's Whodozhnitza	Ch. Bibarcy's Unemployed	Ch. Bibarcy's Petite Patrice
	Pepper of Standfast Farms	Ch. Charlemange de Harris	Suzette of Standfast Farms
	Radegund du Clos des Cerberes (B)	Sim de Bronchain (B)	Tania du Posty Arlequin (B)
	Rembrant v Marslust (N)	Bica v.d. Rozenheerd (N)	Sonja (N)
	Robertson's Gold Money	Ch. Pouky de l'Ile Monsin (B)	Ch. Angeta Jabbar
	Sassi de l'Ile Monsin (B)	Ch. Pouky de l'Ile Monsin (B)	Ch. Casey Jones
	Shirwal Y Allegra v Riven Rock	Ch. Uriah Bras de Fer	Ch. Deewal Victoria (B)
	Shirwal Yalonne	Ch. Uriah Bras de Fer	Ch. Deewal Victoria (B)
	Shirwal Y Aristide	Ch. Uriah Bras de Fer	Lillie's Xaveria
	Timlor Bairgnhomme	Ch. Deewal Victor (B)	Deewal Ti Ti
	Timlor Bhaleleigh	Ch. Deewal Victor (B)	Deewal Ti Ti

Urana Bab-X de Flamand	Ch. Faustine de Saint Roch	Ch. Bab X de Marquis
Wabouve des Preux Vuilbaards	Rhombus des Preux Vuilbaards	Regine de la Thudinie (B)
Wimhi's Wee Wim	Ch. Blandford's Toby	Samantha v.d. Susannapolder (N)
Windsong's Barnaby	Ch. Wimhi's Wee Wim	Bibarcy's Windsong
Xedra des Preux Vuilbaards	Rhombus des Preux Vuilbaards	Rimini des Preux Vuilbaards
Xenofon des Preux Vuilbaards	Rhombus des Preux Vuilbaards	Rimini des Preux Vuilbaards
Xip de la Grande Maison	Ch. Vif des Preux Vuilbaards	Verite des Preux Vuilbaards
Yana des Preux Vuilbaards	Vol des Preux Vuilbaards	Taquine des Preux Vuilbaards
York de la Grande Maison	Ch. Vif des Preux Vuilbaards	Xarda de la Thudinie (B)
1978 Adele's Alexander (C)	Euro's Marco (C)	Denard's Evil Jewel (C)
Adele's Andy (C)	Euro's Marco (C)	Denard's Evil Jewel (C)
Aia du Posty Arlequin (B)	Xar van de Buildrager (B)	Zonia de la Thudinie (B)
Aida de la Thudinie (B)	Rico de la Thudinie (B)	Yanick de la Thudinie (B)
Alexander de Marquis	Ch. Faustine de Saint Roch	Ch. Xarika de Marquis
April Roma	Ch. Bibarcy's Yankee Peddler	Ch. Elsa's Christina Roma
Aquarius Xabel du Meier	Ch. Xavier du Marquis	Ch. Hanover's Belle Amie
Arnoux du Clos des Cerberes	Ch. Dax du Clos des Cerberes	Ch. Istar du Clos des Cerberes
Astarte du Clos des Cerberes	Orphe du Clos des Cerberes	Xurie de la Thudinie (B)
Barbie Minette	Scrappy Scruffy	Nicola Minette
Beda du Clos des Cerberes	Ch. Yancy du Clos des Cerberes	Ch. Ola du Clos des Cerberes
Bibarcy's Admiral Ben Boo	Ch. Bibarcy's Yankee Peddler	Ch. Bibarcy's Witch of the West
Blandford's Fionne of Norloch	Ch. Blandford's Basko	Hollandia Gold Mist of Norloch (C)
Blandford's Krestel	Ch. Blandford's Basil	Massiah of Marjo
Bon Bon Chub	Varick du Clos des Cerberes	Norina du Clos des Cerberes
Bo Peep Des Ours	Ch. Uris Bras de Fer	Ch. Ruffkell's Inspiration
Bric du Clos des Cerberes CD	Ch. Jasper du Clos des Cerberes	Xurie de la Thudinie (B)
Bronville's Darren	Ch. Blandford's Basko	Bronville's Bonnie (C)
Circee du Clos des Cerberes	Ch. Jasper du Clos des Cerberes	Ch. Radegund du Clos des Cerberes
Dareventure's Darcy Jones CD	Ch. Uriah Bras de Fer	Ch. Casey Jones
Dareventure's Delta Dawn	Ch. Blandford's Rudo	Ch. Casey Jones
Dareventure's Lisa Jones	Ch. Uriah Bras de Fer	Ch. Casey Jones

Year	AKC Champion	Sire	Dam
	Dct Zeb CD	Ch. Yrk du Posty Arlequin (B)	Ch. Bianca du Clos des Cerberes
	Debrich's Zwarta Ansja	Ch. Cal-Grons Baldur Noup v. Dafzicht (N)	L'Esprit Fier's Princess Derbe
	Deewal Amulette	Ch. Urex Bras de Fer CDX	Deewal Zera CD
	Deewal Angie Babee	Ch. Sigurd de la Thudinie (B)	Ch. Deewal Yetta Lass
	Deewal Anndee	Ch. Deewal Victor (B)	Deewal Izziette
	Deewal Aura Argus	Ch. Sigurd de la Thudinie (B)	Ch. Deewal Yetta Lass
	Deewal Banner de Quiche	Ch. Deewal Young Husband	Deewal Lance de la Buthiere (F)
	Delanda's Apollo	Ch. Rufkell's Invincible	Urana des Preux Vuilbaards
	Delanda's D'artagnan II	Ch. Delanda's Oly	Delanda's Tania
	Delanda's Miss Topaze	Ch. Terry du Posty Arlequin (B)	Delanda's Tania
	Delanda's Patience	Ch. Delanda's Garcon Brave	Delanda's Chablis Blanc
	Dim de Bolshoy (C)	Max de Bolshoy (C)	Angela of Abercorn (C)
	Foxfires Zeres	Ch. Yrk du Posty Arlequin (B)	Ch. Croix de Guerre Xena
	High Sierra Amiel de Bolshoy (C)	Black Jeyke de Bolshoy (C)	Tanjaca (C)
	Hollandias First	Cambo's Thorton de la Thudinie	Sirka de la Thudinie (B)
	Humek's Quiar vin Rouge	Bibarcy's Quiar	Bibarcy's Vin Rouge
	Ishtar du Clos des Cerberes	Ch. Jasper du Clos des Cerberes	Tania du Posty Arlequin (B)
	Itchwoot de Yeti	Xeres des Preux Vuilbaards	Yeti Decatur
	Janard's Heineken	Ch. Greycliff's Moses	Ch. Vandermint of Greycliff
	Jillax da du Clos des Cerberes	Ch. Dax du Clos des Cerberes	Ch. Jillene du Clos des Cerberes
	Jolie Chanceuse	Ch. Blandford's Basil	Gypsy Rose Alee Nickerson
	JD's Ozzie	Xeres des Preux Vuilbaards	Delanda's Cinder
	Kocomo's Ricolette	Shawn	Yrisa de la Thudinie (B)
	Koe Hond Fumeux Ourse	Vol des Preux Vuilbaards	Uma des Preux Vuilbaards
	Kutah Ouden Dalerdyk	Ch. Dar	Charte du Soleil
	Lady Capulet Tour de Force	Ch. Duxbury House Ulrich	Colette Tour de Force
	L'Esprit Fier's Yleta of Shirwal	Ch. Uriah Bras de Fer	D'argerac Poco Loco
	L'Esprit Fier's Y'Shirwal	Ch. Uriah Bras de Fer	Ch. Deewal Victoria (B)
	L'Esprit Fier's Yves	Ch. Uriah Bras de Fer	L'Esprit Fier's Windy

L'Esprit Fier's Zachariah	Ch. Yrk du Posty Arlequin (B)	Xurate de la Thudinie (B)
L'Esprit Fier's Zantanier	Ch. Yrk du Posty Arlequin (B)	L'Esprit Fier's Windy
Madrone Ledge Abigail CD	Ch. Madrone Ledge Socrate	Ch. Madrone Ledge Vonnie
Madrone Ledge Agate	Ch. Madrone Ledge Socrate	Ch. Madrone Ledge Vonnie
Madrone Ledge Aggie	Ch. Madrone Ledge Socrate	Madrone Ledge Winterset
Maijeune's Destinee	Ch. Ulfio de la Thudinie (B)	Ch. Maijeune's Alouette
Maijeune's Dulcinee	Ch. Ulfio de la Thudinie (B)	Ch. Maijeune's Alouette
Mariposa Afternoon Delight CD	Ch. Bibarcy's Samson of Acoma	Delanda's Keepsake
Mariposa Miracle Mouchette CD	Ch. York de la Grande Maison	Delanda's Keepsake
M Bonnafont de Silverado	Ch. Dar	Charte du Soleil
Normura Kane Notaro	Ch. Nomura Kane No Tomodachi	Komura Konami
Oomingmaks Liberty Luck (C)	Jubal Leo (C)	V Dody des Preux Vuilbaards
Queue Joyeuse Solo	Ch. Ulfio de la Thudinie (B)	Maijeune's Callisto
Ritalee du Clos des Cerberes	Ch. Jasper du Clos des Cerberes	Ch. Radegund du Clos des Cerberes
Robnick's Zazu Zizani of DCT	Ch. Yrk du Posty Arlequin (B)	Ch. Bianca du Clos des Cerberes
Roma's Andre	Ch. Bibarcy's Yankee Peddler	Ch. Elsie's Christina Roma
Sandy Ridge's True Banshee	Ch. Denard's Davey (C)	Ch. A La Chance
Sharduk du Clos des Cerberes II CD	Ch. Lutteur du Val de Rol (F)	Ch. Aries du Clos des Cerberes
Shirwal Y Lynn Amanda	Ch. Uriah Bras de Fer	Ch. Deewal Victoria (B)
Stormy Day of Tanglewood	Frisia's Black Prince (C)	Maurie Loo (C)
Timlor Erik de Brabant	Ch. Timlor Bairgnhomme	Ch. Wendy de la Tour
Tino Silane v. Dafzicht (N)	Oscy v. Dafzicht (N)	Silane Quarsy v. Dafzicht (N)
Titania du Val St. Michel	Hercules du Clos des Cerberes	Ch. Titia du Posty Arlequin (B)
True Lionheart	Hollandia Thunder (C)	Ch. True Nan
True Nan	Mighty Thor de la Thudinie	True of Windy Hill
Vintage Anatole	Ch. Vangogh des Preux Vuilbaards	Delanda's Margot Bergeman
Vlaanderen's Emilie L'Etoile	Ch. Taquin du Posty Arlequin (B)	Ch. Vlaanderen's I'm Kelli Too
Vlaanderen's Ex Why Zee	Ch. Taquin du Posty Arlequin (B)	Ch. Vlaanderen's I'm Kelli Too
Vulcain du Clos des Cytises	Ringo de la Thudinie (B)	Roxane du Clos des Cytises (F)
Windsong's Buffalo	Ch. Jenbedon's Tuff Tully	Bibarcy's Windsong

Year	AKC Champion	Sire	Dam
	Windsong's Damn Yankee	Ch. Jenbedon's Tuff Tully	Bibarcy's Windsong
	Windsong's Yankee Rogue	Ch. Hollandia Evil of Adele (C)	Bibarcy's Windsong
	Witteburg Allure Dumaas	Ch. Voodoo des Preux Vuilbaards	Ch. Yana des Preux Vuilbaards
	Witteburg Thor of Oakridge	Ch. Trajan des Preux Vuilbaards	Ch. Wacquel Relch du Meier
	Xirocco Rabel du Meier	Ch. Raby du Posty Arlequin (B)	Ch. Hanover's Belle Amie
	Yago van de Buildrager (B)	Ullou de la Thudinie (B)	Upsya de la Thudinie (B)
	Yrk du Posty Arlequin (B)	Usti de Bronchain (B)	Upica du Posty Arlequin (B)
	Yum Yum Traquel du Meier	Ch. Trajan des Preux Vuilbaards	Ch. Wacquel Relch du Meier
	Zaika de Bolshoy (C)	Yulco van de Buildrager (B)	Ula de Bolshoy (C)
	Zarita du Clos des Cerberes	Ch. Jasper du Clos des Cerberes	Tania du Posty Arlequin (B)
	Zarko's Delilah Tornai (C)	Junker D'an Naoned (F)	Hollandia van Zarko (C)
	Zeal of Flanderfield	Ch. Blandford's Basko	Fina de Bolshoy (C)
	Zenith des Preux Vuilbaards	Vol des Preux Vuilbaards	Wyla des Preux Vuilbaards
	Zito Ten Roobos (B)	Xoro Ten Roobos (B)	Vivie Ten Roobos (B)
	Zwarta Ansja Debrich	Ch. Cal-Grons Baldur Noup van Dafzicht (N)	L'Esprit Fier's Princess Derbe
1979	Aviance DuMaas	Ch. Voodoo des Preux Vuilbaards	Ch. Yana des Preux Vuilbaards
	Azuree DuMaas	Ch. Voodoo des Preux Vuilbaards	Ch. Yana des Preux Vuilbaards
	Banshee du Clos des Cerberes	Ch. Lutteur du Val de Rol (F)	Ch. Aries du Clos des Cerberes
	Barbichette Sur Qui Compter CD	Ch. Lutteur du Val de Rol (F)	Ch. Koala du Clos des Cerberes
	Beaucrest Ruffian	Ch. Timlor Bairgnhomme	Bonne Amie du Nomura
	Bedelia du Clos des Cerberes	Ch. Lutteur du Val de Rol (F)	Ch. Aries du Clos des Cerberes
	Beirhu Des Rive Gauche	Ch. Urus de la Buthiere (F)	Jumbouv du Clos des Cerberes
	Bora de Bolshoy (C)	Ch. Dim de Bolshoy (C)	Gravine de Bolshoy (C)
	Brotilda Beb v. Marslust (N)	Bica v.d. Rosenheerd (N)	Sonja (N)
	Capone du Clos des Cerberes	Ch. Lutteur du Val de Rol (F)	Zoe du Clos des Cerberes
	Chessman Sur Qui Compter	Ch. Lutteur du Val de Rol (F)	Ch. Koala du Clos des Cerberes CD
	Croix de Guerre Yvette	Ch. Sylvan de la Taupiniere	Blandford's Ursula CD
	Dareventure's Deacon Jones CD	Ch. Uriah Bras de Fer	Ch. Casey Jones

Dareventure's Helmar Ceasar	Ch. Denard's Davy (C)	Ch. Pouky Jones CDX
D'argerac Poco Loco	Ch. Blandford's Toby	Ch. Casey Jones
Deewal Amos	Ch. Deewal Victor (B)	Deewal Izziette
Deewal Autumn Dream	Yapo de la Thudinie (B)	Ch. Xideale du Posty Arlequin (B)
Deewal Broosir de Broote	Ch. Deewal Young Husband	Deewal Lance de la Buthiere (F)
Deewal Chaco of Mariposa	Ch. Vulcain du Clos des Cytises (F)	Ch. Deewal Yetta Lass
Deewal Challenger	Ch. Vulcain du Clos des Cytises (F)	Ch. Deewal Yetta Lass
Deewal Nantes d'An Naoned (F)	Jbaa (F)	Idole du Clos des Jeunes Plantes (F)
Dejoy Kedar	Ch. Deewal Victor (B)	Ch. Delanda's Jan'ette Racquel CDX
Dejoy Kelda CD	Ch. Deewal Victor (B)	Ch. Delanda's Jan'ette Racquel CDX
Dejoy Kieron CD	Ch. Deewal Victor (B)	Ch. Delanda's Jan'ette Racquel CDX
Delanda's Bernadette	Ch. Delanda's Garcon Brave	Delanda's Flaxie
Delanda's Cheyenne Buff	Ch. Delanda's Garcon Brave	Delanda's Indian Maiden
Delanda's Kizzie	Ch. Delanda's Apollo	Delanda's Flaxie
Delanda's Utilla Del Oeste	Ch. Ruffkell's Invincible	Urana Des Preux
Dutchess Mieke of Sunset	Hollandia Nair (C)	Moya of Waldorf
Flanderfield Honey Blue (C)	Ch. Bronville's Darren (C)	Princess de Bolshoy (C)
Foxfires Able Luke	Ch. Urex Bras de Fer CDX	Ch. Croix de Guerre Xena
Foxfires Allegria	Ch. Urex Bras de Fer CDX	Ch. Croix de Guerre Xena
Heve de Bolshoy (C)	Black Jeyke de Bolshoy (C)	Gravine de Bolshoy (C)
Ira Midnight Star of Sunset	Ch. Urmin de la Thudinie (F)	Ch. The Duchess Mieke of Sunset
Jay Pico v.d. Ponyhoeve CD (N)	Heros Nero v.d. Zwikshock (N)	Adabella (N)
Jumbouv Benjamin Bear	Ch. Sir Jumbo du Clos des Cerberes	Ch. Ms Juno du Clos des Cerberes (B)
Kercee du Clos des Cerberes	Ch. Jasper du Clos des Cerberes	Tania du Posty Arlequin
Kocomo's Anna Bella	Rayole Napoleon	Ch. Kocomo's Ricolette
Lexy de la Buthiere (F)	Vizir du Clos des Cytises (F)	Vedette de la Buthiere (F)
Madrone Ledge Zege	Ch. Nomura Wave	Madrone Ledge Winterset
Maijeune's Gigi	Ch. Maijeune's D'Artagnan	Ch. Maijeune's Bouttoniere
Maijeune's Ichor	Ch. Maijeune's D'Artagnan	Ch. Maijeune's Calinerie
Maijeune's Mister Gottfried	Ch. Maijeune's D'Artagnan	Ch. Maijeune's Bouttoniere

Year	AKC Champion	Sire	Dam
	Maijeune's True Glory	Ch. Maijeune's D'Artagnan	Ch. Maijeune's Bouttoniere
	Marike du Timlor	Ch. Timlor Bairgnhomme	Ch. Wendy de la Tour
	McDades Mighty Thor	Bouche's Minette	Leddy's Greta
	Merveille des Rouheuses CD	Ch. Urus de la Buthiere (F)	Julia de la Buthiere (F)
	Michelle du Plateau	Ch. Madrone Ledge Taussant CD	Deewal Gilly
	Moorelane's Dutch Dandy	Ch. Avanti Zorro	Ch. Stormy Day of Tanglewood
	Moorelane's Fredrico	Ch. Avanti Zorro	Ch. Stormy Day of Tanglewood
	Nelly du Clos des Jeunes Plantes (F)	Quarl du Clos des Jeunes Plantes	Vixie du Clos des Jeunes Plantes (F)
	Norloch's Rhea van Dijk (C)	Ch. Blandford's Basco	Hollandia Gold Mist of Norloch (C)
	Nuit Amour de Beaucrest	Ch. Timlor Bairgnhomme	Ch. Madrone Ledge Tosca CD
	Quelly du Plateau	Ch. Timlor Bairgnhomme	Ch. Michelle du Plateau
	Quiche's Buffis (C)	Ch. Denard's Davey (C)	Denard's Chickee Sonya (C)
	Robertson's Ali	Ch. Pouky de l'Ile Monsin (B)	Ch. Angeta Jabbar
	Shirwal Yves Takarevau CD	Ch. Uriah Bras de Fer	Lilles Xaveria
	Standfast Recaro	Ch. Deewal Victor (B)	Ch. Pepper of Standfast Farms
	Taursula's Lone Star	Ch. Taurus du Clos des Cerberes	Ch. Hanover's Beatrix
	Thunderbuff's Butler	Ch. Sigurd de la Thudinie (B)	Ch. Deewal Thunderbuff UD
	Timlor Brandywyne	Ch. Timlor Bairgnhomme	Ch. Wendy de la Tour
	True Zeus	Ch. Jumbouv's Ygor	Ch. True Nan
	Vlaanderen's Easy Does It	Ch. Taquin du Posty Arlequin (B)	Ch. Vlaanderen's I'm Kelli Too
	Vlaanderen's Eris Tri Hardin	Ch. Taquin du Posty Arlequin (B)	Ch. Vlaanderen's I'm Kelli Too
	Von Hoffman's Bourguignon	Ch. Trajan des Preux Vuilbaards	Ch. Sassi de l'Ile Monsin (B)
	Warlo de la Thudinie	Cambo's Tapin de la Thudinie	Upolu de la Thudinie (B)
	Wilbets Ms Zig Zag	Vabu des Preux Vuilbaards	Bibarcy's Velours de Coten
	Wimhi's Naughty Wilhamina	Ch. Wimhi's Wee Wim	Bibarcy's Windsong
1980	Acoma's Festival of Lights	Ch. York de la Grande Maison	Bibarcy's Vengeresse
	Adrianna de Vallombrosa	Ch. Pal-mars Caesar Maximillian	Zonia de la Thudinie (B)
	Alexi du Clos des Cerberes	Twofour du Clos des Cerberes	ShadyLady's Tasha D'Frisia (C)

Yago van de Buildrager (B)
Ch. Torro van Dafzicht (N)
Ch. Torro van Dafzicht (N)
Bica v.d. Rozenheerd (N)
Ch. Voodoo des Preux Vuilbaards
Ch. Urmin de la Thudinie (B)
Hollandia Kyzer (C)
Ch. Deewal Vic-son de Tornai
Ch. Maijeune's D'artagnan
Ch. Bibarcy's Yankee Peddler
Ch. Bibarcy's Yankee Peddler
Ch. Janard's Heinekin
Ch. Madrone Ledge Taussant CD
Ch. Lutteur du Val de Rol (F)
Ch. Lutteur du Val de Rol (F)
Ch. Veto de la Thudinie (B)
Ch. Lutteur du Val de Rol (F)
Ch. Taquin du Posty Arlequin (B)
Ch. Cosmo Jac de Chehelem
Ch. Cosmo Jac de Chehelem
Ch. Cosmo Jac de Chehelem
Ch. Lutteur du Val de Rol (F)
Prince Khyber de Flamand
Ch. Madrone Ledge Taussant CD
Troubadour du Plateau
Ch. Dareventure's Deacon Jones CD
Ch. Denard's Davey (C)
Ch. Uriah Bras de Fer
Ch. Vulcain du Clos des Cytises (F)
Ch. Deewal Victor (B)
Ch. Deewal Victor (B)

Yrca van de Buildrager (B)
Ch. Aspenglen's Blandford Shaika
Ch. Aspenglen's Blandford Shaika
Astra Roup v. Dafzicht (N)
Ch. Yana des Preux Vuilbaards
Duchess of Kent v.d. Banishock (N)
Topsy of Frisia The Second (C)
Ch. Kutah Ouden Dalerdyk
Ch. Madrone Ledge Aggie
Ch. Elsa's Christina Roma
Bibarcy's Wee Molly Brown
Blandford's Samantha
Coopers Babette des Bibarcy
Ch. Aries du Clos des Cerberes
Ch. Circee du Clos des Cerberes
Ch. Bianca du Clos des Cerberes
April du Clos des Cerberes
Ch. Urana Bab-X de Flamand
Ch. Bora de Bolshoy (C)
Ch. Dominic's Angeline
Ch. Dominic's Angeline
Ch. Circee du Clos des Cerberes
Ch. Xarika de Marquis
Cooper's Babette des Bibarcy
Ch. Brigitta du Plateau
Ch. Pouky Jones CDX
Ch. Casey Jones
Ch. Casey Jones
Deewal Ban-de of Sun Valley
Ch. Xideale du Posty Arlequin (B)
Deewal Izziette

Alfa van Buildrager (B)
Aspenglens Alpha Du Baudouin
Aspenglens Auncy Du Shaika
Andy Astra v. Dafzicht (N)
Avant Gard DuMaas
Avanti Zorro
Banjo (C)
Basha Ouden Dalerdyk
Bearrun's Chanel v. Aggie
Bibarcy's April Love
Bibarcy's Blossom Time
Blandford's Jespeh
Bouchon Wee Babette Trote
Brioche du Clos des Cerberes
Caliphe du Clos des Cerberes
Candy du Clos des Cerberes
Cayce du Clos des Cerberes
Chante E de la Vallon
Chehelem Mountain's Bruin
Chehelem Mt's Charlemagne
Chehelem Mountain's Olsa
Claudette du Clos des Cerberes
Comte Poirot de Marquis
Cooper's Rocky des Bouchon
Dahlia du Plateau
Dareventure's L.C. Jones
Dareventure's Monsieur Etain CD
Dareventure's Rico Jones
Deewal Argent Vainqueur
Deewal Black Baron
Deewal Blue Astra

Year	AKC Champion	Sire	Dam
	Deewal Candidate of Qupei	Ch. Vulcain du Clos des Cytises (F)	Ch. Deewal Yve
	Deewal Cambria Romasto	Ch. Vulcain du Clos des Cytises (F)	Ch. Deewal Yetta Lass
	Deewal Caprice	Ch. Vulcain du Clos des Cytises (F)	Ch. Deewal Yve
	Deewal Charger	Ch. Vulcain du Clos des Cytises (F)	Ch. Deewal Yetta Lass
	Deewal Christie Critters	Ch. Vulcain du Clos des Cytises (F)	Ch. Deewal Yve
	Deewal Dark Shadows	Ch. Vulcain du Clos des Cytises (F)	Ch. Deewal Blue Astra
	Deewal Dejoy Krista	Ch. Deewal Victor (B)	Ch. Delanda's Jan'ette Racquel CDX
	Dejoy Ozette	Ch. Delanda's Jacques Raoul CDX	Ch. Dejoy Kelda CD
	Delanda's Bijou	Ch. Delanda's Garcon Brave	Delanda's Flaxie
	Dominic's Angeline	Ch. Urex Bras de Fer CDX	Ch. Quenouille de Bolshoy CDX
	Dominic's Bold Image	Ch. Urex Bras de Fer CDX	Ch. Quenouille de Bolshoy CDX
	Dominic's Ebony	Ch. Deewal Victor (B)	Ch. Quenouille de Bolshoy CDX
	Dominic's Tre's Jolli	Ch. Urex Bras de Fer CDX	Ch. Quenouille de Bolshoy CDX
	Dranna du Clos des Cerberes	Ch. Veto de la Thudinie (B)	April du Clos des Cerberes
	Dzintar of Sunset	Ch. Hollandia's Evil (C)	Ch. The Duchess Mieke of Sunset
	Fallsburn Judo (C)	Smokey de Bolshoy (C)	Fallsburn Bruges Sierra (C)
	Galbraiths Creme de la Creme	Ch. Urex Bras de Fer CDX	Ch. Croix de Guerre Xena
	Gemstone Brandy	Ch. Taquin du Posty Arlequin (B)	Ch. Deewal Yolanda
	Gold Creek Chartan de Saljo	Ch. Deewal Young Husband	Ch. Deewal Autumn Dream
	Gold Creek Durango	Ch. Zito Ten Roobos (B)	Ch. Deewal Autumn Dream
	Janard's Tres Marias Pandora	Ch. Greycliff's Moses (C)	Ch. Vandermint of Greycliff (C)
	Jillax l'Enjoleur Cannonaro	Ch. Dax du Clos des Cerberes	Ch. Gimra du Clos des Cerberes
	Laird's Dandi Bear	Laird of Bibarcy	Bibarcy's Your the Tops
	Madrone Ledge Bold CD	Ch. Ivan d'as Naoned CD (F)	Madrone Ledge Ursula
	Madrone Ledge Courage	Ch. Yago van de Buildrager (B)	Ch. Madrone Ledge Zolla
	Maijeune's Harmony	Ch. Maijeune's Babiliard	Ch. Maijeune's Bouttoniere
	Maijeune's Izekeal CD	Ch. Maijeune's D'artagnan	Ch. Maijeune's Calinerie
	Marty de Ose Brulot	Ch. Von Hoffman's Cafe Brulot	Xia des Preux Vuilbaards
	Moorelane's Funny Girl	Ch. Avanti Zorro	Ch. Stormy Day of Tanglewood

Nicole du Clos des Cerberes	Ch. Lutteur du Val de Rol (F)	Xurie de la Thudinie (B)
Oden De Ose Brulot	Ch. Von Hoffman's Cafe Brulot	Xia des Preux Vuilbaards
Our Adele's Lucifer (C)	Ch. Hollandia's Evil (C)	Euro's Tausha (C)
Quiche's Barrier (C)	Ch. Deewal Victor (B)	Euro's Quiche Kim (C)
Quiche's Bionic Bam Bam (C)	Ch. Deewal Victor (B)	Euro's Quiche Kim (C)
Shirwal Brandolf	Ch. Yrk du Posty Arlequin (B)	Ch. Deewal Victoria
Thunderbuff's Brianna	Ch. Sigurd de la Thudinie (B)	Ch. Deewal Thunderbuff UD
Thunderbuff's Moody Blue	Ch. Sigurd de la Thudinie (B)	Ch. Deewal Thunderbuff UD
Timlor Eeejay	Ch. Beaucrest Ruffian	Ch. Wendy de la Tour
Timlor Ellie	Ch. Beaucrest Ruffian	Ch. Wendy de la Tour
Timlor Evan	Ch. Beaucrest Ruffian	Ch. Wendy de la Tour
Tonnerre du Plateau CD	Algernon du Plateau	Grisette du Plateau
Tocintaq's Witch Kiss (C)	Ringo le Jardin du Etoile (C)	Audace de Tocintaq (C)
Trego de la Buthiere	Ch. Urus de la Buthiere (F)	Ch. Zarko's Delilah Tornai (C)
True Lion's Pride	Ch. True Lion Heart	True Friend of Windy Hill
Vacher's Alpha Centauri CD TD	Ch. Lutteur du Val de Rol (F)	Ch. Yataghan du Clos des Cerberes
Virgo the Solitaires Bova	Ch. Mighty Maxwell Morgan	Leddy's Musette of Carimor
Von Hoffman Cafe Brulot	Ch. Trajan des Preux Vuilbaards	Ch. Sassi de l'Ile Monsin (B)
Von Hoffman Chardonnay	Ch. Trajan des Preux Vuilbaards	Ch. Sassi de l'Ile Monsin (B)
Wiljamark Barney de Jorlee	Ch. Urex Bras de Fer CDX	Ch. Croix de Guerre Xena
Windsong's Rose du Chene Rouge	Ch. Hollandia's Evil (C)	Bibarcy's Windsong
Windsong's Sonja de Gemstone	Ch. Taquin du Posty Arlequin (B)	Ch. Deewal Yolanda
Wingards Briana Noir Ours	Ch. High Sierra's Amiel de Bolshoy (C)	Ch. Zaika de Bolshoy (C)
Zoe du Clos des Cerberes	Ch. Sir Jumbo du Clos des Cerberes	Isis du Clos des Cerberes

Bouviers Certified by the Orthopedic Foundation for Animals, Inc.

Hip dysplasia is a malformation of the hip joints that may occur in any breed but is particularly significant in many of the larger breeds of dogs. A dog may show no outward signs of the condition, and yet it can be detected by x-raying. On the other hand, a dog may show at an early age such outward signs of hip dysplasia as an awkward gait, atrophy or degeneration of muscles in one or both hind legs, an over-development of the forequarters not in proportion to development of the hindquarters, or limping or evidence of pain on arising or after strenuous exercise.

Since much of the research and study of hip dysplasia points to the fact that it is an inherited disorder and polygenetic, only dogs known to be free of hip dysplasia should be used for breeding. Consequently, more and more concerned breeders are having their stock x-rayed, thus assuring that they breed only from dogs whose hip joints will pass certification at two years of age.

Certification is made through the Orthopedic Foundation for Animals, Inc., Dysplasia Control Registry, which is affiliated with the school of Veterinary Medicine at the University of Missouri in Columbia, Missouri. Your veterinarian very likely is informed on the procedure to be followed in x-raying your Bouvier and submitting the radiograph for certification. When the radiograph and the required fee are sent to the Orthopedic Foundation, three qualified veterinary radiologists trained in diagnostic radiography and certified by the American College of Veterinary Radiology evaluate the film. On the basis of their evaluation, a consensus report is issued, and if the dog is found to be clear, he is assigned an OFA registration number. Over three hundred Bouviers have been certified by the Registry to date. The number of films submitted for evaluation of Bouviers is unknown, but many do not meet the certification requirements.

Following is a list of Bouviers certified to date and the OFA number assigned to each. A blank space following a number on the list indicates that the number was assigned to a Bouvier but the owner did not pursue certification after the age for certification was raised to two years.

BF — No.	Name	BF — No.	Name
3	Jez Zaa Bell	63	Ufala Des Preux Vuilbaards
10	Robblynne's Suzyi	64	Ch. Aspenglen's Blandford's
18	Norlock's Rhea Van Dijk		Shaika
20	Ch. Ulfio de la Thudinie	65	Blandford's Jana
21	Ch. Urex Bras de Fer CDX	66	Ruffkell's Invincible
22	Ch. Bibarcy's Tambour de Ville	67	DeLanda's Tania
23	Ch. Bibarcy's Petite Patrice	68	DeLanda's Ida Oeste
24	Ch. Sadine du Posty Arlequin	69	DeLanda's Indian Maiden
25	Ch. Bibarcy's Soldat de Plomb	70	Ch. Wrene Des Preux
26	Ch. Bibarcy's Tourterelle		Vuilbaards
27	Ch. Bibarcy's Cassandra	71	Xola Du Posty Arlequin
28	Duke's Dutchess	72	Vandermint Of Greycliff
29	Ch. Bibarcy's Symphonie	73	The Tanq of Pal-Mar
30	Ch. Blandford's Toby	74	Yapo de la Thudinie
31	Stonehenges Rufus du Plateau	75	Xideale Du Posty Arlequin
32	Hercule du Clos des Cerberes	76	Monjoie Velotee
33	Barbu Hardi Guerrier	77	Ch. Junker Dan Naoned
34	Ch. Bibarcy's Songeuse	78	Gypsy Rose Alee Nickerson
35	Hanover's Brucie	79	Ch. Torro Van Dafzicht
36	Blandford's Molly	80	Diana Van Den Doornakkers
37	Casey Jones	81	Urana Des Preux Vuilbaards
38	Llenbrue's Monique du Plateau	82	DeLanda's Reena Del Oeste
39-T	Chariton Joie De Vivre	83	Akbar of Mission Bell
40	Deewal Victoria	84	Ch. Damar's Appley
41-T	Blandford's Basko	85	Smokey Douglas
42	Ch. Deewal Benjamin	86	Xedra Des Preux Vuilbaards
43	Ch. Deewal Victor	87	Xaldo Van de Buildrager
44	Blandford's Raphaela	88	Baron Hercule Poirot
45-T	Ch. Brentwyn's Myka of	89	Ch. Xchequer De La Grande
	Renwoods		Maison
46	Ch. Niro of Bolshoy	90	Xavier De Marquis
47	Ch. Silette de la Thudinie	91	Glanford's Phaedrak
48	Urus de la Buthiere	92	
49	Veta de la Thudinie	93	
50	Gaillard du Plateau	94	
51	Quenouille De Bolshoy	95	Ch. Sigurd de la Thudinie
52	Kirk of Troy	96	
53	Ch. Deewal Thunderbuff CD	97	
54	Ch. Pouky Jones	98	
55	Bibarcy's Witch of the West	99	C. Noles Sabu
56	Pedrohm's Whodozhnutza	100	Kell Marc's Petit Ours Ami
57	Bibarcy's Johanna du Plateau	101	Sassi De l'Ile Monsin
58	Ch. Elsa's Christina Roma	102-T	Ch. Ivan D'An Naoned CD
59	Donald Von Der Bungener	103	Ch.Bibarcy's Yerma
	Heide	104	Kapu Van Koppelpoort
60	Kristinik's Baron Von Baldur	105	Denards Davey
61	Pal-Mar's Coup De Grace	106	Kim of Zoon Monere
62	Deewal Icon D'Argent Nuit	107	L'Esprit Fier's Mustique

BF—No.	Name	BF—No.	Name
108	Xia des Preux Vuilbaards	156	Niki of Brierwood
109	Koala du Clos des Cerberes	157	Yonna LeGard' Elegant
110	Euro's Garth	158	Black Iris
111	DeLanda's Dartagnan II	159	Bric du Clos des Cerberes
112	Croix de Guerre Xerif	160	Laroche's L'Imance Ours Noir
113	Hanovers Elsa Yandanne	161	Dareventure's Lisa Jones
114	DeLanda's Aristaeus	162	Madrone Ledge Highregard Zoe
115	Ch. Timlor's D'Artagnan CD	163	Chariton Alexandria
116	Ch. Jenbedon's Tuff Tully	164	Hester Du Llenbruc
117	Ch. Deewal Young Husband	165	Ch. Blandford's Bartholomew
118	Ch. Deewal Yetta Lass	166	Frisia's Candice
119	Ch. Roc de la Montagne	167	Ch. Shirwal Y'Lynn Amanda
120	Brandy	168	Ch. Yrk du Posty Arlequin
121	Deewal Ti-Ti	169	Sweet Meadows Dominic Sienna
122	Ch. Wendy de la Tour	170	Ch. New Dawn Thobiase de
123	Ch. Shirwal Yankee Doodle		Tornai
124	Ursa of Halfdan	171	Ch. Deewal Alexander August
125	Ch. Bibarcy's Yankee Peddler	172	Bibarcy's Daisy Mae
126	Bibarcy's Yesterday's Dream	173	Minnie Poo de Melville
127	Luttuer du Val de Rol	174	Cambo's Buster Bob
128	Orphe du Clos des Cerberes	175	New Dawn's de Tornai
129	Ch. Deewal Yolanda	176	Arnoux du Clos des Cerberes
130	Zonia de la Thudine	177	Blandford's Hillde
131	Delanda's Benjamin Rainier	178	Zarko's Delilah Tornai
132	Babouche Rude de Tornai	179	Ajax of Rivendell
133	Debrich's Zwartz Ansja	180	Ch. Pal Mar's Caesar
134	Ch. Whizbang de la Tour		Maximillian
135	Ch. Yancy du Clos des Cerberes	181	L'Esprit Fier's X Classique
136	Hickory Nut of Flanderfield	182	Zito Ten Roobos
137	Dim de Bolshoy	183	Banshee's Chico Desimone
138	Ch. Deewal Yue	184	Ch. Wittebrug Thor of Oakridge
139	Gimra du Clos des Cerberes	185	Brandy 3rd
140	Fody Flanderfield	186	Oula Duval St. Michel
141	Dareventure's Delta Dawn	187	Leddy's Vanessa
142	Zurate de la Thudinie	188	The Duchess Mieke of Sunset
143	Deewal Zendalyn	189	The Duchess Joke of Sunset
144	Zorrolo de la Thudinie	190	Shirwal Yo Sooner
145	Zorlane de la Thudinie	191	Tashia Mercia of Gina
146	Cooper's Babette des Bibarcy	192	Avant' Zorro
147	Ch. Dominic's LeDuc	193	Shah Jahan of Rivendell
148	Yum Yum Traquel Du Meier	194	Madrone Ledge Aggie
149	Madrone Ledge Acacia	195	Ch. Grisette Barry VD Sylverhof
150	Timlor Bairgnhomme	196	April Roma
151	Jumbouv Rok Clos des Cerberes	197	Clarte Du Soleil
152	Ch. Nicholas Ouden Dalerdyk	198	Ch. DeLanda's Jacques Raoul
153	Ch. Alexis' Zexealia		CDX
154		199	Deewal Noah
155	Ch. Madrone Ledge Tamboryn	200	DCT Zeb
	CDX		

BF — No.	Name	BF — No.	Name
201	True Thunder	248	Flander Field's Weardo
202	Ch. Vulcain du Clos des Cytises	249	Deewal Banner de Quiche
203	Ace Number One Boo	250	Quiche's Buffis
204	Nicholette Ouden Dalerdyk	251	Croix de Guerre Yvonne
205	Ch. Janard's Heineken	252	Wittebrug Athena of Oakridge
206	Bibarcy's April Love	253	Beowulf du Clos des Cerberes
207	Bibarcy's Alabama Pride	254	Le Chien Valeureux's Tillie
208	Samantha Pricilla	255	Max de Bear
209	Joy-A-Len's Holla Hendrika	256	Ch. Sharduk du Clos des
210	Dareventure's Bubba Jones		Cerberes
211	Aviance Du Maas	257	Croix de Guerre Yvette
212	Deewal Autumn Dream	258	Croix de Guerre Xavier
213	Ch. Roma's Andre	259	Beauvoir du Clos des Cerberes
214	Jillax Pi du Clos des Cerberes	260	Deewal Alluring Moon Shadow
215	Lady Nadarko	261	Gypsee du Clos des Cerberes
216	Robinick's Zazu Zizani of DCT	262	Kipann's Able Aggression
217	Shirwall Yves Takarevau	263	Amika de Vallonbrosa
218	Goldeden's Morning Mist	264	Deewal Bonjou Co Du Djbouti
219	L'Espirit Fier's Z. Malama	265	Kerry Dants Moselle
220	Winni La Kinkeyou	266	Delanda's Flaxie Boy
221	Deewal Andee	267	Dareventure's Jo Jo Jones
222	Andy Astra V Dafzicht	268	Bruno
223	Ch. DeLanda's Topaz	269	Dominic's Bold Image
224	Lavender Blue Dilly	270	Tara Merika
225	Ch. Bibarcy's Samson	271	Ch. Shirwal Yorick
226	Zou Zou de Bolshoy	272	Deewal Blue Astra
227	Ghislaine La Grande	273	Dominic's Angleine
228	Delcarjero's Katrinka	274	Ch. Barbichette Sur Qui
229	Chausey's Po-An Bojak Supreme		Compter CD
230	Madrone Ledge Vim En Vigore	275	Highsierra's Biella
231	Brioche du Clos des Cerberes	276	Calgrons Senta Van Dafzicht
232	Aspenglen's Astra du Shaika	277	Thunderbuff's Moody Blue
233	Bibarcy's Admiral Ben Boo	278	Quiche's Barrier
234	Madrone Ledge Bold	279	Quiche's Brilliant Blossom
235	Le Chien Valeureux's Monique	280	Amie de Broussaileux
236	Verdedeger's Vuilbaard	281	Ch. Delanda's Cheyenne Buff
237	Banshee du Clos des Cerberes	282	Ch. Fox Fire's Able Luke
238	Aliage DuMaas	283	Yvonne
239	Dareventure's Deacon Jones	284	Von Hoffmans Cafe Brulot
240	Le Chien Valeureux Tyrus	285	Deewal Bruno
241	Crookhaus Foxy Lady CD	286	Taursula's Lone Star
242	Panda of Oomingmak	287	Ch. Quelly du Plateau
243	Ch. Xirocco Rable Du Meier	288	Greycliff's Michelle
244	Ch. Zarko's Kark V. D.	289	Sha Sheen's Bruno
	Sylverhof	290	Ch. Deewal York
245	DeLanda's Samson	291	Sacul Olivia
246	Ch. DeLanda's Garcon Brave	292	October Bear of Ridgewood
247	Star of Moon Ridge	293	Shyman's Nesslie Quick

Pedigree Section

In this section are pedigrees and photographs of all Bouviers that have won the National Specialty, have won Best in Show, and/or have placed First in the Group in AKC Shows from the time the breed was accepted by The American Kennel Club through December 31, 1980. Leading American and European breeding lines are represented here.

Through the study of these pedigrees, breeders and exhibitors can evaluate the breeding programs that have produced top winning dogs. It will be noted that some of these winners are inbred, others are examples of outcrosses, and many are closely line-bred. In some instances, because dogs appear in more than one pedigree, it will be possible to reconstruct and study many generations of a particular line.

The dogs are presented in alphabetical order, and no distinction is made here as to placings or number of wins. Reference to the listing on page 254 and the charts on pages 262 through 269 will show which were National Specialty Winners, which were Best-in-Show winners, and which placed First in the Group.

In some cases ownership may have changed later, but information concerning ownership shown in this section refers to the particular time that the dog was on the show circuit and made the National Specialty win, the Best-in-Show win, and/or the Group First placement.

Ch. Adele's Alexander, WD628852, 2-6-76. Breeder: C. Vander Muren. Owners: William and Sue Miller.

			Cambo's Thorton de la Thudinie
		Euro's Gus	
			Marya's Cindy of Hollandia
	Euro's Marco		
			Nic de la Thudinie
		Quitte de La Valle Du Lay	
			Orphee de La Valle Du Lay
CH. ADELE'S ALEXANDER			
			Cambo's Thorton de la Thudinie
		Ch. Hollandia's Evil of Adele	
			Sirka de la Thudinie
	Denard's Evil Jewel of Adele		
			Cambo's Thorton de la Thudinie
		Euro's Lucky Sonya Denard	
			Quitte de la Valle Du Lay

308

Ch. Argus de la Thudinie. Breeder: J. Chastel. Owner: Fred H. Walsh.

			Azor de la Boheme
		Quasimodo	
			Meg de la Boheme
	Volpi de la Vallee de l'Escaillon		
			Quarl
		Sapho	
			Rapsie de la Planque
CH. ARGUS DE LA THUDINIE			
			Joris du Ble d'Or
		Soprano de la Thudinie	
			Mirette de la Thudinie
	Ucaba		
			Kiou del Roque de Moulin
		Rakina de la Thudinie	
			Mirette de la Thudinie

Ch. Beaucrest Ruffian, WE101433, 2-19-78. Breeders: Roy and Pat
Schiller. Owners: Roy and Pat Schiller.

CH. BEAUCREST RUFFIAN

```
                                                              Int. Ch. Tapin de la Thudinie
                                       Am. & Can. Ch. Deewal Victor
                                                              Ch. Silette de la Thudinie
                   Ch. Timlor Bairgnhomme
                                                              Ch. Quair de la Thudinie
                                       Deewal Ti Ti
                                                              Ch. Hilprize Kelli Sandra

                                                              Ch. Madrone Ledge Viking
                                       Ch. Nomura Kane No Tomodachi
                                                              Deewal Kobe
                   Bonne Amie du Nomura
                                                              Ch. Prudhon des Preux Vuilbaards
                                       Nomura Kona-Me
                                                              Deewal Kobe
```

Ch. Bibarcy's Soldat de Plomb, WB497697, 7-6-69. Breeders: Arthur and Mary Pedersen. Owners: Arthur and Mary Pedersen.

			Heros du Posty Arlequin
		Kous de la Thudinie	
			Belg. & Am. Ch. Irca de la Thudinie
	Ch. Deewal Homer		
			Ch. Noceur de la Thudinie
		Perrette de la Thudinie	
			Nolette de la Thudinie
CH. BIBARCY'S SOLDAT DE PLOMB			
			Ch. Hion de la Thudinie
		Belg. & Am. Ch. Job de la Thudinie	
			Hulotte de la Thudinie
	Ch. Bibarcy's Job's Daughter		
			Ch. Argus de la Thudinie
		Ch. Deewal Argusette	
			Ch. Faussette l'Ideal de Charleroi

Ch. Bo Peep Des Ours, WD483044, 12-23-75. Breeder: Tim Wray. Owners: Dr. and Mrs. Murray Horowitz, Hilgrand Kennels, Reg.

```
                                              Ch. Marc de la Thudinie
                           Ch. Prudhon des Preux Vuilbaards
                                              Ch. Nota du Posty Arlequin
         Ch. Uris Bras de Fer
                                              Ch. Prudhon des Preux Vuilbaards
                           Ranni Bras de Fer
                                              Oriane des Preux Vuilbaards
CH. BO PEEP DES OURS
                                              Ch. Marc de la Thudinie
                           Ch. Prudhon des Preux Vuilbaards
                                              Ch. Nota du Posty Arlequin
         Ch. Ruffkell's Inspiration
                                              Flanette Ruff
                           Ch. Ruffkell's Delight
                                              Ch. Hilprize Kelli Sandra
```

Ch. Boris v.d. Ouden Dijk CD, 3-26-65. Breeder: Julia Van Vorst. Owner: Agnes Miller.

Ch. Chanterie Vicaire, WC134894, 3-6-72.   Breeders: Jay and Harriet Arnold.   Owners: Dr. and Mrs. Horowitz.

Ch. Prudhon des Preux Vuilbaards

               Lais du Posty Arlequin

     Ch. Nota du Posty Arlequin

               Lola du Posty Arlequin

CH. CHANTERIE VICAIRE

               Ch. Marc de la Thudinie

     Ch. Prudhon des Preux Vuilbaards

               Ch. Nota du Posty Arlequin

   Ch. Ripeau Bras de Fer

               Belg. & Am. Ch. Job de la Thudinie

     Oriane des Preux Vuilbaards

               Mouche du Posty Arlequin

314

Left: Ch. Coquin de la Thudinie, W605220, 10-10-53. Breeder: J. Chastel. Owner: Robert Butts, Jr.

                                        Joris du Ble d'or
                          Soprano de la Thudinie
                                        Mirette de la Thudinie
              U'falon de la Thudinie

                          Albione de Biercee

CH. COQUIN DE LA THUDINIE
                                        Jaf due Chateau de Villers
                          Samos des Tro is Iles
                                        Rita de la Gueulardiers
              Wanda des Coudreaux
                                        Ravachol
                          Ch. Uada du Gratte-Saule
                                        Silane de la Thudinie

315

Ch. Deewal Candidate of Qupei, WE125436, 8-4-78. Breeder: Deewal Kennels. Owners: Judi Kramer and Deewal Kennels.

		Ch. Quiar de la Thudinie
	Ringo de la Thudinie	
		Nolette de la Thudinie
Ch. Vulcain du Clos Des Cytises		
		Navarro de la Thudinie
	Roxane du Clos des Cytises	
		Nathalie du Clos des Cytises

CH. DEEWAL CANDIDATE OF QUPEI

		Ch. Prudhon des Preux Vuilbaards
	Am. & Can. Ch. Urex Bras de Fer, C.D.X.	
		Ranni Bras de Fer
Ch. Deewal Yve		
		Belg. Ch. Rico de la Thudinie
	Ch. Silette de la Thudinie	
		Quelly de la Thudinie

Ch. Deewal Lorenzo. Breeder: Deewal Kennels, Reg.
Owner: William Currie.

Ver l'Ideal de Charleroi
Bonzo l'Ideal de Charleroi
Xanthane
Hardy l'Ideal de Charleroi
Bonzo l'Ideal de Charleroi
Civette l'Ideal de Charleroi
Kimenie l'Ideal de Charleroi
CH. DEEWAL LORENZO
Volpi de la Vallee de l'Escaillon
Ch. Argus de la Thudinie
Ucaba
Ch. Deewal Argusette
Bonzo l'Ideal de Charleroi
Ch. Faussette l'Ideal de Charleroi
Asta l'Ideale de Charleroi

317

Ch. Deewal Victor, WC275903, 8-10-72. Breeder: J. Chastel. Owners: Charles and Claire McLean.

<pre>
                                            Ch. Quiar de la Thudinie
                        Ringo de la Thudinie
                                            Nolette de la Thudinie
        Int. Ch. Tapin de la Thudinie
                                            Lais du Posty Arlequin
                        Nina de la Thudinie
                                            Lina du Gratte-Saule
AM. & CAN. CH. DEEWAL VICTOR
                                            Belg. Ch. Olaf de la Thudinie
                        Belg. Ch. Rico de la Thudinie
                                            Maya de la Thudinie
        Ch. Silette de la Thudinie
                                            Belg. Ch. Olaf de la Thudinie
                        Quelly de la Thudinie
                                            Lina du Gratte-Saule
</pre>

Ch. Deewal Young Husband, WC879261, 9-3-74. Breeder: Deewal Kennels, Reg. Owners: Charles and Claire McLean.

<table>
<tr><td></td><td></td><td></td><td>Ch. Marc de la Thudinie</td></tr>
</table>

                                               Ch. Marc de la Thudinie

                         Ch. Prudhon des Preux Vuilbaards

                                               Ch. Nota du Posty Arlequin

Am. & Can. Ch. Urex Bras de Fer, C.D.X.

                                               Ch. Prudhon des Preux Vuilbaards

                         Ranni Bras de Fer

                                               Orianne des Preux Vuilbaards

CH. DEEWAL YOUNG HUSBAND

                                               Belg. Ch. Olaf de la Thudinie

                         Belg. Ch. Rico de la Thudinie

                                             Maya de la Thudinie

             Ch. Silette de la Thudinie

                                               Belg. Ch. Olaf de la Thudinie

                         Quelly de la Thudinie

                                             Lina du Gratte-Saule

Ch. Delanda's Garcon Brave, WD528309, 3-12-76. Breeders: Jorge and Shirley Landa. Owners: Jorge and Shirley Landa.

                                              Ch. Marc de la Thudinie
                        Ch. Picard des Preux Vuilbaards
                                              Ch. Nota du Posty Arlequin
        Ch. Ruffkell's Invincible
                                              Flanette Ruff
                        Ch. Ruffkell's Delight
                                              Ch. Hilprize Kelli Sandra
CH. DELANDA'S GARCON BRAVE
                                              Rico de la Thudinie
                        Ch. Terry du Posty Arlequin
                                              Praline du Posty Arlequin
        Delanda's Reena del Oeste
                                              Ch. Schandor du Clos des Cerberes
                        Moza du Clos des Cerberes
                                              Gaez du Clos des Cerberes

Ch. Delanda's Jacques Raoul CDX, WD246000, 7-12-75. Breeder: S. Landa. Owner: Dennis Criss.

```
                                                      Ch. Marc de la Thudinie
                               Ch. Prudhon des Preux Vuilbaards
                                                      Ch. Nota du Posty Arlequin
           Ch. Ruffkell's Invincible
                                                      Flanett Ruff
                               Ch. Ruffkell's Delight
                                                      Ch. Hilprize Kelli Sandra
CH. DELANDA'S JACQUES RAOUL, C.D.X.
                                                      Ch. Marc de la Thudinie
                               Rhombus des Preux Vuilbaards
                                                      Ch. Nota du Posty Arlequin
           Urana des Preux Vuilbaards
                                                      Ch. Marc de la Thudinie
                               Rachea des Preux Vuilbaards
                                                      Pollie des Preux Vuilbaards
```

Ch. DeNey's Grosser Knabe. Breeder: James Neylon. Owner: W. L. Thiele, Jr.

			Ch. Urmin du Gratte-Saule
		Cendrillo de l'Ile Monsin	
			Tamia de l'Ile Monsin
	Ch. Hion de la Thudinie		
			Ch. Argus de la Thudinie
		Demoiselle de la Thudinie	
			Canaille de la Thudinie
CH. DENEY'S GROSSER KNABE			
			Fricko de Belgique
		Ike de Belgique	
			Erna de Belgique
	Ch. Remado's Jasmine		
			Ch. Ely
		Irisa de l'Ile Monsin	
			Ch. Balta de l'Ile Monsin

CH. DUXBURY HOUSE'S ULRICH
BOUVIER DES FLANDRES

Ch. Duxbury House Ulrich, WB905124, 6-1-71. Breeders: J. B. and G. O. Smith. Owner: Dr. Herschel Copeland.

<table>
<tr><td></td><td></td><td></td><td>Belg. & Am. Ch. Job de la Thudinie</td></tr>
<tr><td></td><td></td><td>Ch. Marc de la Thudinie</td><td></td></tr>
<tr><td></td><td></td><td></td><td>Remado's Kitty</td></tr>
<tr><td></td><td>Ch. Prudhon des Preux Vuilbaards</td><td></td><td></td></tr>
<tr><td></td><td></td><td></td><td>Lais du Posty Arlequin</td></tr>
<tr><td></td><td></td><td>Ch. Nota du Posty Arlequin</td><td></td></tr>
<tr><td></td><td></td><td></td><td>Lolo du Posty Arlequin</td></tr>
<tr><td>CH. DUXBURY HOUSE ULRICH</td><td></td><td></td><td></td></tr>
<tr><td></td><td></td><td></td><td>Belg. & Am. Ch. Job de la Thudinie</td></tr>
<tr><td></td><td></td><td>Ch. Marc de la Thudinie</td><td></td></tr>
<tr><td></td><td></td><td></td><td>Remado's Kitty</td></tr>
<tr><td></td><td>Ch. Ronni des Preux Vuilbaards</td><td></td><td></td></tr>
<tr><td></td><td></td><td></td><td></td></tr>
<tr><td></td><td>Onega des Preux Vuilbaards</td><td></td><td></td></tr>
</table>

Ch. Foxfire's Abel Luke, WD865537, 6-6-77. Breeder: Bridget Guy. Owners: Tom Spann and Ron Buxton.

Ch. Marc de la Thudinie
Ch. Prudhon des Preux Vuilbaards
Ch. Nota du Posty Arlequin
Am. & Can. Ch. Urex Bras de Fer, C.D.X.

Ranni Bras de Fer

CH. FOXFIRE'S ABLE LUKE

Ch. Uriah Bras de Fer
Ch. L'Esprit Fier's Wilhelm
Ch. Bianca du Clos des Cerberes
Ch. Croix de Guerre Xena

Ch. Babka de Saint Roch
Blandford's Ursula, C.D.X.
Algelique de Ver

Ch. Hion de la Thudinie, WA222559, 12-2-58. Breeder: J. Chastel. Owner: Deewal Kennels, Reg.

			Tito
		Urmin du Gratte-Saule	
			Silane de la Thudinie
	Cendrillo de l'Ile Monsin		
			Quinto
		Tamia de l'Ile Monsin	
			Reine de lac-Aux Dames
CH. HION DE LA THUDINIE			
			Volpi de la Vallee de l'Escaillon
		Ch. Argus de la Thudinie	
			Ucaba
	Demoiselle de la Thudinie		
			Ygor des Coudreaux
		Canaille de la Thudinie	
			Zolla de la Thudinie

Ch. Hollandia's Evil, WD100151, 12-11-71. Breeder: David Westra. Owner: Carlos Vander Muren.

<pre>
                                                Ch. Noceur de la Thudinie
                            Ch. Picolo de la Thudinie
                                                Nolette de la Thudinie
            Ch. Cambo's Thorton de la Thudinie
                                                Ch. Marc de la Thudinie
                            Oursonne de la Thudinie
                                                Mabelie de la Thudinie
AM. & CAN. CH. HOLLANDIA'S EVIL OF ADELE
                                                Belg. Ch. Olaf de la Thudinie
                            Rino de la Thudinie
                                                Naia de la Thudinie
            Sirka de la Thudinie
                                                Ch. Marc de la Thudinie
                            Oula de la Thudinie
                                                Nina de la Thudinie
</pre>

326

Ch. Jasper du Clos des Cerberes, WB809389, 6-29-70.
Breeder: E. F. Bowles. Owner: E. F. Bowles.

```
                                          Ch. Marc de la Thudinie
                         Ch. Picard des Preux Vuilbaards
                                          Ch. Nota du Posty Arlequin
        Brabo du Clos des Cerberes
                                          Ike de Belgique
                         Ch. Remado's Katleen
                                          Irisa de l'Ile Monsin
CH. JASPER DU CLOS DES CERBERES
                                          Ch. Chef de Truffe
                         Ch. Schandor du Clos des Cerberes
                                          Ch. Remado's Katleen
        Ch. Altair du Clos Des Cerberes
                                          Ch. Telstar du Clos des Cerberes
                         Ch. Aurega du Clos des Cerberes
                                          Deewal Marzie's Lamb
```

327

Ch. Job de la Thudinie, WA364802, 8-8-60. Breeder: J. Chastel. Owner: Deewal Kennels, Reg.

			Urmin du Gratte-Saule
		Cendrillo de l'Ile Monsin	
			Tamia de l'Ile Monsin
	Ch. Hion de la Thudinie		
			Ch. Argus de la Thudinie
		Demoiselle de la Thudinie	
			Canaille de la Thudinie
BELG. & AM. CH. JOB DE LA THUDINIE			
			Ver l'Ideale de Charleroi
		Bonzo l'Ideale de Charleroi	
			Xanthane
	Hulotte de la Thudinie		
			Ch. Argus de la Thudinie
		Flambee de la Thudinie	
			Canaille de la Thudinie

328

Ch. Konard du Rotiane, WA419253, 5-27-61. Breeder: R. Adams. Owner: James Neylon.

			Soprano de la Thudinie
		Ver l'Ideal de Charleroi	
			Reine l'Ideal de Charleroi
	Bonzo l'Ideal de Charleroi		
			Salvin
		Xanthane	
			Ugenia
INT. CH. KONÁRD DU ROTIANE			
			Ch. Argus de la Thudinie
		Ch. Erlo de la Thudinie	
			Zolla de la Thudinie
	Hosca l'Ideal de Charleroi		
			Bonzo l'Ideal de Charleroi
		Civette l'Ideal de Charleroi	
			Kimenie l'Ideal de Charleroi

Ch. Madrone Ledge Socrates, WB550661, 12-2-69. Breeders: Mr. and Mrs. Ray Hubbard. Owners: Ray and Marion Hubbard.

```
                                              Belg. & Am. Ch. Job de la Thudinie
                          Ch. Marc de la Thudinie
                                              Remado's Kitty
          Ch. Naris du Posty Arlequin
                                              Bonzo l'Ideal de Charleroi
                          Johane du Posty Arlequin
                                              Eliane de la Thudinie
CH. MADRONE LEDGE SOCRATES
                                              Ch. Marc de la Thudinie
                          Belg. Ch. Olaf de la Thudinie
                                              Remado's Lisbeth
          Ch. Pepita du Posty Arlequin
                                              Belg. & Am. Ch. Job de la Thudinie
                          Linouche du Posty Arlequin
                                              Idole du Posty Arlequin
```

Ch. Maijeune's D'artagnan, WD349595, 2-26-76. Breeders: Gladys and Carl May. Owners: Niron and Mary Conrad.

```
                                              Ringo de la Thudinie
                          Int. Ch. Tapin de la Thudinie
                                              Nina de la Thudinie
            Ch. Ulfio de la Thudinie
                                              Rico de la Thudinie
                          Sola de la Thudinie


AM. & CAN. CH. MAIJEUNE'S D'ARTAGNAN
                                              Ch. Marc de la Thudinie
                          Ch. Prudhon des Preux Vuilbaards
                                              Ch. Nota du Posty Arlequin
            Ch. Maijeune's Alouette
                                              Ch. Madrone Ledge Socrates
                          Ch. Madrone Ledge Venus
                                              Madrone Ledge Tigrette
```

Ch. Marc de la Thudinie. Breeder: J. Chastel.
Owner: R. Abady.

                                        Cendrillo de l'Ile Monsin
                        Ch. Hion de la Thudinie
                                        Demoiselle de la Thudinie
        Belg. & Am. Ch. Job de la Thudinie
                                        Bonzo l'Ideale de Charleroi
                        Hulotte de la Thudinie
                                        Flambee de la Thudinię
BELG. & AM. CH. MARC DE LA THUDINIE
                                        Fricko de Belgique
                        Ike de Belgique
                                        Erna de Belgique
        Remado's Kitty
                                        Ch. Ely
                        Irisa de l'Ile Monsin
                                        Balta de l'Ile Monsin

Ch. Moorelane's Fredrico, WE096016, 3-8-78. Breeder: Ila Yeo. Owner: Ila Yeo.

Int. Ch. Tapin de la Thudinie

Ch. Urmin de la Thudinie

Ch. Silette de la Thudinie

Ch. Avanti Zorro

Duchess of Kent v.d. Banishock

CH. MOORELANE'S FREDRICO

Frisia's Black Prince

Ch. Stormy Day of Tanglewood

Maurie Loo

Ch. Naris du Posty Arlequin, WB6157, 8-27-64. Breeder: F. Grulois. Owner: Chester F. Collier.

                                                Ch. Hion de la Thudinie

                       Belg. & Am. Ch. Job de la Thudinie

                                                Hulotte de la Thudinie

             Ch. Marc de la Thudinie

                                                Ike de Belgique

                       Remado's Kitty

                                                  Irisa de l'Ile Monsin

CH. NARIS DU POSTY ARLEQUIN

                                              Ver l'Ideal de Charleroi

                       Bonzo l'Ideal de Charleroi

                                              Xanthane

             Johane du Posty Arlequin

                                              Ch. Argus de la Thudinie

                       Eliane de la Thudinie

                                          Canaille de la Thudinie

Ch. Nelly du Clos des Jeunes Plantes, WE011100, 2-4-77. Breeder: Gelineau. Owners: Carol Gillespie and Claire McLean.

Fricko de Belgique

Karl de l'Ile Monsin

Florida de l'Ile Monsin

Belg. Ch. Quarl du Clos des Jeunes Plantes

Iraky de l'Ile Monsin

Ninon des Casseaux

Jassy du Maine Giraud

CH. NELLY DU CLOS DES JEUNES PLANTES

Belg. Ch. Rico de la Thudinie

Senior de la Thudinie

Quelly de la Thudinie

Vixie du Clos des Jeunes Plantes

Iraky de l'Ile Monsin

Ninon des Casseaux

Jassy du Maine Giraud

Ch. Nomura Wave, WC678290, 12-6-73. Breeder: Lawrence Cox. Owners: Dr. and Mrs. Horowitz.

			Ch. Marc de la Thudinie
		Ch. Prudhon des Preux Vuilbaards	
			Ch. Nota du Posty Arlequin
	Ch. Madrone Ledge Viking		
			Moka de la Thudinie
		Ch. Odelette du Posty Arlequin	
			Liska du Posty Arlequin
CH. NOMURA WAVE			
			Ringo de la Thudinie
		Int. Ch. Tapin de la Thudinie	
			Nina de la Thudinie
	Deewal Vlinder		
			Belg. Ch. Rico de la Thudinie
		Ch. Silette de la Thudinie	
			Quelly de la Thudinie

Ch. Odelette du Posty Arlequin, WA997400, 10-7-66. Breeder: F. Grulois. Owner: Ray and Marion Hubbard.

```
                                              Ch. Hion de la Thudinie
                         Belg. & Am. Ch. Job de la Thudinie
                                              Hulotte de la Thudinie
         Moka de la Thudinie
                                              Heros du Posty Arlequin
                         Kania de la Thudinie
                                              Demoiselle de la Thudinie
CH. ODELETTE DU POSTY ARLEQUIN
                                              Ch. Hion de la Thudinie
                         Belg. & Am. Ch. Job de la Thudinie
                                              Hulotte de la Thudinie
         Liska du Posty Arlequin
                                              Ch. Argus de la Thudinie
                         Eliane de la Thudinie
                                              Canaille de la Thudinie
```

Ch. Picolette du Posty Arlequin, WB399902, 10-25-66. Breeder: F. Grulois. Owners: Ray and Marion Hubbard.

			Belg. & Am. Ch. Job de la Thudinie
		Ch. Marc de la Thudinie	
			Remado's Kitty
	Ch. Naris du Posty Arlequin		
			Bonzo l'Ideal de Charleroi
		Johane du Posty Arlequin	
			Eliane de la Thudinie
CH. PICOLETTE DU POSTY ARLEQUIN			
			Belg. & Am. Ch. Job de la Thudinie
		Moka de la Thudinie	
			Kania de la Thudinie
	Ch. Odelette du Posty Arlequin		
			Belg. & Am. Ch. Job de la Thudinie
		Liska du Posty Arlequin	
			Eliane de la Thudinie

Ch. Prudhon des Preux Vuilbaards, WA846769, 11-3-66. Breeder: R. Abady. Owners: Frank and Lil Mees.

		Ch. Hion de la Thudinie
	Belg. & Am. Ch. Job de la Thudinie	
Ch. Marc de la Thudinie		Hulotte de la Thudinie
		Ike de Belgique
	Remado's Kitty	
CH. PRUDHON DES PREUX VUILBAARDS		Irisa de l'Ile Monsin
		Belg. & Am. Ch. Job de la Thudinie
	Lais du Posty Arlequin	
Ch. Nota du Posty Arlequin		Idole du Posty Arlequin
		Belg. & Am. Ch. Job de la Thudinie
	Lolo du Posty Arlequin	
		Eliane de la Thudinie

Ch. Raby du Posty Arlequin, WB516426, 8-13-68. Breeder: F. Grulois. Owner: Chester Collier.

			Ch. Marc de la Thudinie
		Ch. Naris du Posty Arlequin	
			Johane du Posty Arlequin
	Ch. Quiar de la Thudinie		
			Lais du Posty Arlequin
		Naia de la Thudinie	
			Ketty de la Thudinie
CH. RABY DU POSTY ARLEQUIN			
			Ch. Hion de la Thudinie
		Belg. & Am. Ch. Job de la Thudinie	
			Hulotte de la Thudinie
	Lolo du Posty Arlequin		
			Ch. Argus de la Thudinie
		Eliane de la Thudinie	
			Canaille de la Thudinie

Ch. Rostan du Clos des Cerberes, W915224, 5-22-58. Breeder: E. F. Bowles. Owner: E. F. Bowles.

		Belco
	Ch. Marius du Clos des Cerberes	
		Ch. Lisa
Bel Ami du Clos des Cerberes		
		Ch. Baska Aleida du Zaanhoeve
	Ch. Ellyrdia	
		Silta
CH. ROSTAN DU CLOS DES CERBERES		
		Jan du Clos des Cerberes
	Dombey	
		Inga
Si Jolie du Clos des Cerberes		
		Samos des Tois Isles
	Wandru des Coudreaux	
		Ch. Uada du Gratte-Saule

Ch. Shirwal Yankee Doodle, WD121878, 3-3-75. Breeders: W. Seger and C. McLean. Owner: Gloria Molik.

		Ch. Marc de la Thudinie
	Ch. Prudhon des Preux Vuilbaards	
		Ch. Nota du Posty Arlequin
Ch. Uriah Bras de Fer		
		Ch. Prudhon des Preux Vuilbaards
	Ranni Bras de Fer	
		Oriane des Preux Vuilbaards
CH. SHIRWAL YANKEE DOODLE		
		Ringo de la Thudinie
	Int. Ch. Tapin de la Thudinie	
		Nina de la Thudinie
Ch. Deewal Victoria		
		Belg. Ch. Rico de la Thudinie
	Ch. Silette de la Thudinie	
		Quelly de la Thudinie

Ch. Sir Jumbo du Clos des Cerberes, WB841460, 2-8-71. Breeder:
Edmee F. Bowles. Owners: Bob and Ingrid Kornheiser.

Ch. Marc de la Thudinie

Ch. Picard des Preux Vuilbaards

Ch. Nota du Posty Arlequin

Brabo du Clos des Cerberes

Ike de Belgique

Ch. Remado's Katleen

Irisa de l'Ile Monsin

CH. SIR JUMBO DU CLOS DES CERBERES

Ch. Coquin de la Thudinie

Ch. Chef de Truffe

Ch. Draga de la Thudinie

Ch. Eliane du Clos des Cerberes

Ike de Belgique

Ch. Remado's Katleen

Irisa de l'Ile Monsin

343

Ch. Tamara Bras de Fer, WB568319, 1-2-70. Breeder: Frank J. Mees. Owners: Frank and Lil Mees.

```
                                          Belg. & Am. Ch. Job de la Thudinie
                            Ch. Marc de la Thudinie
                                          Remado's Kitty
             Ch. Prudhon des Preux Vuilbaards
                                          Lais du Posty Arlequin
                            Ch. Nota du Posty Arlequin
                                          Lola du Posty Arlequin
CH. TAMARA BRAS DE FER
                                          Ch. Hion de la Thudinie
                            Belg. & Am. Ch. Job de la Thudinie
                                          Hulotte de la Thudinie
             Oriane des Preux Vuilbaards
                                          Lais du Posty Arlequin
                            Mouche du Posty Arlequin
                                          Johanne du Posty Arlequin
```

Ch. Taquin du Posty Arlequin, WC223600, 6-6-70. Breeder: F. Grulois. Owner: Chester F. Collier.

                                              Ch. Marc de la Thudinie
                          Belg. Ch. Olaf de la Thudinie
                                              Remado's Lisbeth
          Belg. Ch. Rico de la Thudinie
                                              Lais du Posty Arlequin
                          Maya de la Thudinie
                                              Hulotte de la Thudinie
CH. TAQUIN DU POSTY ARLEQUIN
                                              Kous de la Thudinie
                          Belg. Ch. Nicko du Posty Arlequin
                                              Linouche du Posty Arlequin
          Praline du Posty Arlequin
                                              Belg. & Am. Ch. Job de la Thudinie
                          Liska du Posty Arlequin
                                              Eliane de la Thudinie

Ch Thunderbuff's Butler, WD779653, 7-14-77. Breeders: Don and Connie Pruitt.
Owner: Anita James.

```
                                         Belg. Ch. Olaf de la Thudinie
                           Belg. Ch. Rico de la Thudinie
                                         Maya de la Thudinie
             Am. & Can. Ch. Sigurd de la Thudinie
                                         Belg. Ch. Olaf de la Thudinie
                           Quelly de la Thudinie
                                         Lina du Gratte-Saule
AM. & CAN. CH. THUNDERBUFF BUTLER
                                         Ch. Naris du Posty Arlequin
                           Ch. Quair de la Thudinie
                                         Naia de la Thudinie
             Ch. Deewal Thunderbuff, U.D.
                                         Ch. Deewal Lorenzo
                           Flanette Jemima
                                         Ch. Deewal Claudette
```

Ch. Timlor Bairgnhomme, WD327339, 9-8-75. Breeder: Loryce
Heisel. Owner: Loryce Heisel.

```
                                            Ringo de la Thudinie
                            Int. Ch. Tapin de la Thudinie
                                            Nina de la Thudinie
            Am. & Can. Ch. Deewal Victor
                                            Belg. Ch. Rico de la Thudinie
                            Ch. Silette de la Thudinie
                                            Quelly de la Thudinie
CH. TIMLOR BAIRGNHOMME
                                            Ch. Naris du Posty Arlequin
                            Ch. Quiar de la Thudinie
                                            Naia de la Thudinie
            Deewal Ti Ti
                                            Belg. & Am. Ch. Job de la Thudinie
                            Ch. Hilprize Kelli Sandra
                                            Ch. Deewal Hardiesse
```

Ch. Uriah Bras de Fer, WB997569, 5-22-71. Breeder: Dan
Rosenberg. Owner: Carole Wyatt.

<pre>
                                        Belg. & Am. Ch. Job de la Thudinie
                        Ch. Marc de la Thudinie
                                        Remado's Kitty
        Ch. Prudhon des Preux Vuilbaards
                                        Lais du Posty Arlequin
                        Ch. Nota du Posty Arlequin
                                        Lolo du Posty Arlequin
CH. URIAH BRAS DE FER
                                        Ch. Marc de la Thudinie
                        Ch. Prudhon des Preux Vuilbaards
                                        Ch. Nota du Posty Arlequin
        Ranni Bras de Fer
                                        Belg. & Am. Ch. Job de la Thudinie
                        Oriane des Preux Vuilbaards
                                        Mouche du Posty Arlequin
</pre>

Ch. Wallou des Preux Vuilbaards, WC753034, 3-7-73. Breeder: Robert Abady. Owners: John and Janet Malanovits.

Belg. & Am. Ch. Job de la Thudinie

Ch. Marc de la Thudinie

Remado's Kitty

Rhombus des Preux Vuilbaards

Lais du Posty Arlequin

Ch. Nota du Posty Arlequin

Lolo du Posty Arlequin

CH. WALLOU DES PREUX VUILBAARDS

Ch. Naris du Posty Arlequin

Ch. Quiar de la Thudinie

Naia de la Thudinie

Regine de la Thudinie

Ch. Noceur de la Thudinie

Pia de la Thudinie

Nolette de la Thudinie

Ch. Wiljamark Barney de Jorlee, WD995437, 4-28-78. Breeder: Willie Hasson. Owner: Jordan P. Davis.

```
                                              Ch. Marc de la Thudinie
                             Ch. Prudhon des Preux Vuilbaards
                                              Ch. Nota du Posty Arlequin
            Am. & Can. Ch. Urex Bras de Fer, C.D.X.
                                              Ch. Prudhon Des Preux Vuilbaard
                             Ranni Bras de Fer
                                              Oriane Des Preux Vuilbaards
CH. WILJAMARK BARNEY DE JORLEE
                                              Ch. Uriah Bras de Fer
                             Ch. L'Esprit Fier Wilhelm
                                              Ch. Bianca Du Clos Des Cerberes
            Ch. Croix de Guerre Xena
                                              Ch. Babka D. Saint Roch
                             Blandford's Ursula
                                              Angelique De Ver
```

350

Ch. Yrk du Posty Arlequin, WD135154, 12-8-74. Breeder: F. Grulois. Owners: Shirley Seger and Carole Wyatt.

<pre>
                                        Belg. Ch. Rico de la Thudinie
                        Ch. Taquin du Posty Arlequin
                                        Praline du Posty Arlequin
        Usti de Broachain
                                        Belg. Ch. Olaf de la Thudinie
                        Sianne de Bronchain
                                        Querida de la Thudinie

CH. YRK DU POSTY ARLEQUIN
                                        Belg. Ch. Olaf de la Thudinie
                        Sim de Brochain
                                        Querida de la Thudinie
        Upica du Posty Arlequin
                                        Ch. Quiar de la Thudinie
                        Roquepine du Posty Arlequin
                                        Liska du Posty Arlequin
</pre>

These Denlinger books available in local stores, or write the publisher.

YOUR DOG BOOK SERIES

Illustrated with photographs and line drawings, including chapters on selecting a puppy, famous kennels and dogs, breed history and development, personality and character, training, feeding, grooming, kenneling, breeding, whelping, etc. 5½ x 8½.

YOUR AFGHAN HOUND
YOUR AIREDALE TERRIER
YOUR ALASKAN MALAMUTE
YOUR BASENJI
YOUR BEAGLE
YOUR BORZOI
YOUR BOXER
YOUR BULLDOG
YOUR BULL TERRIER
YOUR CAIRN TERRIER
YOUR CHIHUAHUA
YOUR DACHSHUND
YOUR ENGLISH SPRINGER SPANIEL
YOUR GERMAN SHEPHERD
YOUR GERMAN SHORTHAIRED POINTER
YOUR GREAT DANE
YOUR LHASA APSO

YOUR MALTESE
YOUR MINIATURE PINSCHER
YOUR MINIATURE SCHNAUZER
YOUR NORWEGIAN ELKHOUND
YOUR OLD ENGLISH SHEEPDOG
YOUR PEKINGESE
YOUR POMERANIAN
YOUR POODLE
YOUR PUG
YOUR SAMOYED
YOUR SHIH TZU
YOUR SILKY TERRIER
YOUR ST. BERNARD
YOUR VIZSLA
YOUR WELSH CORGI
YOUR YORKSHIRE TERRIER

OTHER DOG BOOKS

A GUIDE TO JUNIOR SHOWMANSHIP
  COMPETITION & SPORTSMANSHIP
THE BELGIAN TERVUREN
THE BLOODHOUND
THE BOSTON TERRIER
BOUVIER DES FLANDRES
BREEDING BETTER COCKER SPANIELS
THE CHESAPEAKE BAY RETRIEVER
CHINESE NAMES FOR ORIENTAL DOGS
THE CHINESE SHAR-PEI
DOGS IN PHILOSOPHY
DOGS IN SHAKESPEARE
THE DYNAMICS OF CANINE GAIT
GAELIC NAMES FOR CELTIC DOGS
GERMAN NAMES FOR GERMAN DOGS
GREAT DANES IN CANADA

GROOMING AND SHOWING TOY DOGS
THE IRISH TERRIER
THE ITALIAN GREYHOUND
THE KERRY BLUE TERRIER
THE LABRADOR RETRIEVER
MEISEN BREEDING MANUAL
MEISEN POODLE MANUAL
MR. LUCKY'S TRICK DOG TRAINING
RAPPID OBEDIENCE & WATCHDOG TRAINING
DOG TRAINING IS KID STUFF
DOG TRAINING IS KID STUFF COLORING BOOK
HOW TO TRAIN DOGS FOR POLICE WORK
SKITCH (The Message of the Roses)
THE STANDARD BOOK OF DOG BREEDING
THE STANDARD BOOK OF DOG GROOMING
YOU AND YOUR IRISH WOLFHOUND

To order any of these books, write to Denlinger's Publishers, P.O. Box 76, Fairfax, VA 22030

For information call (703) 631-1500.   VISA and Master Charge orders accepted

New titles are constantly in production, so please call us to inquire about breed books not listed here.

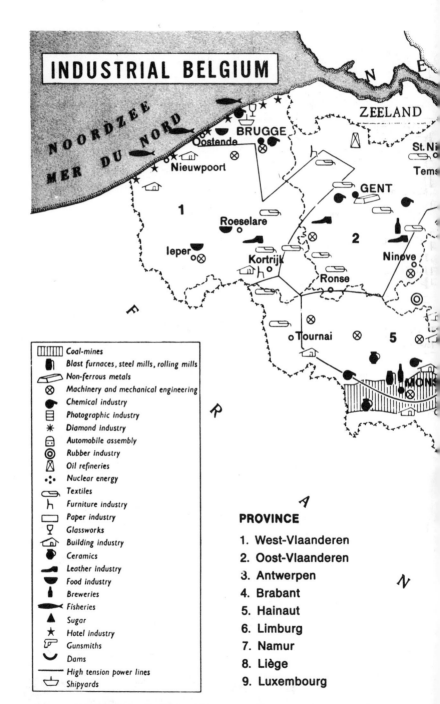

INDUSTRIAL BELGIUM

NOORDZEE
MER DU NORD

ZEELAND

Oostende

BRUGGE

Nieuwpoort

St. N

Tems

GENT

1

Roeselare

2

Ieper

Kortrijk

Ninove

Ronse

Tournai

5

MONS

	Coal-mines
	Blast furnaces, steel mills, rolling mills
	Non-ferrous metals
⊗	Machinery and mechanical engineering
	Chemical industry
	Photographic industry
✳	Diamond industry
	Automobile assembly
◎	Rubber industry
	Oil refineries
•:•	Nuclear energy
	Textiles
⌐	Furniture industry
	Paper industry
	Glassworks
	Building industry
	Ceramics
	Leather industry
	Food industry
	Breweries
	Fisheries
▲	Sugar
★	Hotel industry
	Gunsmiths
⌣	Dams
—	High tension power lines
	Shipyards

PROVINCE

1. West-Vlaanderen
2. Oost-Vlaanderen
3. Antwerpen
4. Brabant
5. Hainaut
6. Limburg
7. Namur
8. Liège
9. Luxembourg